Snake Oil, Hustlers
and Hambones

Snake Oil, Hustlers and Hambones

The American Medicine Show

Ann Anderson

FOREWORD BY HEINRICH R. FALK

McFarland & Company, Inc., Publishers
Jefferson, North Carolina, and London

Library of Congress Cataloguing-in-Publication Data

Anderson, Ann, 1951–
    Snake oil, hustlers and hambones : the American medicine show /
Ann Anderson ; foreword by Heinrich R.
Falk.
      p.   cm.
    Includes bibliographical references and index.   ∞
    ISBN 0-7864-0800-6 (illustrated case binding : 50# alkaline paper)
    1. Quacks and quackery — United States — History — 19th century.
2. Medicine shows — United States — History — 19th century.
3. Healers — United States — History — 19th century.   4. Patent
medicines — United States — History — 19th century.   I. Title.
R730.A54   2000
615.8'56'09034 — dc21   00-30486

British Library cataloguing data are available

Manufactured in the United States of America

*McFarland & Company, Inc., Publishers
  Box 611, Jefferson, North Carolina 28640
  www.mcfarlandpub.com*

To my mother

Table of Contents

Foreword

Theatre studies have come a long way since Aristotle. For centuries theatre was treated as literature on a stage. The idea of theatre as something performed, with or without literary pretensions, did not fully emerge until the twentieth century. Even today, theatre as performance in the absence of a written text is frequently relegated to the margins of scholarly attention and interest.

Studies of popular theatre and entertainment often adopt one of two general approaches. There are popular studies, which present an entertaining story with scant attention to the underlying scholarship; and there are scholarly monographs, which often squeeze all that is popular out of the telling of the story. Popular studies lack substance; scholarly studies lack interest and excitement. Frequently neither approach to popular theatre contextualizes the phenomenon within its broader historical and social framework.

The following treatment of the medicine show in America combines careful scholarship with a presentation that reflects the interest and excitement inherent in this popular entertainment. Because the medicine showmen appropriated elements from many of the contemporary popular entertainments, including the circus, wild west shows, minstrel shows, and even vaudeville, this book examines the medicine show within the broader context of popular theatre as well as social history. Medical practices, commerce, and advertising are explored in relation to the history of the rise and eventual demise of the medicine show in America.

Snake Oil, Hustlers and Hambones reminds us that the entertainment we watch every night on television is simply the hook for the offers during the intervals to cure our real and imagined aches and pains — the sweet spoonful that tricks us into drinking the medicine down.

Heinrich R. Falk
Santa Barbara, CA
May 2000

1

Origins and Influences

"How much is your health worth, Ladies and Gentlemen? It's priceless, isn't it? Well, my friends, one half-dollar is all it takes to put you in the pink. That's right, Ladies and Gents, for fifty pennies, Nature's True Remedy will succeed where doctors have failed. Only Nature can heal and I have Nature right here in this little bottle. My secret formula, from God's own laboratory, the Earth itself, will cure rheumatism, cancer, diabetes, baldness, bad breath, and curvature of the spine."

At the turn of the twentieth century, such claptrap was heard on street corners all across America. The great American medicine show "doc" operated on the premise that people long to believe in a magic bullet that will cure their pains in an instant. He told his audiences what they wanted to hear, and they rewarded him with medicine purchases. His rapid-fire spiel was a theatrical mix of circus, wild west show, minstrelsy, vaudeville, and popular drama. Equal parts entertainment, ser-

mon, and doctor's house call, medicine shows were samplers of American popular theater in the nineteenth and early twentieth centuries. Dog-and-pony shows, magic tricks, pie-eating contests, mediums, and menageries put audiences in a buying mood. Anything entertaining or attention-getting made its way onto the medicine show platform. In the history of marketing, medicine shows were the link between the medieval European mountebank who told stories and sold potions in the village square, and today's television commercial. The medicine show is now extinct, but its primary principle survives: Give the folks free entertainment and they'll buy anything you've got.

Before the advent of electronic media, the presentation of amusement and remedies to the North American populace was perforce a live event. From roughly 1800 to 1940, the medicine-show pitchman traversed the continent from end to end, promising health in a bottle.[1] His cure-all was bogus, but his show delivered what it advertised—a diversion from the tedium of daily life. From one year to the next, he provided the only entertainment to be had for isolated village dwellers, farmers, miners, loggers, and oil-field workers.

Medicine showmen have existed all over the world and in every age, including ancient Egypt and classical Greece.[2] In many parts of Asia, medicine shows are in use today to draw crowds and demonstrate the efficacy of a potion.[3] The American traveling medicine show, however, was a unique theatrical phenomenon. A hybrid of popular culture and confidence game, the shows were as varied as the medicines and as brash and energetic as America itself.

Medieval Origins

The traditions of the American medicine show came from Europe and were invented some time during the Middle Ages (A.D. 600–1350), when performing was discouraged. Before that, at the height of the Roman Empire and during its long decline, there was plenty of work for actors, singers, dancers, and jugglers. The demise of performing as a legal profession began in A.D. 410 when a barbarian army sacked Rome. Germanic tribes had their own kind of mimes and singers, but thought Roman theater effete and decadent. The new rulers of Rome allowed theater to continue only as a consolation to the vanquished.

In addition to barbarians, performers had another foe: the Christian Church had opposed the gladiatorial bloodbaths, animal massacres, and lewd pantomimes of the Romans for centuries. In A.D. 568, the church finally succeeded in banning theaters and circuses throughout Europe.[4] Between secular and church authorities, performers were doubly out of favor, but by the time restrictions were in place, Roman culture was far too ingrained in Europe to die out. Mimes and jugglers didn't settle down quietly and become farmers, bakers, and butchers. Instead, under great duress, they became a whole new class of workers who were forced to travel to eke out a living. Comic actors, magicians, and tumblers flouted the law and continued to work wherever they could convert a crowd into an audience—typically a castle courtyard or marketplace.[5] In the face of constant opposition from church and state, performers sprang into action, collected whatever pay they could, and left town in a hurry.

One day an unknown entertainer had the bright idea to do tooth extractions as a part of his act, and the medicine show was born.[6] This innovator and the other fleet-footed dancers, acrobats, and mimes who followed his lead started a line of performers that extended to the nineteenth-century American medicine showmen.

Italy

A performer who trafficked in potions and dentistry was known as a *mountebank*, which literally means "he who jumps on a bench." Nowhere in Europe was the mountebank more prevalent than in Italy, and nowhere in that country was he a more common sight than in Venice. In fact, the term *Venetian mountebank* came to mean any mountebank.

The word *mountebank* is often used interchangeably with *charlatan*, from the Italian *ciarlatano*, or "one who sells salves or other drugs in public places, pulls teeth and exhibits tricks of legerdemain."[7] *Charlatan* later came to mean a chattering con artist, one who impersonates an educated man and knowingly sells fake medicine. (Some medicine sellers were sincere but misinformed, and some accidentally stumbled upon a potion that did sufferers some good. Still others knew a little about medicine and simply enjoyed showing off their learning in public. The difficulty for consumers, then and now, lies in identifying the phonies.)

Some charlatans hired a troupe of performing assistants, whose physical antics weakened sales resistance. When

the time came to close the sale, however, the mountebank was on his own. He had to make each listener hear what he or she wanted to hear — a powerful magic trick indeed.[8]

The Renaissance (1350–1600) produced favorable conditions for charlatans. Old ways of thinking were cast aside, and it seemed that anything was possible. A semiliterate village dweller might have been aware of a new discovery, but he or she was probably not sufficiently educated to distinguish fact from fiction. Charlatans could not have flourished without the support of a willing, naïve audience.[9] According to historian Grete de Francesco, "The extraordinary power of impostors is therefore only to be understood after a consideration of the minds and circumstances of their gullible victims, the crowds who sought them out, half convinced before a word was spoken."[10] If charlatans had

Charlatans in Paris, early seventeenth century. Bibliothèque Nationale de France, Paris.

not existed, villagers would have invented them.

The Enlightenment of the eighteenth century was notable for increased scientific curiosity. Before then, science was inaccessible to ordinary people, but at that time, new scientific theories were in wide circulation. Charlatans made use of newly minted technical terms to impress and bewilder their listeners.[11] De Francesco says of the charlatan's influence:

> The charlatan achieves his great power by simply opening a possibility for men to believe what they already want to believe. His choicest audience would be composed of the semiliterate, those who had exchanged their common sense for a little distorted information and had encountered science and education at some time, though briefly and unsuccessfully. This was the audience, easily intoxicated by visions, that sought the charlatan quite as eagerly as he looked for it: the half educated wanted no really learned leader, nor would they listen to one wholly ignorant. Their needs were ideally met by the counterfeiter of knowledge, who served up a rehash of science in a form that suited their appetite. A half-educated man need not be a charlatan, but most charlatans have been half-educated men.[12]

Owen Tully Stratton, a medicine man who operated in the Pacific Northwest at the turn of the century, corroborates de Francesco's theory. Stratton found that his two years of pharmacy school and one in medical school hampered his ability to make a convincing sales pitch. He was in awe of his uneducated partner, who, "in his ignorance of physiology, *materia medica*, and therapeutics, could make [his pitch] ring like a twenty dollar gold piece."[13]

It was in the mountebank's interest to appear more powerful than his audience of ignorant peasants. Charlatans played up their supposed occult powers in order to insulate themselves from challenges. After all, who would dare argue with a man with divinely inspired knowledge or ability?[14] Cultivating a powerful image for the peasantry was a risky tactic, however, because it generated hostility from aristocrats. Nobles feared that mountebanks might actually have supernatural powers. Certain tricks, especially ones that simulated physical injury, were popular with audiences, but looked suspiciously like sorcery. Thomas Coryat, an English traveler, observed the methods of a typical, tricky Venetian mountebank in 1608:

> The musicke is a preamble and introduction to the ensuing matter: in the meane time while the musicke playes, the principall Mountebank which is the Captaine and ringleader of all the rest, opens his truncke and sets abroach his wares; after the musicke hath ceased, he maketh an oration to the audience of halfe an houre long, or almost an houre. Wherein he doth most hyperbolically extoll the vertue of his drugs and confections....
> Though many of them are very counterfeit and false. Truely I often wondred at many of these naturall Orators. For they would tell their tales with such admirable volubility and plausible grace, even extempore, and seasoned with that singular variety of elegant jests and witty conceits, that they did often strike admiration into strangers that never heard them before. After the chiefest Mountebanks first speech is ended, he delivereth out his commodities little by little.... Also have I seene a Mountebank hackle and gash his naked arme with a knife most pitifully to beholde, so that the blood hath streamed out in great abundance,

and by and by after he hath applied a certaine oyle unto it, wherewith he hath incontinent both stanched the blood and so thoroughly healed the woundes and gashes, that when he hath afterward showed us his arme again, we could not possibly perceive the least token of a gash.[15]

The preceding scenario illustrates three important aspects of the mountebank's performance that were carried on by his American counterpart centuries later. First, he manipulated the supply. By providing his wares "little by little," he created the perception that there might not be enough medicine for everyone. As Robert Cialdini notes in his excellent study of the psychology of persuasion, "As a rule, if it is rare or becoming rare, it is more valuable."[16]

Mountebanks made good use of this "limited number" tactic. (And so do modern advertisers.) Second, a lengthy, hypnotic patter — "almost an houre" in this case — wore down sales resistance and kept the audience in a receptive frame of mind. Third, a demonstration of the product incorporated a magic trick. The cut and healed arm was an interesting trick by itself, and when used in a medicine show, it sold the goods.[17]

For many in the audience, the mountebank's tales of faraway places fed their imaginations long after the show had gone. His stories transformed washtubs into sailing ships and plow horses into Arabian steeds. He brought magic into the workaday lives of ordinary people. Most villagers hadn't been anywhere or seen anything, so the mountebank

Card advertising Warner's Safe Yeast.

was an authority figure by virtue of his broad experience. If there was trouble with the law, he simply left town to take his chances with bad weather, bad roads, and bandits.[18] Often his departure was very hurried, for while news traveled slowly by our standards, it was improving rapidly and no mountebank wanted a bad reputation to precede him to the next village.[19]

Upon his arrival in a new town, the mountebank put up handbills in the local tavern to announce his show. The handbills mentioned his exotic travels to get the reader's attention, and provided some knowledge of current events through illustrations.[20] Forward-looking mountebanks employed advance men, announcers who arrived at a town a day or two beforehand to put up the fliers and whip up anticipation.[21] Later, in the United States, handbills and colorful illustrated cards were used to promote medicine shows and the medicine itself. The cards were collected by rural folk who had no other access to pictures. If they wanted artwork, they had to accept commerce, too.[22]

As time went on and the competition among mountebanks became more intense, their presentations became even more lively and creative. Dwarfs and midgets, talking parrots, apes, lizards, horoscopes and fortune-telling became part of the mountebank's show. The odd, mysterious, and grotesque are medicine show traditions.[23]

As the medicine show evolved, the mountebank's role as performer became more important than his role as medical expert, although the two aspects of his persona intermingled. The performances sometimes consisted of a playlet in which he played the role of a doctor. Afterward, he would come to the front of the platform (if there was one) to sell his ointment while still in character, blurring the line between theater and sales pitch. (A modern example is the commercial copy that reads, "I'm not a doctor but I play one on TV.")

All sorts of popular entertainment were used by mountebanks. Some Italian charlatans traveled with a *commedia dell'arte* troupe and were the leader and focal point of the show. *Commedia*, a type of Italian street theater, grew out of the practices of the displaced Roman mimes of the Middle Ages and flourished in the sixteenth and seventeenth centuries. The dialogue was improvised around set scenarios and the action took place in a portable booth.

The booth was a multipurpose bit of staging. First, it delineated a performance space. Second, in the middle of a busy marketplace, it afforded privacy to the poor soul who went behind the curtain to deliver himself up to the ministrations of the quack. Third, it provided an on-site lab for mixing potions. The performers could sell the available supply while the mountebank went to the back to whip up a fresh batch.[24]

Commedia scenarios were posted backstage to remind the actors which storyline they were performing that day. Each scenario left lots of room for *lazzi*, or comic business, usually physical comedy like catching and eating flies or spitting cherry pits in someone's face. Here is part of a typical *commedia* scenario about a rich man with money problems:

BRIGHELLA, *a servant*: enters, looks around, sees no one, calls

PANTALONE, *an old man*:   frightened, enters
BRIGHELLA: wants to quit his job
PANTALONE: pleads with him to stay
BRIGHELLA: relents and promises to help
PANTALONE: (in a stage whisper) confides that he's broke and his creditors (especially Truffaldino) are after him
TRUFFALDINO: enters, demands payment, comically angry scene ensues[25]

Commedia actors played stock characters: the miserly old man, called Pantalone; his pedantic friend in black robes, the Dottore; the swaggering Spanish soldier; and the clown, to name a few. The actors wore leather masks that identified the characters.[26] Clowns, or zanni in Italian (from which we get our word *zany*), put the crowd in a good mood and directed attention away from the mountebank. *Zanni* never made a direct reference to the mountebank's pitch or his wares. The sale was made after the show, when the crowd was warmed up, the theory being that a sucker who is made to wait is a sucker who is compelled to buy.

Italian mountebanks flourished well into the nineteenth century. P.T. Barnum (discussed in more detail later) went to Florence in the 1820s and saw Christoforo, the most famous charlatan in Italy at the time. Barnum recognized that Christoforo's show was the prototype for the American performing quack and wrote of him:

> He understood human nature ... its superstitions, tastes, changefulness, and love of display and excitement. He has done no harm, and given as much amusement as he has been paid for.... I dare say his death will cause more sensation and evoke more tears than that of any better physician in Tuscany.[27]

Italian mountebanks influenced the American medicine show, whether the latter-day practitioners of the craft knew it or not. The improvisational techniques of the *commedia dell'arte* traveled particularly well across the Atlantic Ocean.

English Quacks

American medicine shows were influenced not only by Italian street performers but also by English nostrum sellers, usually referred to simply as quacks or stage quacks. (The word *quack*, to state the obvious, means to make a noise like a duck. A nostrum is a medicine made by the person who recommends it.)

London, like Venice, was a center for street healers, and there were many similarities between Italian *ciarlatani* and English quacks. Like his Italian colleague, who understood that a performer must establish his space, the English quack sold medicine from the back of a cart. If he didn't have a cart, a horse would provide some height and, if necessary, a quick getaway. English quacks were also known for their serious, lengthy speeches as well as their jokes.

The English quack's clown assistant was called a Merry Andrew. It was his job to commend his master to the crowd, and he may have fashioned his remarks thus:

> Gentlemen. Tho' I am an English Fool yet my Master has the Honour to be a High-German physician, who in his travels around the Universe, has cured twelve Foreign Ministers of State of those Twin Plagues, Bribery and Infidelity; six kinds of Tyranical

Fevers, the whole Conclave of Cardinals of Pride, Laziness and Hypocrisy and the present Pope of the Anti-Christian evil![28]

A High-German doctor, a specific type of quack, was a serious version of the comic Italian Dottore. These somber fellows were seldom seen without a long black coat, human skull, and Latin tomes. Their affected accents made their medical nonsense more plausible to the crowd.

English quacks also mastered tricks that simulated physical injury. Stabbing oneself in the stomach was a crowd-pleaser. The trick required a false stomach, a bladder of animal blood, and a protective metal plate. A convincing agonized scream was also a must. One unfortunate trickster did the trick a bit too realistically, according to Reginald Scot, a seventeenth-century student of magic:

> A juggler caused himself to be killed at a taverne in cheapside, from whence he presentlie went into Powles churchyard and died. Which misfortune fell upon him through his owne Follie, as being then drunken, and having forgotten his plate, which he should have had for his defense.[29]

The English ruling class, as in Italy, was wary of magicians. There is a story about King Henry VIII's favorite juggler, a Mr. Brandon, who nearly got into serious trouble on account of a trick. Brandon approached a wall upon which a dove perched. He drew a picture of the dove on the wall and then struck the drawing with a knife point. The real dove keeled over dead. His audience was horrified and Brandon was ordered never to repeat the stunt. Scot wrote that if an old woman had done the trick, she would have been burned as a witch.[30]

One of the first laws prohibiting quacks was enacted in England in 1511, during the reign of Henry VIII. The peeved tone of the statute indicates how vexing quack doctors had become:

> Forasmuch as the science and cunning of physick and surgery, is daily within this realm, exercised by a great multitude of ignorant persons, of whom the greater part have no manner of insight in the same, nor any other kind of learning; that common artificers as smiths, weavers and women, boldly and accustomably take upon them great cures and things of great difficulty in which they partly use sorcery and witchcraft, partly apply such medicines unto the disease as to be noxious and nothing meet, therefore to the High displeasure of God, great infamy to the Faculty, and the grievous hurt and damage and destruction of many of the King's liege people.[31]

Quacks persisted and flourished in spite of the Act. They operated openly and with increasing audacity as time went on. Face-to-face harangues were the method of drumming up business until the Restoration period (1660–88). At that time, quacks adopted the practice of papering a new location with handbills, called "quackbills" in London. Advertising quickly caught on as an efficient method of reaching a wide audience. Tavern walls were covered with quackbills that directed the reader to a specific practitioner. Some fliers were models of advertising savvy. John Case, a quack who worked the London streets around 1660, was an especially gifted copywriter:

> All ye that are of Venus Race
> Apply yourselves to Dr. Case

Who, with a Box or two of PILLS
Will soon remove your painful ILLS

The rhyme not only embeds the good
Doctor's name in the reader's mind, it
implies his discretion with the phrase *of
Venus Race*— a polite reference to venereal disease. Case's quackbills also
offered free legal and astrological con-
sultations. One of his fliers advertised
"fourteen pills for thirteen pence," a
phrase with an irresistible bargain-base-
ment ring.[32]

Quacks understood the psychology
of persuasion, using a mixture of "as-
surance, hyperbole and bombast."[33] The
audience was put in the role of congregation: receptive and passive. Quacks
likewise had no compunctions about
linking their pitches to religion: "You
will say you committed yourself to Providence as well as Prunes."[34]

By the seventeenth century, London
was a hotbed of medical malpractice.
The medical profession, if it could be
called that, was a diverse, unorganized
crew of astrologers, nostrum makers,
beauty specialists, bone setters, tooth
pullers, midwives, magicians, con artists,
and folk healers. A more respectable
class of so-called regular doctors was divided into three categories: the apothecary, who mixed remedies; the surgeon,
who did the messy stuff; and the doctor,
who made diagnoses and prescribed
medicine, but never got his hands
dirty.[35] The modern physician had not
yet evolved. King James I attempted to
legislate against medical impostors, but
only the truly egregious frauds were ever
brought before the magistrate and usually only in London. Those who cam-
paigned against quackery seldom pre-

vailed in courts of law. Judges felt that
the principle *caveat emptor* (buyer be-
ware) was as applicable to medicine as
any other business, and juries resented
physicians who attempted to control the
marketplace.[36]

Publicly, the quack was always
someone else. The term was invective to
be hurled at the competition, whether he
was a fellow mountebank or a "regular"
doctor who attended the rich. A quack
was, in Ben Jonson's colorful phrase, a
"turdy-facy, nasty-paty, lousy-fartical
rogue."[37] Although "quack" was an all-
purpose insult that applied to any profession, it was consistently directed at
"those who cried up their goods in the
market, surrounded by zanies and monkeys, jokes and buffoonery, those who
pasted bills upon walls, who puffed their
wares in newspapers, who circuited the
nation, who mass-marketed cure-alls
and catholicons."[38] Actually, most medical practitioners advertised in some way.
Quackishness was a matter of degree and
subjectivity. John Pechy, an Oxford University graduate and licensee of the
College of Physicians, was accused of
"quackish practices" because he not only
put up handbills but also offered his services at a cut rate.[39]

Therein lies the essence of the
quack's appeal: He was a healer of the
people, the champion of the working stiff
who couldn't afford a court physician
but who had a few pence to spare on a
potion. The peasant class usually re-
sorted to folk healers, and the upper
classes used physicians and surgeons.
The great mass of people in the middle
paid for the occasional bone setter or
tooth drawer, but, more often than not,
they diagnosed and treated themselves

with nostrums. In an age rife with lethal diseases, it was obvious that the regular doctors' treatments weren't very effective. Doctors had no special status in premodern England. They were employees, like a stable hand or cook. Neither was medical knowledge thought to be anything out of the ordinary. Anyone was capable of mixing a poultice from herbs grown in the kitchen garden or "breathing" (opening) a vein.[40]

"People apply to quacks," wrote William Wadd, "because like drowning men, when honest practitioners give no hope, they catch at every twig. Thus the love of life, on the one hand, and the love of gain on the other, create a tolerably good correspondence between the quack and the public."[41] Although quacks were often denounced by the regular doctors, ordinary folks could appreciate the argument that the university was no rival for the school of life.[42]

Doctors were expected to kowtow to their powerful clients. Royal patients, especially, expected their every whim to be indulged. For example, one of George III's daughters became ill. The princess asked the doctor for ice cream as she thought "it might greatly refresh her." His Majesty had never heard of ice cream being given in such cases before and expressed concern. The doctor, thinking fast, replied, "Oh, no, please your Majesty, it may well be allowed provided it be taken warm." "Oh well, well doctor," said His Majesty. "Warm ice then, very warm ice."[43] At the other extreme, in 1810, the mentally disordered King George was strapped to a chair, and his head was shaved and blistered — the state-of-the-art treatment at the time for mental illness.[44]

University-trained physicians did not succeed in keeping the upper classes as their exclusive clientele for a simple reason: There was money to be made in the licensing of nostrums. King Charles II favored nostrums and did good business in licensing their manufacture. A royal patent conferred prestige on a medicine, thereby undermining the medical establishment's claims of quackery.[45] To qualify for a patent, a medicine had to be certified as an original formula; whether or not it worked was not an issue. Any mountebank who wished to succeed at the highest level got a royal patent for his formula and cultivated a royal clientele.[46]

In the eighteenth century, a quack's pseudoscientific pitch was considered cultivated entertainment for the English aristocracy. Wealthy malingerers abounded and made a hobby out of visiting both regular doctors and quacks. Fashions in hypochondria came and went: The vapors (a polite name for gas) was the *maladie du jour* for a time, and then biliousness was all the rage.[47] To the horror of the real doctors, the quacks were not only adept at acquiring customers but also actually effected cures in many cases. This may have been due to the power of suggestion, also known as the placebo effect. Or possibly, from time to time, they just got lucky.

It was a truism of Enlightenment ideology that information of any kind ought to be available to the general public. An informed public, it was thought, would reject magic, witchcraft, popery, and quackery. Self-dosing was considered by some to be not only a right but a responsibility. Consumers were encouraged to keep a large stock of herbal remedies at home and to be fully conversant with their use. The well-stocked medicine chest contained several dozen items, from adhesive plaster to valerian root. Furthermore, consumerism was catching on. Instead of moderating one's diet, getting enough sleep, and staying clean, the emphasis was on things, which is to say, medicines.[48]

Marketing was revolutionized in the eighteenth century by the advent of newspaper advertising and brand names. Every English person who sat with morning tea and the newspaper was assailed with ads for Godfrey's Cordial, Hooper's Female Pills, Dr. James' Powders, and scores of other remedies supposed to be infallible.[49] In its turn, the American economy would later be affected dramatically by patent-medicine advertising.

Old-world attitudes and trends traveled to the American colonies and had a tangible impact on the performers who wandered up and down the Eastern Seaboard. Medicine-show operators inherited Italian and English traditions of performing, advertising, and selling, and then, as we shall see, wove those traditions into the fabric of American culture.

The American Colonies

It's not clear when European charlatans first came to North America, but by the eighteenth century, the colonies were infested with them. Despite a pervasive antipathy toward performers of any stripe, the colonists supported an army of wandering showfolk. Enter-

tainment-starved settlers sometimes went to great lengths to catch a show. In 1771, for example, a group of 120 people traveled from New York to Long Island just to see a quack put on his presentation. Unfortunately, it is not known whether they enjoyed the show, because the boat sank on the way home. Undaunted, New Yorkers continued to patronize performing quacks whenever they could.

American mountebanks used the same conventions that worked so well in the old country, according to this anonymous medicine show actor:

> We traveled with a booth; the performers paraded outside, as they did at the fairs in England; then a drama played in which "Dr." Greenberg appeared as the hero; and at the end of the play, before the audience dispersed, the "Doctor" made a flamboyant speech recommending an ointment they had for sale, and while he was eulogizing the ointment the members of his company had to go among the audience and sell it. I had four weeks with "Dr." Greenberg, earning 25 dollars a week for my acting, and a percentage on the amount of ointment I sold.[50]

Performers peddled English or homemade herbal potions along with their magic tricks and animal displays. A typical bill in the late eighteenth century might have included a balloon ascension, free tooth extraction ("No Cure, No Pay"), a magic trick involving the reattachment of a severed chicken head, tricks on the slack wire, and exotic costuming. Medicine showfolk borrowed from any and all popular entertainment forms. Everything from ventriloquism to banjo picking and melodrama was presented.[51] Medicine-show fare was strictly for fun: The privations of the road and the rural character of the audience mitigated against serious drama or original playwriting. In her discussion of early American theater, Constance Rourke writes,

> The best acting — and many gifted players traveled over the country — could offer little more than sheer theatricals. With transient audiences and scratch companies and the hardships of travel there was small chance for intensification and depth; even the elder Booth concentrated only on single scenes. The pioneer theater was coarsened and haphazard. No drama came out of this broad movement: nothing can be clearer than the fact that drama as a powerful native form did not appear in America at this time or even throughout the entire nineteenth century.[52]

Nevertheless, even sophisticated New Yorkers couldn't get enough of quack performers. A cheap magic trick was evidently much better than no entertainment at all.[53]

In 1757 one William Smith wrote, "Quacks abound like Locusts in Egypt, and too many have recommended themselves to full Practice and profitable Subsistence. This is the less to be wondered at, as the Profession is under no Kind of Regulation."[54] Regulation was a factor that doomed the medicine show, but not until much later. The medicine-show doctor operated unimpeded until the beginning of the twentieth century. Even the Connecticut Act for the Suppressing of Mountebanks, passed in 1772, did little to stop this burgeoning industry. The law was harsh, unequivocal, but ultimately ineffective. It read, in part:

> That no mountebank, or person whatsoever under him, shall exhibit or cause to be exhibited on any publick stage or place whatsoever within this Colony, any games, tricks, plays, juggling or feats of uncommon decsterity and agility of body, tending to no good and useful purposes, but tending to collect together numbers of spectators and gratify vain or useless curiosity. Nor shall any mountebank, or person under him, at or on any such stage place offer, vend, or otherwise dispose of, or invite any person so collected to purchase or receive any physick, drugs, or medicines, commended to be efficacious and useful in various disorders.[55]

It is a testament to the persistence of both the peddlers and the colonists that shows grew and flourished despite such legislation. The colonists may not have approved of performers on principle, but neither did they like to be told what to consume or how to spend their precious free time. On the other hand, the medicine hustler had a long way to go before he was entirely welcome on Main Street. He was even lower on the social scale than a so-called legitimate stage actor.[56]

What the government could not accomplish, the clergy attempted. Preachers, especially Calvinists, inveighed against

> various wandering companies, bands, troupes, mostly comic and vulgarly theatrical … flaunting their handbills on the streets and seducing vulgar crowds to attend on their mimicries. Usually the characters of the actors comport with the scenes. Such coarse buffoonery, set off by stale songs and monkey dances, only degrades and corrupts the spectators.[57]

The clergy's attitude was understandable. Actors have tended to earn their perennially bad reputation. Early circus types, especially, were trouble. You could bank on fistfights, bad debts, and "a train of low and dissipated memories" whenever they were in town.[58] Despite official and religious opposition, traveling performers did pretty much as they pleased; without knowing it, they set the stage for the medicine shows.

Their behavior offstage may have been predictable; onstage, however, their performances began to take on new characteristics.

All-American Influences

The Yankee Peddler

Early American traveling performers employed old-world conventions. As time went by, however, performers were influenced by homegrown customs and attitudes; in turn, these performers became cultural influences themselves.

A seminal influence on the medicine show was the Yankee peddler. A character both real and legendary, he became an American archetype: a lanky loner with a pack full of notions, herbs, pots, shoes, and clocks. He did not display his wares in the village square; rather, he carried his goods deep into the frontier, to one cabin door at a time. To announce his arrival, he often played an instrument, or to amuse the backwoods housewives, he did a magic trick. Some peddlers specialized in the sale of medicines and packaged their own herbs — sassafras, bergamot, wormwood, and the like — or bought them from one of the patent medicine firms in Philadelphia. The peddler often repackaged those

medicines under his own label and recommended them for entirely different illnesses. A clever peddler, costumed in a frock coat, tall silk hat, and fake diamond jewelry, could persuade his customers that he actually knew something about medicine. Before long, every herb salesman in New England was called "Doctor," just as every Southern gentleman with a beard was "Colonel."[59]

Irish immigrants who settled in New England brought their supernatural creatures with them, so the Yankee imagination ran to witches and ghosts. Fairies and hobgoblins also slipped into Colonial folklore. The Yankee peddler wove these characters into his tales and cloaked himself in an aura of mystery.[60] He bartered his goods and told stories; for his trouble, he was fed and put up for the night. In the morning, he disappeared, whistling, over the next hill.

The Yankee peddler was seen not only in New England but also all through the colonies, and at the farthest reaches of the frontier. Divisive regional sentiments pervaded America until the 1830s, but the peddler eventually made the name Yankee synonymous with American. "The word Yankee is no longer a term of reproach," wrote newspaperman John Neal in 1833. "It is getting to be a title of distinction."[61] The Yankee embodied many qualities of the national character: shrewdness, ingenuity, independence and humor. He was, above all, a wanderer — a person eminently capable of realizing that supremely American ideal, self-invention.

Tall Tales and Medicine Sales

Selling patent medicines is an exercise in exaggeration. Yankee peddlers who trafficked in cure-alls were abetted by a cultural predilection for tall tales. During the Colonial period and until about 1830, several legendary Yankee characters took hold in the popular imagination. One such character was Brother Jonathan. He was perhaps named for a friend of Washington Irving (also an author of fantastic stories). The fictional Jonathan was variously a peddler, sailor, storekeeper, or simple Green Mountain boy. He appeared in short stories and essays and later was the lead character in many early American plays. His character was dynamic, clever, unlettered, and above all sincere. Unless portrayed as a sailor, he appeared in a blue long-tail coat, a white bell-crowned hat, and red and white striped trousers — an unmistakable prototype for Uncle Sam. He was the symbolic American — an ebullient practical joker deliberately crafted as a contrast to the British fop.[62] In some respects, he was a lout, but he was *our* lout.

Other popular Yankee characters were Jack Downing, who satirized the workings of our new democracy; Sam Slick, a clock peddler, whose popularity in periodicals lasted for three decades; and Hezekiah Bigelow, who spoke in rhyme. These characters were exemplars of the Yankee traits of good-natured lying masked by an impenetrable reserve — the components of any good medicine sales pitch.

If the Yankee was the dominant figure during the American Revolution, then the fabled backwoodsman of Ohio and Kentucky ruled after the War of 1812. The tall tale was folklore taken to its most imaginative extreme, and the backwoodsman was its centerpiece. The Yankee peddler and Brother Jonathan told stories of larger-than-life characters; the backwoodsman was himself a gigantic figure: "I'm a regular tornado, tough as hickory and long-winded as a nor'wester. I can strike a blow like a falling tree, and every lick makes a gap in the crowd that lets in an acre of sunshine."[63] Cunning was the Yankee's stock in trade; the backwoodsman conveyed size and strength, which was a response to the harshness of the frontier. The forest was full of terrors, but there was nothing — hostile tribesman or hungry bear — that the woodsman could not tame in spectacular fashion.

The most famous real-life backwoodsman was Davy Crockett. His adventures, actual and fictional, circulated throughout the nation's newspapers.[64] Crockett did as much as anybody to magnify his image. "I'm the darling branch of old Kentuck," he boasted. "I can hold a buffalo out to drink and put a rifleball through the moon." His legend grew even larger after his death: He could make lightning by hitting his own eye, ride a tornado, strike a fire with his knuckles, and ride Niagara Falls on an alligator. Legend placed him in California, Texas, and even Japan and the South Seas.[65] He was the author, as well as the subject, of many tall tales.

Close cousin to the backwoodsman was the boatman. Mike Fink, the first white man to take a flatboat over the falls of the Ohio River, was the most famous of all. Endless stories were told of his feats: He wrestled and drowned a she-wolf who swam out to attack him, and rode a moose like a horse for miles through the woods.

"Child of nature" was the appellation

affixed to the likes of Crockett and Fink. This theme of first battling then becoming one with the landscape was taken up late in the nineteenth century by many medicine pitchmen. Sporting fringed buckskins and spouting legends of their own invention, pitchmen like Diamond Kit and Nevada Ned (whose careers will be described in later chapters), took up where Crockett and Fink left off.

By the 1830s, the tall tale had become an American art form. Stories of such larger-than-life characters, as Pecos Bill, Paul Bunyan, and numerous others enlivened social gatherings and filled newspapers. Traveling actors told tall tales from makeshift stages in taverns and meeting houses. Stories were serialized in periodicals or took the form of dime novels. Many stories had to do with hunting, but others had the whiff of scientific discovery — exploring the moon or the depths of the ocean. Tall tales exploded the English language with words like *absquatulate, slantendiclur, catawampus,* and *tarnacious.*[66]

Americans had come to expect overblown public discourse. For example, a Mississippi congressman spoke these words in praise of John Calhoun:

> And how, sir, shall I speak of him, he who is so justly esteemed the wonder of the world, the astonisher of mankind? Like the great Niagara, he goes dashing and sweeping on, bidding all created things give way, and bearing down, in his restless course, all who have the temerity to oppose his onward career. [67]

The same sort of verbal excess is evident in this pitch for the cure-all Banyan:

> Is there some way you can delay that final moment before your name is

PHINEAS T. BARNUM,
Proprietor of the largest Traveling Exhibition in the World.

Portrait of P.T. Barnum from a pamphlet advertising his "Great Traveling Museum, Menagerie, Caravan and Hippodrome" (1872).

> written down by a bony hand in the cold diary of death? Of course there is, and that is why I have travelled over great wastes of stormy seas, to ask that you let me help you to good health, vigour and a long life, with the aid of the remarkable carton I now hold in my hand.[68]

Rhetoric was far more whimsical and ornate in the nineteenth century than it is today. A medicine pitchman could get away with telling an audience that a doctor "will cut out your umbilicus and remove your tweedium." Here is an example of an original fable concocted for Princess Lotus Blossom (a.k.a. Violet McNeal), for the purpose of selling medicine:

> A visiting prince came to go on a tiger

Barnum's "Feejee mermaid," an illustration from the *Sunday Herald*.

hunt with my family. When he was in the back country he wounded a tiger, which mauled him badly. The tiger was killed by one of the retainers. There was no medicine available and when infection set in, the prince's life was despaired of. One of my relatives had the tiger skinned and cut up. He took the backbone of the Royal Bengal Tiger, chopped it up, put it in a pot, and rendered the fat and the marrow. With this substance he anointed the injured prince, who made a miracu-

lous and rapid recovery. Further investigation of this Tiger Fat was made, and it was discovered to be of great value for cuts, bruises, burns, rheumatism, backache, and other ailments. The price of Tiger Fat is one dollar. To everyone who buys the Tiger Fat, we are going to make a present of the five dollar package of Vital Sparks, so you all can discover for yourselves what they will do.[69]

Tiger Fat contained petroleum jelly and not one molecule of tiger. It was a big seller for Violet McNeal — an ordinary Caucasian woman who passed herself off as a Chinese princess. The medicine pitch, part tall tale and part popular science, embodied the national bent for embellishment. Americans loved oratory as well as fables. In the nineteenth century, it wasn't enough to converse; anything worth saying was declaimed. Alexis de Tocqueville said, "An American cannot converse, but he can discuss…. He speaks to you as if he were addressing a society."

> The age abounded in talk — in court, legislature and pulpit; at public meetings and private clubs; in schools, societies, and organizations. Since schoolchildren learned orations and declamations and spoke them on "elocution days," famous speeches were part of the cultural equipment of all literate Americans.[70]

The medicine pitchman's spiel was the nexus of oratory, theater, and marketing.

P.T. Barnum

In America, modern marketing and entertainment began in earnest with Phineas Taylor Barnum (1810–91) the quintessential Connecticut Yankee. An

American folk hero (or perhaps anti-hero), Barnum and his feats have become as legendary as Crockett's. He was a master charlatan who managed to make his audiences feel good about being taken.

Barnum had many businesses before he hit it big with his Greatest Show on Earth. In the 1820s, P.T. Barnum was a medicine pitchman. With a German partner named Proler, Barnum sold Proler's Bear Grease from a colorful wagon throughout New England. Neither the product (which guaranteed hair growth on the baldest pate) nor the venture was successful. In fact, Proler was probably the only person to put one over on Barnum: After a few desultory months on the road, he absconded with the funds and went back to Europe. However, no experience was ever wasted on Barnum, who always learned from his mistakes. He was learning, perhaps better than anyone before or since, the art of combining salesmanship with showmanship.[71]

"Any idiot can attract attention," says advertising scholar James Twitchell, "but it is a talent to hold an audience still." What keeps an audience from walking away is a promise — of something new, different, entertaining, informative, outrageous, or useful. In today's parlance, a false promotion is hype. Nineteenth-century audiences called it humbug. "Creating humbug was Barnum's life's work," says Twitchell. "He knew that in the hands of a master, humbug becomes more than claptrap spun around a product. When it worked, what you sold was both the product and the humbug, the steak and the sizzle."[72] Selling "the steak and the sizzle," or in

the case of medicine shows, the medicine and the promise of a result, is the very heart of the matter.

Author of the maxim "There's a sucker born every minute," Barnum was born into a community of dedicated practical jokers. "A joke was never given up in Bethel [Connecticut] until the very end of it was unravelled," he wrote in his autobiography.[73] Indeed, the nineteenth century, writes historian A.H. Saxon, "was the age par excellence of the practical joke, and contemporary newspapers and memoirs abound in accounts of those 'practiced' by others."[74] Humbug, according to Barnum, the self-appointed Prince of Humbugs, was the most practical of practical jokes — it got the consumer's attention. Some of Barnum's most notorious humbugs were the Feejee [*sic*] Mermaid, which was a monkey head grafted onto a fish; Joice Heth, supposedly George Washington's 116-year-old nurse, who lived to be no more than eighty; and the dwarf called General Tom Thumb who was made to look older and smaller than he was and was never in an army. The deceptions were all in fun, and Barnum gave value for money paid — visitors to his exhibits had a good time.[75]

Barnum was the first showman to understand that entertainment is a commodity that can be packaged and sold to a mass audience. His American Museums drew crowds from all economic strata, and were proportionally more popular, in their day, than Disney World is now. "The great defect in our American civilization," he wrote, "is a severe and drudging practicalness — a practicalness which is not commendable, because it loses sight of the true aims of life, and concentrates itself upon dry and technical areas of duty, and upon a sordid love of acquisition."[76]

Barnum himself was devoted to acquisition, but that was only one aspect of his complex character. He was also devoted to Christianity as practiced in the Universalist Church. Unlike Calvinists, who preached that each person is preordained to eternal salvation or damnation, Universalists, a minority sect in Barnum's day, preached that salvation was available to all — even circus performers and actors. Barnum fought a continuous battle for respectability in a country steeped in Calvinist doctrine. According to this rather severe view of Christianity, entertainers were first on God's list for eternal damnation. Saxon writes:

> The hostility ... was real enough, a carryover from the days of the English Reformation when "players" and other shiftless caterers to public amusement were officially declared to be "rogues, vagabonds, and sturdy beggars" and subject to public whipping as just chastisement for their shameless way of life. The Puritans transplanted to America the hatred of such entertainers, whose activities were prohibited by law in several New England states, including Connecticut, until well into the nineteenth century.[77]

As Saxon suggests, even after legal prohibitions to performing had been rescinded, there was still a lot of hostility and distrust to be overcome. Barnum went to great pains to establish his unwavering integrity and Christian faith; he also made sure his presentations were inoffensive family fare. Arguing that his shows were highly instructive and moral, he went so far as to draw a parallel between attending his American Museum and church-going. It was a stroke of marketing genius. One patron was overheard to say before a showing of *The Drunkard*, "Are services about to begin?" The manager replied, "Yes, the congregation is now going up."[78]

Barnum tended to sermonize whenever he spoke publicly. He was such an electrifying speaker that he was invited on several occasions to speak from the pulpit at gatherings of the First Universalist Society in Bridgeport, Connecticut. His neighbors, in all seriousness, took to calling him Reverend Barnum, an ad hoc ordination to which he did not demur. He would have had us believe, and perhaps he believed himself, that uplifting the American public was foremost in his mind. A Reverend Dr. Hopper remarked, "What a spiritual showman he would have made; how he would have exhibited the menagerie of the heart, in which ferocious beasts, in the form of fiery passions, prey upon the soul."[79] Barnum's own pastor wrote, "If being made for a thing is a divine call to that thing, then Mr. Barnum was divinely called to be a showman."[80] Barnum had a ministry, and the gospel he preached was entertainment. His religious feeling appears to have been genuine, but at the same time he was not averse to parlaying his reputation as a man of faith into ticket sales. Scores of medicine pitchmen who posed as clergy trod a trail first blazed by Barnum.

Barnum was the pitchman's pitchman. "Contemporaries sensed that he was a representative American," writes historian Neil Harris, "not simply because of his enterprise and energy, but because of a special outlook on reality, a peculiar and masterly way of manipulating other people and somehow making them feel grateful for being the subjects of his manipulation."[81] Medicine showmen borrowed from Barnum every time they held a parade, advertised, used an attention-getting gimmick, or passed themselves off as preachers. If a pitchman came up with a way to put over a sale, chances are that Barnum did it first. Modern advertising and promotion, marketing, and show business were fused into the American medicine show; and all of them, it will be shown, began with Barnum.

2

Colonial and Pioneer Medicine Set the Stage for the Patent-Medicine Industry

Medicine-show people were able to make a living because they were competitive, scientifically and economically, with their contemporaries in the medical field. Given the state of the medical arts in the nineteenth century, self-dosing with a proprietary medicine was as reasonable a treatment as any other. In order to paint an accurate picture of the medicine show phenomenon, one must include the development of the American medical profession, and the growth of the patent medicine industry. In this chapter and the next, those two topics will be discussed.

We take for granted much of today's medical technology — anesthesia, antibiotics, scanning devices, and so on. In the history of medicine, however, these advances are very recent; the twentieth century has seen unprecedented scientific development. Until the first few decades of the nineteenth century, the body of medical knowledge was slim indeed. Various diseases had been identified, but their causes were unknown. Most medical practitioners subscribed to one of three theories: disease was an imbalance of the four humors — blood, bile, phlegm, and water; it was due to a loss of body heat; or it was due to either too much tension or too much relaxation.[1]

Germ theory was unknown, as was knowledge of cancer cells, cholesterol, or most other causes of illness.

Colonial and Pioneer America, or Home (Sick) on the Range

In Colonial times, professional medical treatment was not only primitive, it was largely unavailable. In 1775, there were only 400 doctors with university degrees in the colonies, and they lived in cities of the Eastern Seaboard.[2] Even if there had been enough doctors to serve the population, they wouldn't have done much good. So often did doctors kill their patients that they were said to be God's nutcrackers — they opened the corporeal shell to let the soul escape.

The English practice of specializing the professions of pharmacist, doctor, and surgeon had to be abandoned in the colonies. Specialization works only where there is sufficient population to support it, and this was not the case in the New World. There were no guilds or professional associations to standardize and regulate the profession, so men who had formerly been apothecaries or apprentices in England were free to call themselves physicians in America. In the seventeenth century, several attempts were made to license physicians, but this was to recommend rather than permit. Licensing was meant to encourage excellence among those who undertook to heal the sick, not to exclude those who lacked knowledge or skill. Those without a license, often called domestic practitioners, were free to operate as they chose. If a cure or two were effected, a person was often made a doctor by approbation. One such person

> was a fellow with a worsted cap and great black fists. They stiled him doctor. Flat [the innkeeper] told me he had been a shoemaker in town and was a notable fellow in his trade, but happening two years agoe to cure an old woman of a pestilential mortal disease, he thereby acquired the character of a physitian, was applied to from all quarters, and finding the practice of physick a more profitable business than cobling, he laid aside his awls and leather, got himself some gallipots, and instead of cobling soals, fell to cobling human bodies.[3]

Anyone with a flair for healing was given their due. In the seventeenth century, before the formation of medical schools and societies, women doctors were not subject to gender bias. A Sarah Alcock of Roxbury, Massachusetts, was "very skilled in physick and chirurgery," and was praised "within the gates." In the same state in 1663, the good people of Rehoboth lured Mrs. Bridget Fuller away from the neighboring town of Plymouth so she could serve the community as midwife.[4]

After 1760, there was a shift in medical practice. Men traveled to Edinburgh, Scotland, or went to Philadelphia College for a degree. Graduates of these august institutions began to form a medical elite. Once again, a trend toward regulation arose, and it lasted for a decade or so. Various colonies passed regulations for medical practice, but all such regulations were eventually abolished. It was not yet possible or practical to separate scientific knowledge from mere empiricism.[5] It would be many decades before the medical profession was organized and licensed.

After the American Revolutionary War and the War of 1812, Americans saw medical regulation as a loathsome holdover from England. Americans had not fought and won two wars against the British in order to emulate them. Doctors themselves, like their fellow Americans, didn't want a hidebound medical profession any more than they wanted primogeniture, a monarchy, or any other hierarchical British form of social organization.[6] Furthermore, "the physical immensity of the country and the abundance of free land frustrated every attempt to graft European institutions onto American society."[7] Anyone with a medical problem was free to seek treatment from any available source. Accepted protocols were a mix of superstition, apochrypha, case histories, and anything that seemed like a good idea at the time.

The Colonial doctor built his practice by inspiring confidence, but few doctors could claim a truly confidence-inspiring record. Some physicians published testimonials or encouraged favorable word of mouth. The most honest thing that could be said of a doctor was that he had a knack. Hardly anyone claimed to produce consistent results, even those who had been to college.

The most respected physician in the Colonial era was Dr. Benjamin Rush, a signer of the Declaration of Independence. Rush went to Edinburgh for his degree and was a professor at the College of Philadelphia. He was a rationalist whose thinking was consonant with the eighteenth-century Enlightenment. He believed that superstition had no place

in medicine and that the secrets of the universe could be unlocked with applied study. While that may seem like a commendably modern approach, Rush's medical theories were unfortunately both archaic and lethal. Rush believed in the one-cause-fits-all model of disease, namely "morbid excitement caused by capillary tension."[8] In other words, the patient must be bled. He wielded his lancet with a fervor, and even as his patients turned into corpses, he was not dissuaded from his theory. When a yellow fever epidemic killed 4,000 Philadelphians (10 percent of the population) in 1793, Rush's patients died by the score. Rush bled his patients so thoroughly that the sticky stream often overflowed the containers placed to catch it. Yellow fever is spread by mosquitoes, and as blood dripped to the floor, mosquitoes swarmed. In all probability, many of Rush's patients would have died anyway, but some might have had a chance had they kept their bloodstream intact. It was plain to Rush's detractors that bleeding did nothing to stanch the epidemic, but Rush held his ground and his lancet.

Rush's post-epidemic reputation was somewhat diminished, but he continued to represent the best the profession had to offer. Among the doctor's victims over the course of his long career were his own sister, three apprentices, and George Washington. As the father of our country lay dying with a nonspecific infection, Rush relieved him of thirty-two fluid ounces of blood, more or less ensuring Washington's demise. When Rush wasn't draining his patients (he never really knew for certain how much blood the human body contained), he was either blistering or purging them.

Blistering succeeds only in causing un-necessary pain, and purging causes de-hydration.[9]

Another medical torture inflicted by Rush and his contemporaries was calomel — a tasteless white powder of mercury chloride that produces at least as much suffering as the ailment for which it is prescribed; and in the Colonial era, it was prescribed frequently. "The doctor comes with good free will, but ne'er forgets his calomel," went a popular rhyme.[10] Calomel causes a heavy flow of saliva, bleeding gums, mouth sores, tooth loss, and an unfettered, bloody evacuation of the bowels. Patients hated it, and those who prescribed it hardened themselves for the messy business of doctoring. "We went into it with our sleeves rolled up," said one physician.[11] Early medical treatment was not for the faint of heart, neither patient nor doctor. It was assaultive, invasive, full of revolting effluvia, and often useless.

The few hospitals that existed in Colonial times had little to offer. Conditions were far from antiseptic, and one could easily be bled or purged at home. Patients deemed morally unfit were not admitted. The designation generally applied to unwed mothers, those with venereal disease, and vagrants.[12]

Doctors were not entirely to blame for the morbidity of the population. Ignorance of the causes of disease and workings of the body made for some appalling conditions. There was no sanitation because there was no perceived need for it. Sewage was dumped into the streets, sometimes right onto the heads of unfortunate passersby. What didn't flow into the gutters was consumed by

swine, which were in turn consumed by people. Salt pork was eaten in enormous quantities, and vegetables were eaten hardly at all. The water supply was impure; in fact, there were no municipal water systems until the mid–1800s. On farms, outhouses were located near wells, and clothing was caked with manure and worn until it fell apart. Even the beds of the wealthy were infested with vermin. Bathing was considered an eccentricity. Night air was thought to be poisoned.

Almost everyone, even children, drank oceans of liquor. Madeira, rum, cider, applejack, sherry, rye, and whiskey were popular beverages. Alcohol was consumed at every meal, in between meals, at polling booths, barn raisings, weddings, and funerals. It was partial pay for soldiers, *de rigeur* as a token of hospitality, the pick-me-up of choice on work breaks, and an ingredient in folk remedies. It wasn't until late in the nineteenth century, when the temperance movement gained momentum, that alcohol consumption slackened. In the first half of the nineteenth century, Americans drank twice the amount we do today, and further courted illness with nonexistent sanitation and poor nutrition.[13]

Epidemics raged through the country in the first half of the nineteenth century, as well. Yellow fever–bearing mosquitoes took the lives of many who could have been saved by proper sanitation, fresh air, and fluid replacement. The disease was terrifying, and vulnerable citizens fought it with the best information at hand — superstition. Cannons were fired to scare it, amulets of garlic and pieces of tar were carried, as were handkerchiefs soaked in vinegar; but swamps were not drained and rain barrels were not covered.[14]

Another terrible disease, cholera, decimated the population in 1832, 1849, and 1866. The relentless worldwide 1832 epidemic of Asiatic cholera made its way from India into every population center in the United States. It swept through city slums, bolstering the widely held notion that illness was the just reward of an immoral life — immorality being equated with poverty in Calvinist philosophy. Death from cholera ensued quickly, followed by panic and despair among the living. In Chicago, everyone who could leave did; in Detroit, funeral bells that had been ringing ceaselessly were banned for their demoralizing effect; in New Orleans, the disease claimed 300 victims a day:

> It was not so much the number of cases and high fatality of the disease, but the mysteriousness and suddenness with which it struck that filled people with a dread and fear that often reached panic. Persons in excellent health were suddenly stricken with a feeling of uneasiness and shortly were consumed with inward burnings and a craving for cold drinks; then came vomiting, intestinal spasms almost as severe as in tetanus cases, and finally, general debility, slow circulation, sunken eyes, cold lifeless skin, and collapse. The fate of many victims was decided within a few hours.[15]

Cholera is a bacterial infection that usually spreads through contaminated water or milk. During the nineteenth century, however, its cause was unknown. Many erroneous theories were considered, such as comets, poisoned air, and fumes from the ground. One rumor averred that licking postage stamps caused the disease. No new remedy was considered too offbeat or misguided to try; sulfur pills were thought to prevent the disease, and one Alabama doctor administered tobacco-smoke enemas as a sure cure. A doctor named Drake almost deduced the real cause of cholera: He believed in the presence of animalculae, creatures too tiny to see — an idea that came close to germ theory. Although the disease still occurs, cholera is relatively easy to cure if the patient can get antibiotic and fluid injections.[16] Unfortunately for cholera victims in earlier times (and for some third-world populations today), those life-saving items were not available.

The pioneers of the midwestern states did not fare much better with health than their city cousins. Until the twentieth century, 90 percent of Americans lived in the country, and few doctors dwelt among them. If a pioneer wanted shelter, he had to build it; if he wanted food, he had to grow it; and if he needed clothing, he (or she) had to make it. Women worked as hard as men, and children worked as hard as they could. Every aspect of daily life required effort. Short-handed, poorly trained prairie doctors fought an uphill battle to control illness in an exhausted population. When sickness descended, and it did so with depressing regularity, nothing got done. Winters were harsh, summers were stifling, and to make things worse, the pioneer diet abetted the onset of illness. Midwestern settlers ate mostly salted meat and fat. Even teething babies were given bacon rinds to chew. Tobacco was chewed and expectorated with no regard for sanitation, much less aesthetics. As in the cities, milk and water supplies on the farm were often contaminated. Alcohol flowed. It was reported in the Medical Repository early in the century:

> The inhabitants are almost constantly in a state of repletion, by stuffing and cramming, and by the use of stimulating drink. The consumption of animal food is probably much greater in the Fredonian [United] states, than in any other civilized nation; and it ought likewise to be observed, that the quantity of ardent spirits drank by our people, exceeds everything of the kind, that the world can produce; the appetite for inebriating drink seems to be increasing and insatiable.[17]

The middle of the continent, long before it was paved over with housing developments and shopping malls, was a mosquito-infested swamp. The land around the Great Lakes was known for its sickliness, as was the land adjoining the Erie Canal. The postcolonial settlers of Kentucky and Ohio complained of epidemic fevers and influenzas. In 1807, for example, malaria raged through the Ohio Valley. Settlers identified a chain of cause and effect between stagnant, putrid water and malaria, but their analysis was off the mark — it was mosquitoes, not swamp gas, that carried the disease. Michigan residents, Native Americans included, battled malaria every summer. In Michigan, after the land was plowed in the spring, it was observed that

> the malarial gases set free, that country became very sickly. Crops went back into the ground, animals suffered for food, and if the people had not been too sick to need much to eat they, too, must have gone hungry. The pale,

sallow, bloated faces of that period were the rule; there were no healthy faces except of persons just arrived.[18]

Ohio, Illinois, and Indiana were plagued with yellow and spotted fevers, scarlatina, whooping cough, and diphtheria. A nonspecific infection killed one-eighth of the population in Indianapolis in 1821. A wave of typhoid and pneumonia hit in 1838 and wiped out half of Elkhart County, Indiana. "Bilious" fevers were rampant. Ohio journalist and lawmaker James Kilbourne said, "Respecting the healthfulness of this country, I have to repeat that it is in fact sickly in a considerable degree."[19]

The diseases of the East Coast traveled west with no impediment: Measles, small pox, mumps, and scarlet fever attacked frontier settlements. Influenza and erysipelas, also known as black tongue, were epidemic. Skin rashes affected whole villages at a time; rheumatism was common, perhaps due to the habit of allowing wet clothing to dry on the body. Children often came down with croup. Bad dental hygiene permitted various infections to take hold.[20] On the other hand, heart disease and other degenerative diseases of the liver and kidneys were largely unknown — because few people lived long enough to develop them.[21]

Of all the ailments that plagued the region, the most common was a malaria-like infection called ague. It struck so frequently that it was barely worth a mention: "He's only got the ager," it would be said of a sufferer. Some types of ague caused chills and shaking so severe it was impossible to hold a tool. It was reported in 1836 that an Illinois family had to stop shingling the cabin roof for fear their shaking would cause them to fall off. Other types of agues were feverish; some caused alternating fevers and chills. Typical symptoms were

> yawning and stretching, a feeling of lassitude, blueness of the fingernails, then little cold sensations which increased until the victim's teeth chattered in his jaws and he "felt like a harp with a thousand strings." As the chills increased, the victim shivered and shook "like a miniature earthquake." After an hour or so, warmth returned, then gradually merged into raging heat with racking head pains and an aching back. The spell ended with copious sweating and a return to normal.[22]

Someone who knew the symptoms all too well wrote:

> You felt as though you had gone through some sort of collision, thrashing-machine or jarring machine, and came out not killed, but the next thing to it. You felt weak, as though you had run too far after something, and then didn't catch it. You felt languid, stupid and sore, and was down in the mouth and heel and partially raveled out. Your back was out of fix, your head ached and your appetite crazy. Your eyes had too much white in them, your ears, especially after taking quinine, had too much roar in them, and your whole body and soul were entirely woebegone, disconsolate, sad, poor, and good for nothing. You didn't think too much of yourself and didn't think other people did, either; and you didn't care. You didn't quite make up your mind to commit suicide, but sometimes wished some accident would happen to knock either the malady or yourself out of existence. You imagined that even the dogs looked at you with a kind of self-complacency. You thought the sun had kind of a sickly shine about it. About this time

you came to the conclusion that you would not accept the whole state of Indiana as a gift; and if you had the strength and the means, you picked up Hannah and the baby and your traps, and went back "yander" to "Old Virginny," the "Jerseys," Maryland or "Pennsylvanny." [23]

Sickness was thought to be unavoidable. Even when vaccinations were available, many farmers rejected them as contrary to the will of God. Persuading a patient to submit to treatment was no easy task. One country doctor remarked, "Among the most disagreeable things attending the practice of medicine, are the prejudices the physician must constantly meet with, either in the mind of the patient, or in those of his friends. It is easier to cure the body complaint of a hundred persons than to eradicate the prejudices from the mind of one."[24] A widely held prejudice was that one's health was determined by providence alone. The Indian Doctor's Dispensary, published in Cincinnati in 1813 says, "If the Lord will, I shall get well by this means or some other."[25]

Folk Remedies

Pioneer women were responsible for running the home, and that duty included medical care. It was assumed that a wife knew her family better than any doctor could.[26] A doctor, even if one could be located, was usually a last resort and was only called for in serious cases. Before a doctor was summoned, it was likely that a pioneer wife had first tried a folk remedy. She might have used her own recipe, or one suggested by another woman, who was, perhaps, the local midwife. If there were no knowledgeable neighbor, then a Native American medicine man or local botanist might have been relied on to offer a cure. The local *materia medica* was a combination of plants, animals, and superstition.[27] A remedy was given credence only if it tasted like hell — "one bad devil to drive out another."[28] Some recipes were, by today's standard, absurdly complicated, time consuming, and definitely not for the squeamish. The following recipe is for a massage oil to ease the pain of rheumatism:

> Take a young fat dog and kill him, scald and clean him as you would a pig, then extract his guts through a hole previously made in his side, and substitute in the place thereof, two handfuls of nettles, two ounces of brimstone, one dozen hen eggs, four ounces of turpentine, a handful of tanzy, a pint of red fishing worms, and about three-fourths of a pound of tobacco, cut up fine; mix all those ingredients well together before deposited in the dog's belly, and then sew up the whole [*sic*], then roast him well before a hot fire, save the oil, anoint the joints and weak parts before the fire as hot as you can bear it.[29]

Whether the recipe was good for the patient is not known — it most certainly was not good for the dog.

Dozens of home remedies were jotted down in family albums, passed along in conversation, or published in newspapers. For tapeworm, drink pumpkinseed tea; treat rheumatism with bear or rattlesnake oil; draw out measles with saffron; cure an itch with soft soap applied with a corn cob, followed by sulfur and lard. Goose grease was prescribed for just about everything.[30] Pioneer women spent a good deal of their time identifying, cultivating, and gathering ingredients for home cures. For some, it was an avocation, for others a necessity. Recipes were handed down and self-help medical almanacs were consulted.

The first European settlers of the New World brought their herbal recipe books from England. *Bancke's Herbal*, first published in 1525, was popular, as was *Culpepper's Complete Herbal and English Physician*, published in 1652. Because different species of plants grow here than did in England, many recipes were rendered useless. Herbs had to be shipped from the Old Country, which was expensive and impractical in the case of a full-blown disease. Some ingredients were grown here; Paul Revere's garden in the north end of Boston was a re-creation of an English kitchen garden. Colonists tended to ignore the profusion of indigenous healing plants that grew right under their noses.

Native Americans, to those who cared to acknowledge the obvious, were onto something regarding health and hygiene. A Dutch settler observed, "It is somewhat strange that among these barbarous people, there are few or none who are cross-eyed, blind, crippled, lame, hunch-backed, or limping men; all are well-fashioned people, strong and sound of body, well-formed, without blemish." Even though Indian remedies tended to be simpler and more effective than those of the white settlers, it took a long time for them to gain acceptance. The Continental Army had a list of forty-eight plant remedies, and only three were made from native plants. Little by little, however, white Americans overcame their Eurocentrism. Native American cures, especially in the midwest, where English botanicals were unavailable, became very popular. Indigenous medicine, as discussed later, eventually had a big influence on the American patent-medicine industry.[31]

Who Is a Doctor?

The formation of the American medical profession was a chaotic affair. For decades, everybody pointed a finger at everybody else and screamed, "Quack!" In America, as in the mother country, "Quacks were other people. Everybody felt happy in execrating the quack, because, everybody could agree, the quack was someone else."[32] Only those who worked with their hands were worthy of respect in a culture where everything was homemade. A pioneer doctor had to supplement his uncertain income with farming, blacksmithing, or another trade. Doctors were as low on the social scale as their leeches. They were regarded as parasites who lived off the labor of real men. On the rare occasions when a doctor's services were called for, he had to ride long distances on muddy tracks and create his own pharmacy on site.[33]

There were a few medical schools in the nineteenth century, but they were not adequate to serve a rapidly expanding nation. Americans were too busy subduing the continent to spend time on such frivolities as a protracted education. The only schooling deemed necessary was that which could be applied to an immediate, practical result — say, setting broken bones. Doctors were not

often called for the treatment of infectious diseases, even after germ theory had been accepted in the late nineteenth century. As the country expanded, and distances between settlements grew, educational standards dropped. By the middle of the nineteenth century, there were several medical schools, but knowledgeable consumers rightly regarded them as degree mills. Medical schools were run with an eye to profitability, not excellence.[34] A typical course of study lasted four or five months. Schools had no books, no exams, and no labs. Instruction was given in the form of lectures, dry discourses handed down to the entire class with no opportunity for questions or discussion.[35] Neither were there opportunities for clinical practice.

Many pioneer doctors were illiterate. The dean of a medical college in 1870 declined to give written exams because so few students could read.[36] Illiteracy did not further damage a doctor's low standing, because book learning was highly suspect. For many pioneer doctors, an apprenticeship was the best way to enter the profession. An aspirant would live in a doctor's home, roll pills, mix powders, take care of the horse, and if he could, he would "read medicine." After a few years of keeping a discreet distance on house calls, the young doctor might venture an opinion or tie a splint. When he was deemed fit to practice by his mentor, the young man went his own way.[37] Medical training came into the modern era in 1893, with the establishment of the Johns Hopkins School of Medicine. The school required a college degree for entrance and was the first to have a well-equipped lab and a teaching hospital. It was decades before this prototype of medical training was widely copied.[38]

In the meantime, scientifically dubious practitioners multiplied in number and type. There were hydropaths, homeopaths, botanico-medical, physio-medical, uroscopian, electric, eclectic, hygeo-therapeutic, faith, and many other "healers." The midwest harbored quacks as manure does flies. Indiana was called "a sink-hole in medical practice," and Ohio "a paradise for the incompetent."[39] It was a freewheeling medical environment in which the medicine showman with his tall silk hat and folksy manner could operate unrestrained.

The Thomsonians

One of those old, discredited methods of healing was especially influential in preparing the way for the nostrum seller in America. The Thomsonians, believers in the teachings of Samuel Thomson, promoted herbal self-medication and rejected the "riglar" doctor with the religiosity of the converted. Thomson was an unlettered, self-taught herbalist. His system of diagnosis and cures sold for twenty dollars and conferred the right on the purchaser to practice it. His method was so simple that he believed a medical profession would soon be obsolete. Thomson's theory of disease was as simple as it was wrong-headed: According to him, all illness is caused by a deficiency of body heat. Restore the body's capacity to warm itself, Thomson asserted, and disease will vanish. To that end, Thomson relied heavily on steam baths and the ingestion of *Lobelia inflata*, commonly known as puke weed. Thom-

son regularly steamed his patients to the point of fainting, and then administered *Lobelia* or some other herb guaranteed to flush the system with alarming speed. He claimed to cure "dropsy, cancer, humors, mortifications, 'felons,' dysentery, consumption, rheumatism, 'scalt' head, venereal diseases and fits."[40] Thomson was once arrested for murder in Salisbury, Massachusetts, after one of his patients died, allegedly from a *Lobelia* overdose. Thomson was acquitted. In 1813, he went to Washington, D.C., where he obtained a patent. (Patents were issued at that time, although not for originality or usefulness.)

Thomsonians themselves formed societies for moral support and the exchange of information. Groups sprang up like puke weeds. Their motto was "To make every man his own physician."[41] Thomsonian "irregulars" waged a propaganda and legislative war against the "regular" doctors. Regulations that had hindered the Thomsonians were repealed, and the medical establishment was humiliated. Thomsonians were convinced they were fighting for true medical principles, and the abolition of a monopoly on health care. Their unscientific approach horrified the regulars, who saw in Thomsonianism a threat to both public health and their personal finances.

Thomson gathered a wide following. Between 1830 and 1840, an estimated one-sixth of the American population practiced his method.[42] By 1840, 100,000 patent rights had been sold.[43] Thomsonians made the process of quack identification easy: The enemies of health were the doctors who spoke Latin. They "are not of the people, but arrayed against the people, and bent on killing them with rat's bane…. They bleed us to fainting, blister us to wincing, stupefy us with opium…. Go among their patients and labor to overthrow a long established confidence! Denounce them as mercenary! Break down the aristocracy of learning and science!"[44] This sort of rant was in accordance with the prevailing philosophy of Jacksonian democracy: No one was above anyone else. A call to the healing profession was more important than a degree.[45] After 1840, the Thomsonian movement splintered, creating more choices for consumers — and more confusion as well. The Thomsonians were in disarray, but they had inculcated an ethic of self-care in American culture.

The midwestern pioneer was a plum to be picked by anyone with a homespun approach. Midwesterners had a strong regional self-identity. Foreign ways, such as speaking Latin, were suspect. Even the customs of the more civilized east-coast states were considered effete. "At all times, the pioneer reserved the sovereign right to try to make the science of medicine conform to his concept of democracy, to criticize, complain, refuse to regulate, do his own doctoring, or none at all."[46] The proud unlearned pioneer, in his effort to resist a con, fashioned himself into the most compliant sucker imaginable. The medicine show doc, with his populist appeal, couldn't have had a more receptive audience.

In self-defense, regular doctors formed medical societies. The various groups struggled to survive, but many disbanded. There was constant internecine warfare among the schools, licensing agencies, and societies. This was consistent with a general rejection of British institutions. Societies came and went until the formation of the American Medical Association in 1846. Even for decades after that medical watershed, you were a doctor simply if you said you were.[47] The operative principle in American medicine was *laissez-faire*. Thus, the stage was set for the unprecedented growth of the patent-medicine industry.

3

Patent Medicines: Good for What Ails You

Medicine showmen stalked the American landscape from Colonial times until the first few decades of the twentieth century because the medicines they sold in between soft-shoe dances and comedy routines were what their customers craved. Male and female, old and young, rich and poor, Americans of all types wanted proprietary remedies. (The terms *patent* and *proprietary* are often used synonymously.)[1] In the previous chapter, we saw why the population doctored itself. Now we will examine why patent medicines were often the remedy of choice. The popularity of medicine shows was directly related to the importance of patent medicines in American culture.

Nostrum makers saw a need and set out to meet it. Their collective effort made factory-made medicine one of the first successful industries in the United States.

Medicine manufacturers did not collect orders and then fill them, as was the practice with other goods. Rather, they created a steady supply of a product and then generated the demand. This was an entirely new way of doing business. In other words, patent medicines brought manufacturing, advertising, and distribution into the modern era.

Before 1800, there was no need for marketing because there were no surpluses. Everything that was made was either used at home, bartered for some other goods or service, or sold immediately. One pound of sugar was as good as the next, so, staple goods were largely interchangeable. A farmer in the market for a wagon, for instance, would price the few available models and get the best one he could for the lowest price.[2] Patent medicines, on the other hand, had become so numerous that manufacturers needed customers to ask for their products by name.

American colonists favored British proprietaries over domestic remedies. When the inventory of imports was low, clever Colonial apothecaries made their own medicine batches and poured them into British-made bottles without telling their customers.

During and after the Revolutionary War, anti–British feeling predictably ran high in America, and supply lines to England were cut. Americans ended their dependence on British remedies, and the American medicine industry took hold.

One of the first American products was Widow Read's Ointment for itching and lice, invented by Benjamin Franklin's mother-in-law. Franklin designed advertisements for the salve that appeared in the *Pennsylvania Gazette*.

Citizens of the new nation were disposed to "buy American." Products with names like Dr. John Hill's American Balsam, promoted as being made from indigenous herbs (for the cure of whooping cough and hypochondria), gave the customer the satisfaction of supporting a homegrown industry.[3] By the 1830s, the American patent-medicine industry was in full swing.

The Medicines

By the 1850s, patent medicines had saturated the market. In 1858, one patent-medicine catalog listed 1,500 nostrums.[4] Advertising copy promised relief of vague ailments like "general debility," "catarrh of the heart, liver, appendix and kidneys," and "dyspepsia."

Nostrum sellers often made wildly inflated claims for cures: One label offered relief for "every ailment known to man, woman and child."[5]

Some remedies may have been helpful, although those consisting of sugar water and flavoring were useless, aside from the placebo effect. Medicines containing digitalis, quinine, ipecac, and phenolphthalein may have had medical value, provided they were taken in the right doses for the appropriate ailment. However, because both manufacturers and purchasers had limited medical knowledge, the probability of misprescribing was very high.

Herbal remedies often contained multiple ingredients. The misnamed Seven Barks, for example, contained hydrangea, poke root, Culver's root, dandelion, Lady's slipper, colocynth, bloodroot, blue flag, stone root, goldenseal, mandrake, black cohosh, butternut, aloes, capsicum, sassafras, and ginger.[6] It was the buckshot approach to medication: Blast the target with multiple pellets and perhaps something will hit the bulls-eye.

Users of formulas containing herbal laxatives and diuretics experienced an obvious effect and were satisfied that the medicine was doing *something*. In addition to the natural credulity of their customers, makers of patent medicines had biology in their favor: In 80 percent of all cases, the body will heal itself with no medication at all. Between the placebo effect and the body's natural healing ability, nostrum makers had an enormous advantage —*post hoc, ergo propter hoc* (after this, therefore because of it) was the logical error that resulted in sales.[7]

BELLE
Dyspepsia Tablets

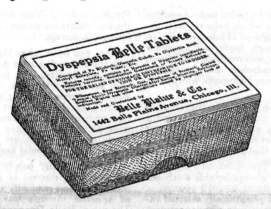

Composed of

Po. Rhubarb

Oleoresin
Cubeb

Po.
Glycyrrhiza
Root

Methyl
Salicylate

Po. Sugar

Nature's
Remedy

Contains no
Narcotic or
Hypnotic
Ingredients

Perfectly
Harmless

Satisfaction
Guaranteed

For the Relief of Stomach Distress
Due to Indigestion or Dyspepsia

Flatulence "Gas", Nausea, Vertigo, Biliousness, Sour Stomach, Colic,
Cramps, Palpitation, Pain, Weakness of Stomach, Acid Fermentation,
Mal-assimilation of Food, Heartburn, Stomach Distress, Vomiting, Fullness
of Stomach, Coated Tongue, Atonic Dyspepsia, Frog in Throat, Offensive
Breath, Acid Stomach, Distress After Eating, Dizziness, Sick Headache,
Bad Taste in Mouth, Bloating, Belchings, Sour Risings, restless nights
and other conditions caused by improper food or indigestion. Will nor-
malize and cure indigestion, improve the appetite and if taken in time
will instantly relieve a slight cold or attack of indigestion.

Chew a few Pleasant Tablets | Laboratories | **PRICE** $1 00
Instant Stomach Relief! | 1442 Belle Plaine Ave. | **Per Box**

MADE AND GUARANTEED BY

Belle Plaine & Co.   22 Quincy Street
CHICAGO, ILL.

Advertisement for Belle Dyspepsia Tablets.

Doctors argued that seriously ill patients who self-dosed with nostrums
were endangering themselves: Delaying
proper treatment could result in death.[8]
Sellers of patent medicines had a per-
suasive rebuttal: Regular doctors were
selfish and too small-minded to recog-

nize a medical breakthrough when they
saw one. Doctors, said the proprietary
makers, didn't want patent medicines
because they didn't want competition.
Furthermore, "[the doctor's] therapy
was brutal, his was mild. Their treatment was costly, his was cheap. Their

prescriptions were in Latin, his could be read by all. Their approaches were cumbersome, his were simple."[9] Proprietary makers had to condemn doctors and assume an air of scientific authority at the same time. Even though Americans had ostensibly rejected English influence, when it came to patent remedies, the dynamic of the Old World was still in play. Manufacturers claimed that doctors had nothing special to offer, and in the nineteenth century, that was a reasonable argument.

Many of the liquid proprietaries contained alcohol, morphine, opium, laudanum, or cocaine. Consumers believed the remedies were effective because the narcotics produced a feeling of well-being. Many nostrums were advertised for relief of "that run down feeling," and a swig or two of a narcotic-laden mixture was just the thing for that. Not surprisingly, many consumers of proprietaries became addicted. The following small sample indicates the availability of proprietary narcotics in the nineteenth century:

- Seth Arnold's Cough Killer — morphine
- Boschee's Syrup — morphine
- Dr. Bull's Cough Syrup — heroin
- Farney's Teething Syrup — morphine and chloroform
- James' Soothing Syrup–heroin
- Jayne's Expectorant — opium, digitalis
- Mrs. Winslow's Soothing Syrup — morphine
- One Day Cough Cure — cannabis indica
- Petit's Eye Salve — morphine[10]

Some medicines contained up to 40 percent alcohol. Manufacturers claimed that the alcohol was necessary to preserve the herbs. For a time, more alcohol was consumed in the form of patent medicines than in liquor. Many medicines were admixtures of ingredients that were harmful, helpful, and neutral:

- Nutriol — a general tonic. It contained calcium, iron, manganese, potassium, fish oil, alcohol, and strychnine.
- Lungardia — contained kerosene, turpentine, some alcohol, clove oil, sugar, and water. It was advertised for relief of deep-seated coughs and colds, but was probably better suited for stripping the finish off a piece of furniture.
- Tuberculene — creosote, rock candy syrup, glycerin, and wild cherry. Advertised as a cure for tuberculosis, it was declared a fraud in 1926 and removed from the market.
- Pul-BroTu — potassium iodide and arsenic. It did not cure tuberculosis, as claimed, and was declared a menace by the Portland City Council.

The list is endless. In addition to the usual herbal/alcohol emulsions, there are countless combinations of narcotics, poisons, emetics, toxins, and paint-thinners.[11]

Toward the end of the nineteenth century, technology captured the popular imagination. The human body and the universe were viewed as machines that ran according to a grand schematic. In the logic of the time, it took a machine to fix a machine; therefore, medical gadgetry was a big seller. Items purporting to harness the healing power of electricity were especially popular. Numerous electrical devices using metal pads and salt water were marketed for the relief of everything from cancer to arthritis. There were electric salves, hairbrushes, corsets, plasters, ointments, and even electric food.[12] The kidneys and liver were thought to be especially in need of a few energizing volts. Health belts, which supposedly supplied healing electricity to the midriff, were hawked by pitchmen with great success. Health belts were made of felt, a bit of copper, and capsicum — red pepper, which burned the skin and provided the illusion of electrical current. "All the wearer ever got out of his belt was a dream — and a blister."[13]

The Manufacturers

Like any other industry, the patent-medicine trade had its stars. First to make their mark were the four Lees. Samuel Lee, Jr., of Windham, Connecticut, sold Bilious Pills for the cure of jaundice, dropsy, worms, yellow fever, and "female complaints." So did Samuel H.P. Lee of New London. The former Lee claimed his pills were superior to the latter's as they contained no calomel. From the very beginning of the industry, the fight was on for brand identification and market share. Later, two other Lees came on the scene, Michael of Baltimore and Richard of New York.[14]

The first American patent-medicine baron was Thomas W. Dyott. He was an apothecary's apprentice in England who later owned a pharmacy in Philadelphia. Dyott's agents, working out of Cincinnati and New York, created the first nationwide market for a mass-produced item. His Robertson's Infallible Worm Destroying Lozenges were of questionable medical value, but they generated $250,000 — a fortune in the 1820s. Dyott sold his remedies at half-price to the poor, but some of his other business practices were less altruistic; the Dr. Robertson of Edinburgh that he claimed as his grandfather was fictional, as was the medical degree he conferred upon himself. (Business picked up when his labels read "Dr." Dyott.) English-style glassware was popular in his day, so Dyott built his own glass factory to make medicine bottles. In a fit of grandiosity, he built Dyottville, a model town for his factory workers. His employees were obliged to eschew liquor, swearing, lying, and gambling. (Dyott didn't mind that his workers laced his nostrums with alcohol and printed falsehoods of his own invention on labels.) Bathing and Sunday school attendance were also compulsory for Dyottville residents. Dyott's empire dissolved in the bank panic of 1837, and he did jail time for fraud. After an early release, he managed to make another fortune before his death in 1861.[15]

"Dr." Benjamin Bandreth, another English-born entrepreneur, made a fortune with his Vegetable Universal pills, an herbal cathartic. He was worth $200,000 in 1839. By 1870, he owned several blocks in downtown Manhattan. In that same year, his factory in Sing-Sing turned out two million boxes of pills. Henry T. Hembold was another successful manufacturer. In 1871, he built a Temple of Pharmacy on Broadway. Its perfumed fountains, caged canaries, and floor-to-ceiling mirrors were for the benefit of such wealthy clients as Jacob Astor, Commodore Vanderbilt, and Jay Gould.[16] High society consumed patent medicine, but shunned patent-medicine makers. The fortunes of Henry Hembold and James Ayer were "new money," and therefore not worthy of respect among the upper classes. Hembold hobnobbed with President Ulysses S. Grant, but that "was traceable to [Mrs. Hembold's] excellent family connections rather than to her husband's profuse expenditure and display."[17]

Lydia Pinkham, purveyor of potions for female health.

One of the most successful manufacturers was Lydia Pinkham, whose motherly Victorian countenance decorated the bottle. Her face was so well known that at the time of her death in 1883 she was said to be the most famous woman in America.[18] She was an ordinary New England housewife who concocted an herbal remedy "for female complaints and weakness" in her kitchen. She dispensed it free to neighborhood ladies, thereby cornering a demographic niche. (Pinkham's neighborhood was notable for powerful women; both Susan B. Anthony and Mary Baker Eddy lived nearby.) Pressed by economic necessity, the family put the remedy on the market and the product took off. She called it Lydia Pinkham's Vegetable Compound in order to capitalize on vegetarianism, a fad at the time. Mrs. Pinkham, a vocal temperance supporter, added alcohol to her mixture as a preservative. Women were encouraged to write to Mrs. Pinkham, and she responded personally with letters addressed, "Dear Friend," and signed, "Yours for Health." Mrs. Pinkham became a cross between Betty Crocker and Dear Abby, an iconic nurturing mother figure, whose nasty-tasting medicine and good advice would fix what ailed you. In an age of "ideal womanhood," when "the curse" really was one, Mrs. Pinkham provided more than a remedy, she provided understanding. As she said, "Only a woman can understand another woman's ills."[19] Letters continued to pour in to Mrs. Pinkham even after her well-publicized death.[20] Such is the power of a well-honed corporate image.

Why Patent Medicines?

Necessity dictated that a prairie wife doctor her own family, a difficult and time-consuming job. Patent remedies became "mother's little helper." Rather than grow, dry, chop, and mix their own herbs, women had only to reach for a bottle. Packaged nostrums, therefore, provided something almost as important as the medicine itself: convenience. Doctors asserted the superiority of their treatments, but for patients living in isolated areas, the point was moot. Rural America could not support many doctors or pharmacies, but most villages had a general store that carried an array of bottled medicines.[21] It was the male population, however, that turned occasional self-dosing into a daily habit.

Dependence on narcotic and alcoholic nostrums was exacerbated by the War Between the States. The Civil War (1861–1865) further debilitated a population already weakened by chronic ill health and established patent medicines in the American economy. Among the 620,000 soldiers who died in the Civil War were 400,000 victims of disease. Malaria, dysentery, and typhoid, nicknamed "General Summer," did much of the soldier's work for him. Alcohol rations had been abolished in the army in 1832, so liquor-laden proprietaries were eagerly consumed by sick and healthy soldiers alike. Further, during the war, liquor was taxed, but medicine was not, making proprietaries a more economical purchase for both civilians and the military. Union supply sergeants bought Hostetter's Bitters, a brand containing 43 percent alcohol, by the case.[22] Army patronage created an $18 million fortune for Colonel Hostetter and an intractable problem for soldiers: Narcotic addition was so prevalent that it became known as "the army disease." At the war's end, many surviving combatants were inveterate self-dosers and introduced the habit to their families. Peruna, which contained 19 percent alcohol, created an army of "Peruna drunks." After the war, it was marketed to women as a bust enlarger, although the only body part it was likely to enlarge was the liver.

Members of the Women's Christian Temperance Union, militant anti-alcohol activists, broke up saloons by day and got loaded on patent medicine at night, with no acknowledged contradiction. Demon alcohol was forbidden, but a "dose" was permissible.[23] Abuse of one patent medicine often led to another. One advertised product was for the purpose of kicking "the Peruna habit." Sears catalog offered a "Cure for the Opium and Morphine Habit." An alcoholism "remedy" that evidently relied on the "hair of the dog" theory contained 41.6 percent alcohol.[24]

Advertising

Medicine shows connected nineteenth-century medical technology, entertainment, and advertising. The entertainment was a marketing tool that persuaded the audience to buy the advertised products. Just as television programs induce us to watch commercials, medicine-show acts "got the suckers into the tent." The actors made the medicine available to consumers, but perhaps more important, they made the consumer available to the advertiser. "In the case of many nostrums it is fair to say that there was no demand at all for the product until it was created by advertising."[25]

Any outdoor surface — a rock, a tree, or even a barn door — would do for a slogan or logo. Outdoor advertising was inexpensive and easy to place. Farmers let medicine companies put logos on their barns, provided the entire structure was given a fresh coat of paint. The countryside became the advertiser's canvas. A British visitor observed in 1882:

> America is daubed from one end of the country to the other with huge white-paint notices of favorite articles of manufacture, with an endless array of advertisements puffing off the medicines of pretentious quacks.... it is one of the first things that strikes the stranger as soon as he has landed in the New World: he cannot step a mile into the open country, whether into the fields or along the high roads without meeting the disfigurements.... at length he becomes quite accustomed to the sight and is able to look upon it with complacency and expect "Bitters," "Gargling Oil," "Horse Powders," etc. at every turn of the path.[26]

Newspapers

The proprietary medicine industry was supported by expanded rail lines, inexpensive mass-produced bottles, and low postal rates. But more than any other factor, the invention of cheap, wood-pulp paper had a significant impact on the growth of the industry. Paper meant advertising space, and the products most often advertised were patent medicines. "In America, newspaper publishing and patent-medicine advertising were born together, grew up side by side, and have been boon companions to this day."[27]

In Colonial times, newspapers were printed on expensive rag-based paper imported from Britain. Clothing was worn until it was threadbare and then made into rag rugs. By the time it was ready for recycling into paper, there was very little to go around. Big-city newspapers often had only 300 sheets of paper a day. After the Revolutionary War, paper was even more scarce, and advertisements were crammed into one-inch columns of six-point type. A change came about as an unintended benefit of the Civil War: Shortages that resulted from the war forced the invention of wood-based paper. Soon newspaper executives had all the pages they could fill. An abundant paper supply meant more advertising space, and therefore, more advertising revenue.

Outdoor advertising could be had for nothing (or for the cost of the paint), but newspapers were the most efficient medium for establishing a trademark. In the early 1800s, nostrum advertising generated more than one-third of the profits for the newspaper business.[28] In 1847, 2,000 newspapers ran eleven million medicine ads.[29] Repetition was the key to embedding the product name in the customer's mind.[30] One manufacturer ran an ad for his pill thirty-seven times in the same newspaper issue. Other advertisers ran the same column-inch ad for years, without changing a word of copy.[31] By the Civil War, half of all newspaper advertising revenues were from medicine.[32] Manufacturers included a "red clause" (printed in red ink) in their advertising contracts, permitting them to cancel if laws were passed restricting the sale of their products. Newspaper editors adopted a tacit policy of supporting the medicine industry, as they (or their publishers) were loath to criticize their most important source of income. As a result, the public was slow to learn about the dangers posed by many of the formulas.[33]

Now we return to P.T. Barnum. The master showman invented many of the advertising conventions that are still in use today. Barnum touted the salutary effects of his hair restorer with imaginatively designed posters and handbills. He pioneered the use of outlandish typography, testimonials, celebrity endorsement, and wild hyperbole in his medicine ads.[34] Later, he used the same imaginative style to promote his circus. By the Civil War, his advertising techniques were commonplace, not only for

medicine, but for marketing in general. Barnum's methods were later used in theater advertising and appear repeatedly in contemporary television commercials. "The fact that so many of advertising's ways of getting our attention started with patent medicines and then moved with Barnum into circus and theater advertising, has caused what must be an unfair association in many generations' minds."[35] The association exists, but whether it's unfair is a debatable question.

Testimonials, which were presented as slice-of-life vignettes, were especially popular. Having one's appreciative comments published in an ad was a way for an ordinary person to get attention. As one newspaper editor advised, "If your brains won't get you into the papers, sign a patent medicine testimonial. Maybe your kidneys will." Ministers were assured of having their testimonials

Advertising card for Parker's Tonic.

printed.[36] Manufacturers sold testimonial letters to each other in order to create databases for direct mail advertising.[37]

Dr. James C. Ayer, maker of the best-selling Cherry Pectoral, realized the power of advertising as had no other manufacturer before him. Ads for Cherry Pectoral ran in *every* newspaper in the United States; it was the first saturation campaign. Many manufacturers published colorful lithographed almanacs that were distributed free in country stores and pharmacies. Ayer boasted that his almanac was second only to the Bible in circulation.[38] So successful was the strategy that a small Massachusetts town offered to name itself for Ayer if he would bring his factory there. Other manufacturers followed Ayer's lead. Lydia Pinkham advertised everywhere and sent printer's casts of her face to even the smallest newspapers. In the absence of other pictures, newspapers used her likeness in stories about Sarah Bernhardt, Queen Victoria, and Mrs. Grover Cleveland.[39]

F.G. Kinsman, a proprietary bottler in Augusta, Maine, realized that any blank sheet of paper could be filled with advertising. To that end, he created a religious magazine expressly for the purpose of including ads for his products. In one stroke, he got his message before the public and allied that message with respectability. Religion and medicine proved to be a powerful combination. Families wanted inspirational reading in the home, and soon each denomination wanted its own publication. Kinsman was happy to fill the need. Publishers, aware of Kinsman's phenomenal success, created magazines to sell space to advertisers. *Harper's Magazine* and *Atlantic Monthly* set aside advertising sections. Soon after, *Ladies' Home Journal* and *Cosmopolitan*, among others, integrated ads into the body of the magazines. *Collier's, Saturday Evening Post*, and *Women's Home Companion* took it a step further: They were created specifically as advertising vehicles. "At this point ... the role of publisher changed from being a seller

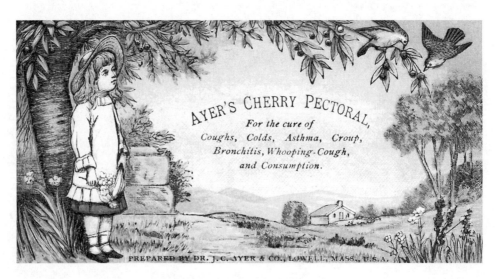

Card for Ayer's Cherry Pectoral.

of a product to consumers to being a gatherer of consumers for the advertisers."[40] By the 1870s, a quarter of all advertising was for proprietary drugs. If advertising and entertainment are wedded in American popular culture, then their courtship began with the promotion of patent medicines.

For the makers of proprietaries, their "literature department" was almost more important than their medicine factories. "The heart of the business were the printing, folding, and binding departments, which ran all year round, turning out circulars and little gems of pain-inducing literature by the millions of copies."[41] Manufacturers inundated the public with handbills, calendars, almanacs, and booklets. In the nineteenth century, one of the most popular advertisements was the trade card—a colorfully illustrated, engraved postcard that

Top and right: Card for Ayer's Sarsaparilla.

A REAL BLESSING.

Ay... Compound Extract of Sarsaparilla is a skilfully prepared combination of the best vegetable alteratives and blood purifiers.

It is composed of the Sarsaparilla root of the tropics, well-known as an alterative of great value, combined with Stillingia, Yellow-Dock and Mandrake, all celebrated for curative qualities. These, chemically united with the Iodides of Potassium and Iron, form a medicine of unsurpassed power, the most efficient of all remedies for scrofulous, mercurial and blood disorders.

By our processes the medicinal principles of the several ingredients are extracted in a manner which draws out and renders available their entire virtues, producing a highly concentrated extract, in which the various medicinal qualities are combined in that nice proportion necessary to give each its full healing and curative influence. Uniformly successful and certain in its remedial effects, **Ayer's Sarsaparilla** produces rapid and complete cures of Scrofula, Erysipelas, Salt Rheum, Tetter, Scald Head, Ring Worm, Sores, Boils, Humors, Pimples, Ulcers, Tumors, Eruptions, and all scrofulous diseases and conditions. For all diseases arising from the impurity or deficient vitality of the blood, or from mercurial poison, it is a powerful, safe and certain remedy. By its invigorating and purifying effects it always relieves and often cures Liver Complaints, Female Weaknesses and Irregularities, Rheumatism, Neuralgia, Jaundice, Dyspepsia, Emaciation and General Debility. It stimulates and enlivens the vital functions, promotes energy and strength, and infuses new life and vigor throughout the whole system. In renovating the blood it clears and quickens the intellect, and thus gives to both mind and body the power of long-sustained, arduous and successful effort. For the cure of the disorders, lassitude and debility peculiar to the Spring, it has proved to be the best remedy ever devised, neutralizing the poisons in the blood, and restoring the vigor of health.

When you are sick, the best medicine that can be obtained is none too good, and is the cheapest, whatever it costs. **Ayer's Sarsaparilla** is a medicine of such concentrated curative power that it is by far the most economical and reliable medicine that can be used, while it is entirely safe for patients of all ages. Physicians know its composition and prescribe it in their practice. It has been widely used for forty years, and has won the unqualified confidence of multitudes who pronounce it in the household **A Real Blessing.**

Prepared by **Dr. J. C. Ayer & Co., Lowell, Mass., U. S. A.**

Sold by all Druggists and Dealers in Medicine.

In every Home much sickness and suffering can be prevented by the discreet use of PARKER'S GINGER TONIC.

PARKER'S HAIR BALSAM.

An elegant dressing, much preferred to all similar articles on account of its exquisite perfume and superior cleanliness and purity. Containing only such ingredients as are beneficial to the scalp, the BALSAM Never Fails to Restore the Youthful Color & Beauty to Gray Hair.

Warranted to stop falling of the hair, to make it soft and silken, and to remove dandruff. Does not stain, not oily. Cures itching and humors.

Sold in large bottles at ONLY **FIFTY CENTS** AND $1,

PARKER'S GINGER TONIC.

The Best Cure for Coughs and Consumption, and all diseases arising from defective nutrition, impure blood and exhaustion. Every mother who once tries this excellent medicine in her family, will feel that she cannot afford to do without it. Asthma, Colds, Bronchitis, Indigestion, Skin Eruptions, Heart troubles, Female Complaints, Rheumatism, Chills, Malaria, Diarrhœa, Colic, Cramps, Kidney and Liver disorders are at times prevalent in every home, and there is no cure that compares with Parker's Ginger Tonic. It frequently saves life. It is your own fault if you suffer when you do not use the remedy that cures.

SOLD IN LARGE BOTTLES AT 50c. & $1.

I have been a great sufferer from a complication of Liver Complaint with other diseases for a number of years. Headache, Nervousness, Excruciating pains, sleeplessness kept me fairly wild day and night. I could obtain no relief from physicians, so in absolute despair I tried Parker's Ginger Tonic. It was simply wonderful in what a short space of time these symptoms disappeared. All the pain and weariness and melancholy have left me. I can't remember of ever feeling so well.
MRS. A. M. HOBBS, Chicago, Ill.

"For 25 years erysipelas broke out in blotches on my face. I could find no cure until I used Parker's Ginger Tonic two years ago. I am 65 years old and it has done me more good than any medicine I have ever taken.   ELIZABETH C. HARPER, Pickinsville, Ala.

HINDERCORNS.

Promptly removes all kinds of Corns, Bunions, Warts, Callouses, &c. Hinders their further growth. Stops all pain. Gives no trouble. Ensures comfort to the feet. Makes walking easy.

Don't suffer any longer from these painful excrescences, but remove them with HINDERCORNS. It cures when everything else fails.

PRICE 15 CENTS.

HISCOX & CO., 163 WILLIAM STREET, NEW YORK.

Sold at the Store Where you received This Card.

carried the manufacturer's name and address and pitched his particular brand of medicine. The cards are a detailed record of clothing, hair, and furnishing styles of the Victorian age. They document period copywriting style as well:

MISERABLE! MISERABLE! Yes, he looks miserable! He is BILIOUS, and biliousness, with its killing complaints— bad unnatural taste, loss of appetite, imperfect sleep, headache, fever, etc.—do not tend to make anyone happy or cheerful. But he wouldn't take HAGER'S CHILL AND AGUE SPECIFIC. O no! He doesn't believe in it. Perhaps, dear reader, you will never believe in it, either, unless you try it…. If you feel badly, try a

Top and left: Parker's Ginger Tonic. These young ladies represent the Victorian ideal of feminine beauty.

bottle of HAGER'S CHILL AND FEVER SPECIFIC, a reliable remedy for all malarial troubles, such as biliousness, Fever and Ague, Dumb Chills, &c.[42]

In modern times, advertisers shy away from topical or controversial subjects. Not so in the patent-medicine era — politicians, suffragettes, and immigrants were lampooned in newspaper ads and almanacs. Darwin's theory of evolution was satirized in trade cards for Merchant's Gargling Oil; Maxham's Combined Remedy had an illustration of New York's Boss Tweed exiting a jail; under a picture of black abolitionist William A. Douglas, a caption read, "Golly, is he going to take Sulphur Bitters for his

THE DATE of Penn's Treaty is in dispute, but it is universally admitted that AYER'S CHERRY PECTORAL prolongs and saves life, and therefore far exceeds in value anything Penn ever offered the natives in exchange for their lands. It rapidly cures Colds, Coughs, Sore Throat, Influenza, Quinsy, Laryngitis, Hoarseness, Bronchitis, Croup, Asthma, and Catarrh. It wonderfully increases the power and flexibility of the voice, strengthens weak lungs, allays pulmonary irritation, and affords the most effectual relief for **Whooping Cough** and **Consumption** in its advanced stages.

It should be noticed that the doses of AYER'S CHERRY PECTORAL consist of a limited number of *drops*, it being of great strength and curative power, making it more economical as a medicine than many other preparations. Its powerful uniform control over all diseases of the throat and lungs makes it the most reliable medicine that can be procured.

Full directions accompany each bottle.

PREPARED BY

Dr. J. C. AYER & CO., Lowell, Mass.

FOR SALE BY

Top and bottom: This card advertising Ayer's Cherry Pectoral combines a brand name with an historical event (Native Americans signing a treaty with William Penn). The back of the card touts the benefits of the medicine, which "far exceeds in value anything Penn ever offered the natives in exchange for their lands."

complexion?" After the Civil War, northern whites were greatly concerned about the influx of African Americans into the labor force. Racial anxiety was expressed openly and often in patent medicine advertising and ingrained stereotypes into the national consciousness.[43]

Readers were hammered with outlandish claims for cure-alls and insidious suggestions that lethal disease lurked in their unmedicated bodies. Anyone with the slightest hypochondriacal tendency was sure he or she was at death's door after seeing lists of symptoms in an unending flow of print ads. Sore muscles, headaches, constipation, or any combination thereof were described in agonizing detail. It was easy to convince readers that these were symptoms of a fatal disease. As one turn-of-the-century advertising executive opined, "I believe most ailing people get a morbid satisfaction from reading vivid descriptions of the symptoms of their sickness."[44] Ad-

vertisers and pitchmen had no compunctions about scaring consumers into a purchase. Ads and labels were full of symbols of death. Skulls and crossbones, tombstones, and the Grim Reaper admonished the frightened customer to look to his health and part with a dollar. Illustrators drew all manner of diseased organs, tapeworms, lesions, men keeling over from a heart attack, cancer victims with their flesh eaten away—nothing was too grisly. Consumers and sellers indulged in an orgy of morbid preoccupation.

If the fear of death didn't work, fear of humiliation was the next best tactic. Bad breath, it was suggested, could kill a friendship or budding romance. Baldness was a character flaw, and eczema would effectively destroy one's social life.[45] This ploy is still much in evidence today. Advertisers have even thought of new body odors to worry about (as if there weren't enough already). The makers of patent medicines invented the

Card for Beals Torrey Shoe reflects racial stereotypes of the day.

oldest advertising trick in the book—create a problem and then solve it.

Some advertisers went so far as to create and tout a product as a cure for society's ills. Popular-culture scholar Griel Marcus writes about Rexall's Americanitis Elixir:

> It's hard to know where to begin with the America depicted in the big broad poster. At the top, in the background, there's a spectacular mountain range, the Rockies crowned with a steeplelike peak and covered with snow down to their lowest foothills, which suddenly turn green and smooth, a sylvan glade. Emerging from a line of great oaks at the base of the hills is a long parade of men, women, boys and girls, all crossing a huge meadow and gathering at "The Fountain of Perpetual Youth." The fountain is made by an enormous bottle of Americanitis Elixir: "Especially Recommended for Nervous Disorders, Exhaustion, and All Troubles Arising from Americanitis." The picture all but screams with self-confidence, optimism and joy, with a celebration of the American small-town utopia generalized into its natural setting.[46]

The Elixir offers a cure for Americanitis but doesn't describe the ailment. On closer examination, the picture reveals some clues: The people don't look at each other or seem connected in any way. They appear both lifeless and restless. One of the children doesn't even look human. Marcus continues:

> Americanitis may have been a trademark, but the condition would have been recognized by everyone.... the writer George Beard, in his book, American Nervousness, traced its causes to industrialization, an unstable economy, "too much freedom of thought," "repression of turbulent emotions," overspecialization and above all, the pressure of time. Ameri-

canitis Elixir went on the market at a time when, to many, America itself was becoming unrecognizable. Between 1880 and 1910 the population of the country doubled, mostly because of immigration. Everywhere you went, there were people who didn't look like you, who didn't speak the same language: people who thought that they, too, were Americans. Just as you couldn't tell the disease from the cure, you couldn't always distinguish who belonged here from those who didn't.[47]

The Victorian age (1840–1900) has been called "the age of the womb" because women were valued primarily for their reproductive function. Ladies warmed to the theme of "female trouble," a phenomenon not unnoticed by copywriters: "Pendleton's Calisaya Tonic Bitters is used by the most delicate females," went one slogan.[48] Nostrum makers did not hold back in their appeals to women:

> INVALID LADIES THIS IS FOR YOU
> There are thousands of females in America who suffer untold miseries from chronic diseases of their sex. ...the physical changes that mark the three eras of womanhood (the maiden the wife and the mother,) have much to do with their sufferings, most of which is endured in silence, unknown by even the family physician and most intimate friends. To all such whose hollow cheeks, pale faces, sunken eyes and feeble footsteps indicate nervous and general debility bordering on consumption, we would earnestly recommend that grand system renovating tonic, BURDOCK BLOOD BITTERS....[49]

Mythological and historical figures were co-opted for the advertisers' purpose. There was a Minerva Pill for venereal disease, a Juno Pill for sterility, and Hercules sold multiple products. Ben

INVALID LADIES!
THIS IS FOR YOU.

There are thousands of females in America who suffer untold miseries from chronic diseasees common to their sex. This is due largely to the peculiar habits of life and fashion, and the improper training of girlhood. Then, too, the physical changes that mark the three eras of womanhood (the maiden the wife and the mother,) have much to do with their sufferings, most of which is endured in silence, unknown by even the family physician and most intimate friends. To all such whose hollow cheeks, pale faces, sunken eyes and feeble footsteps indicate nervous and general debility bordering on consumption, we would earnestly recommend that grand system renovating tonic,

BURDOCK BLOOD BITTERS,

It makes pure, healthy blood, and regulates all the organs to a proper action, cures constipation, liver and kidney complaint, female weakness, nervous and general debility, and all the distressing miseries from which two-thirds of the women of America are suffering. **All Invalid Ladies** should send for our **Special Circular** addressed to **Ladies Only,** which treats on a subject of vital importance.

Address FOSTER, MILBURN & CO., Buffalo, N. Y.

Hur was on hand to cure an ailing kidney, and Ponce de Leon's name was on a tonic for (what else?) youthful appearance.[50] Patriotic symbols such as the bald eagle and Uncle Sam proliferated. Another common device was a foreign association: There were Dr. Lin's Chinese Blood Pills, Turkish Wafers, Incomparable Algerine Medicine, Peruvian Syrup, Hungarian Balsam, and so on. It was the homegrown image of the indigenous American, however, that was most commonly exploited.[51] Further on, we will examine the wild-west type of medicine show.

Some newspaper editors attempted to weed out

Top and left: Card advertising Burdock Blood Bitters, a female tonic.

obvious scams. Obviously, no single medicine could cure poison ivy, cancer, and curvature of the spine. Nostrum advertising, however, was far too lucrative to turn down. One manufacturer spent $100,000 a year on print ads — significant money in 1850.[52] The only thing that's changed in more than 100 years is the quantity of proprietary medicines sold. Today, billions are spent each year on cold remedies that do not remedy, weight-loss products that do not affect weight, digestive cures that strip the intestines, and so on.[53]

All television did was to "get the pitchman off the streets and into our parlors," as a Federal Trade Commissioner remarked off the record.[54] Television advertising generates many more dollars by reaching many more customers than were available to the medicine show doctor, but the psychology of the pitch is essentially the same. The same FTC official also said:

> To the hard-sell spoken word was added visual impression, and proprietary manufacturers became inveterate users of the medium. Reaching back into the ancient days of patent medicine promotion, they revived symbols of evil from the devil's dark domain, and now the fiendish creatures wiggled. Spectators peered inside the body, watched limp intestines undulate with vigor when plied with laxatives, observed the exciting race from stomach to brain, harkened to white-coated actors impersonating doctors.[55]

It was the climate of ongoing egregious fraud that finally set doctors and savvy consumers against the medicine makers and advertisers. None of the proprietary manufacturers were ethical by modern standards, but the context in which they operated should be taken into account. This was, after all, the age of robber barons, stock manipulators, child labor, and exploitation of immigrants. Social Darwinism was the guiding principle in business. Money was the end that justified the means. At the turn of the century, anyone making enormous amounts of money was most likely conducting himself in a way that would now be considered unethical.

Advertising was effective as far as it went. In addition to printed material, however, manufacturers needed traveling agents. Salesmen not only got the product to outlying markets, but also formed relationships with the customers. Hordes of competing salesmen crisscrossed the country with creative sales pitches. Medicine pitchmen needed to establish a distinctive presence in order to build a loyal clientele. Some carried certificates signed by the "doctor" who made the medicine, but others, like their Yankee peddler colleagues, realized that medicines could be bought, repackaged, and sold as one's own.[56] Thus began the great American medicine show: From small-time operator to big-time entrepreneur, the important thing was to get the message and the product in front of the consumer.

4

Museums, Circuses, and the Wild, Wild West

Traveling medicine pitchmen knew that in order to sell, they first had to entertain. Circus routines, minstrel shows, vaudeville acts, and wild west revues appeared on medicine-show platforms. Popular entertainment in the nineteenth century was plentiful, and pitchmen made use of the various forms. Performers migrated easily from one type of show to another. For example, a circus performer might do a season with Barnum, find himself out of work, join a medicine show for a time, and then move on to a carnival or vaudeville company. At the turn of the century, popular entertainment appealed to both the wealthy and working classes, the native-born and the newly arrived. Show business mirrored the process of assimilation that was occurring in American society itself. This and the following two chapters outline the types of popular stage presentations that were featured by medicine pitchmen.

After the American Revolution, the lively arts were better tolerated, as long as they had a demonstrable redeeming quality. Plays were billed as "moral lectures," and theaters were dubbed "opera houses." Middle America clung to the model of "the immediately useful and the practical." Sensible people had no time for purely creative pursuits while there was a continent to subdue. Artists were thought to be hopelessly impractical, but could be countenanced if they justified themselves in financial terms. On the local level, the arts were seen as the province of women, and above all, prevailing standards of morality had to be respected.[1] Amateur theatricals were fine, but there was no niche in village economies for resident performers. All in all, it was better to leave performance to strangers.[2]

Traveling performers visited small-town America at their peril, however.

Carnival grounds and medicine show tents were often scenes of violence. Local thugs thought little of beating or killing "showfolk" for extra amusement. As Barnum noted in his memoir, "When I consider the kind of company into which for a number of years I was thrown I am astonished as well as grateful I was not utterly ruined."[3]

Proprietary Museums

Where could "respectable" folk go for wholesome entertainment? The proprietary museum, found in almost every city, was a venue for family fun. In the first two decades of the nineteenth century, museums were funded by philanthropists who viewed these institutions as agents of cultural and civic progress. The general public, however, was not at all concerned with cultural progress and stayed away from museums in droves. By 1840, due to insufficient ticket sales, showmen had taken over the museum business. The European model of high culture was abandoned, and museums came to be geared toward popular tastes. Proprietary museums contained human and animal freaks of nature, exotic live and stuffed animals, works of art, magicians, lantern shows, wax figures, fossils, and "moral lectures." *Museum* had become the name for any building containing a variety of exhibits and entertainment. Two-headed calves, dwarfs, fossils, and fine art were shown side by side without comment on their relative cultural or scientific importance. Proprietary museums were the perfect Jacksonian institution.[4]

Theater attendance was (and still is)

frowned upon in many fundamentalist and religious-conservative homes. Women who frequented saloons and theaters were suspected of immorality; women who actually worked in those places were presumed to be immoral. There is little evidence that actresses practiced prostitution, but prostitutes frequently solicited customers in and around theaters. Physical proximity between actresses and prostitutes tainted the reputation of the former.[5] In the Victorian age, "no matter how consummate the artist, preeminent the favorite, and modest the woman, the actress could not supersede the fact that she lived a public life and consented to be 'hired' for amusement by all who could command the price."[6] A museum, however, was a place where a single woman could go and not be mistaken for a harlot. For families too poor to buy theater tickets, museums were within financial reach; for immigrants, for whom the English language was a barrier, museum exhibits were comprehensible.[7] Proprietary museums united disparate segments of the population under the museum roof.

Of all the proprietary museums, none was more successful than Barnum's American Museum, which opened on New Year's Day, 1842. Situated on Ann Street in the Bowery, the museum was geographically and symbolically located at the crossroads of working-class and upper-crust New York. Barnum purchased the building and the collection from the estate of John Scudder. Although the five-story building was already filled to bursting at the time of its acquisition, Barnum purchased Charles Wilson Peale's popular collection of odd items and crammed that in, too. Peale's "cabinets of curiosities" contained a five-legged cow, a hairball found in a sow's belly, ancient coins, a tattooed head of a New Zealand chieftain, and numerous insects, skins, and skeletons. Barnum expanded the collection continuously. He even built the first aquarium in the United States, which housed a hapless white whale until its premature death.[8] One of his most celebrated attractions was a five-year-old boy named Charles Stratton, who was only twenty-five inches tall. In typical Barnum fashion, the boy was renamed General Tom Thumb. Stratton maintained a life-long association with Barnum. Two other little people, George Wash-ington Morrison McNutt and Lavinia Bump, also made their livelihood on display for Barnum. He orchestrated a love triangle among the three; when Lavinia declared her preference for the General, their marriage (which lasted twenty years) was attended by 2,000 spectators.[9]

Barnum knew that the key to the museum's success was constant promotion. "Advertising is like learning," Barnum remarked. "A little is a dangerous thing."[10] It was his intention, for the first year of the museum's operation, to spend *all* the profits on advertising. The money came in so quickly, however, that he was hard pressed to find ways to use it. A monument to humbug, the museum building itself was completely covered with "Barnumisms." Flags, banners, paintings of animals, gas lights that spelled *Barnum*, and an illuminated color wheel decorated the structure.[11] He hired a brass band to play on the sidewalk, carefully choosing the worst musicians he could find in the hope that their terrible playing would drive people inside.[12]

Barnum's critics accused him of "profit-driven fakery" and of misinforming people rather than enlightening them. Among actual exotic animals, treasures, dwarfs, and conjoined twins, he also displayed shameless frauds: The "Dog-Face Boy," for

Tom Thumb and Lavinia Bump.

example, was merely a person with excessive facial hair and no actual canine characteristics. But Barnum's admission price was affordable — "twenty-five cents, and no questions asked"— and his museum hours accommodated working people. Furthermore, in the 1860s, African Americans, who were excluded from almost all public amusements, were welcome in Barnum's museum. By the standard of the period, his American Museum was a "bastion of egalitarianism."[13] It was, says Bluford Adams, "a distillation of the very best, and the very worst, the proprietary museum had to offer."[14]

The Ann Street museum, Barnum's first and most successful, was dedicated to temperance, domesticity, Christianity, and money. It was a "non-stop celebration of trade," in which religion and commerce mingled. Barnum displayed posters that portrayed his other unrelated businesses, inviting vicarious participation in his enterprises. The hallways of the building were jammed with phrenologists, palm readers, medicine sellers, and magicians. Plays, or moral lectures, included such fare as *The Christian Martyrs, Joseph in Egypt, The Drunkard,* and *Uncle Tom's Cabin.* While the plays dramatized the rewards of morality and temperance, the curtains and cycloramas that framed them touted the benefits of alcoholic Yahoo Bitters, Horse Liniment, and Ready Relief.[15]

Barnum often turned the 3,000-

The Bearded Girl, another hirsute Barnum attraction.

seat "lecture room" over to ministers for church services. He promised to exclude "anything calculated to corrupt the mind or taint the juvenile imagination."[16] The working-class women in attendance were always addressed as "ladies," a subtle indication that Barnum, if not society in general, included them in the Victorian cult of domesticity.[17]

When the Ann Street Museum burned down in 1865, Barnum built a larger one uptown. He went into partnership with the Van Amburgh Menagerie Company, and the building became an indoor zoo that housed elephants, giraffes, and beluga whales. Before the creation of the Central Park Zoo in the late 1860s, the Museum was the best place to view animals.[18] After the second building burned down in 1868, Barnum got out of the museum business.[19] Barnum is best known for his circus, but he always considered himself to be a "museum man."[20]

In the mid–nineteenth century, New York's elite conducted an acrimonious public debate over the definition of *museum* with businessmen such as Barnum. Wealthy industrialists and socialites wanted their city to be known for world-class collections of fine art rather than tattooed women and shrunken heads. Jacksonian democracy was a popular ideal, but the debate over what constituted a museum reflected the actual class consciousness of the period. Barnum, who pandered to the masses with unprecedented commercial success, infuriated New York's high society and intelligentsia. An anonymous writer in *The Nation* called Barnum's customers "disreputable," "vicious and degraded," and the "worst and most corrupt classes of our people." As Adams notes, "there is no reason to believe that [The American] Museum's predominantly middle- and working-class visitors were any more vicious or corrupt than the gentry who published and read *The Nation*."[21] In fact, Barnum went to great lengths to ensure propriety at his establishment. Eventually, the Museum of Natural History and the Metropolitan Museum of Art, built in the 1860s, supplanted the proprietary museum — but arguably only because, by that time, Barnum's second American Museum had burned down.[22]

Dime and Anatomical Museums

Barnum's American Museums were the largest and most spectacular of their day. No other entrepreneur matched his showmanship and ability to capitalize constant expansion. However, many lesser businessmen made a good, if not princely, living on a lower rung of the museum ladder. The true significance of the American Museum in relation to medicine shows is its later devolution into the dime museum. Dime museums were store-front attractions that peaked in popularity around the turn of the twentieth century. Medicine show veterans often worked in dime museums, which they regarded as indoor venues in which to pitch a cure-all. Dime museums typically provided cheap entertainment, a penny arcade, and a curio hall where "human oddities" were on display. Small museums had theaters for thirty to fifty-minute shows featuring singers, dancers, and comics. Larger museums often had full-length plays. After the show, the announcement, or *blow-off*, "This way out!" cleared the auditorium for the next show, which commenced immediately. If the announcer's blow-off failed to get the patrons out of their seats, the management would resort to a "chaser," that is, presenting the same act two or three times in a row. Variety acts and lectures on "Baby Alice, the Midget Wonder" (she weighed a pound and a half), or the "The Three-Faced Songstress" (an optical illusion), worked equally well on an outdoor medicine platform or indoors in a museum. Like medicine shows, dime museums had a "professor" who lectured on the "one-of-a-kind" acts and unique human beings in the curio hall. Exuding authority and masking a lack of true erudition with bombast, the professor provided exegeses on the bearded lady or the bottled human embryos floating in formaldehyde.[23]

Some dime museums, known as "anatomical museums," were designed specifically as stationary medicine shows. Visitors to these halls of medical horror were lured inside with dramatic window dressing. The Reinhardt brothers' midwestern chain of anatomical museums, for example, had mechanical mannequins portraying a dying General Custer, complete with heaving chest wound. In St. Paul, Minnesota, their storefront was a spectacular jungle scene in which a hunter in a pith helmet was bitten repeatedly by a snake.[24] Another window portrayed doctors treating a syphilitic baby, which was more to the point. The New York Museum of Anatomy owed its success to its great number and variety of diseased body parts. "Here presented," the announcer would intone, "the numerous lesions, contagions, and disorders which infect all parts of this beautiful mechanism — maladies belonging to the skin, the muscles, the joints, the glands, and to all the internal viscera — every disease deranging the functions, corrupting the blood, decomposing the tissues, deforming the structure and defacing the beauty of the human form divine."[25]

Many museums had signs over the entrance reading, "For Men Only." The visitor, once drawn inside, might see a few caged birds and snakes, or perhaps a curvaceous naked female mannequin. Further along the exhibit, in a dim and hushed atmosphere, the true purpose of the establishment unfolded: Glass cases housed ghastly exhibits of diseased and necrotic organs and a variety of skin disorders. The ravages of the "secret vice"— masturbation — were brought home by a picture of a grinning, drooling idiot.[26] In the Victorian mind, disgust was allied with titillation, and exhibitors included waxwork examples of torture and sadism. The emphasis, however, was on the ravages of disease. Models of genitalia eaten up by syphilis or gonorrhea were a special draw. Standing close by was the "doctor," who would steer the terrified viewer into a private room for a consultation and inevitable medicine sale.[27]

The Circus

Museums benefited city dwellers, but small-town residents and farmers did not enjoy permanent exhibits and shows. Rural America, therefore, provided the bread and butter for many traveling performers. One of the first types of itinerant troupes in America was the circus. The first circuses in the New World appeared in Colonial days and were imported from England. They were mostly animal exhibitions, set up in tavern yards and other open spaces. Circus owners often left a trail of angry shell game losers and unpaid feed store owners. To offset bad feelings, they played up the educational aspect of the show, a relatively easy task at a time when there were no such things as zoos, and a non-indigenous creature was an oddity. Curious settlers were eager to see a caged lion or tiger. Records are scanty, but it is known that in the eighteenth century, some colonists were privileged to see at different times a lion, a camel, a polar bear, male and female orangutans, a sloth, a baboon, a tiger, a buffalo, a crocodile, and various birds and reptiles. Tropical beasts were a special favorite with a North American crowd.[28] For most spectators, "the circus was India, Arabia and the jungle."[29] According to one Iowa resident, "It was a compendium of biologic research but more important still, it brought to our ears the latest band pieces and taught us the most popular songs. It furnished us with jokes. It relieved our dullness. It gave us something to talk about."[30]

Hachaliah Bailey, a New York State farmer, bought his elephant, Bet, in 1808 and exhibited her with great success. Old Bet sold a lot of tickets and made her owner very rich until she was shot by an angry farmer in 1816. Bet's popularity started a menagerie mania among the farmers of Dutchess, Putnam, and Westchester counties. Exotic animals became cash cows all up and down the Eastern Seaboard.[31] Medicine pitchmen, with a practiced eye for a successful come-on, frequently used animals to draw crowds for their lectures. They didn't have full menageries as a rule, but one well-placed iguana could gather a street-corner audience quite nicely. The scale of the presentation was smaller, but the principle was the same: A strange-looking creature will draw a crowd.

A circus in the modern sense has no relationship to the chariot races of ancient Rome. Philip Astley's London circus in the 1700s was the first modern circus. It was an equestrian exhibition that included tightrope walking, acrobatics,

and clowning. A riding master named Faulks produced the first American exhibition like Astley's in 1771. Faulks performed his show at the Philadelphia jail for the benefit of the prisoners. According to the advertisement in the local newspaper, Faulks's tricks included standing on the saddle, riding three horses at one time, and playing the French horn while on horseback.[32]

John Bill Ricketts advertised a show for his Philadelphia riding academy in 1793. The show consisted of trick riding; on horseback Ricketts performed a hornpipe, somersaults, poses, and dismounting and remounting at a full gallop. It is known that George Washington himself attended that performance. The show was so successful that Ricketts took it on the road to New York, Boston, and Charleston. He later built an amphitheater in Philadelphia and added clown acts and pantomimes to his show. The amphitheater burned down in 1799. (Although the livestock was saved, Ricketts was despondent. His choice to return to England was an unfortunate one — his ship sank, and all were drowned.)[33]

At the beginning of the nineteenth century, the three primary types of traveling entertainment were the menagerie, the circus, and a combination of the two.[34] Acrobatic and equestrian troupes often joined menageries. Troupes hit the road in every possible combination, sometimes adding a clown or two.[35] Indeed, early circuses even put on melodramas in which horses were featured players.[36]

Upon their introduction to North America, circuses were immediately successful. At their height, there were as many as twenty-six companies on tour.[37] Many circus troupes traveled by water, on steamers or flatboats.[38] The Great Lakes, the Ohio River, and the Mississippi River provided access to thousands of towns and plantations. Small-town audiences especially loved the pageantry.

Medicine shows of all sizes took their cue from the circus. The practice of ballyhoo—attracting a crowd with animals, a street parade, or a band—came directly from the circus, as did spangly costumes, a bombastic announcing style, and a penchant for sideshow grotesquerie.

Naturally, it was Barnum who perfected these crowd-getting techniques. Barnum came out of retirement at age sixty to try his hand at the circus business. He joined William Cameron Coup and Dan Castello, and soon, like the American Museum, their circus got bigger and more popular. In 1874 he bought out his partners and joined James Bailey to create The Greatest Show on Earth. Barnum was in his element. All the advertising tricks he invented for his museum worked beautifully to promote his circus: Parades, bands, handbills, and posters heightened the expectations of his audiences. His best known ballyhoo was Jumbo, a docile African bull elephant, purchased from the London Museum. Twelve feet high at the shoulder and weighing six tons, Jumbo toured the United States and be-

came synonymous with Barnum and the circus. In three and a half years, Jumbo earned $1.75 million, was ridden by three million children, and ate a "mountain" of peanuts. When Jumbo was struck and killed by a train on September 15, 1885, Barnum had the beast's hide mounted on a wooden frame and put on display in a menagerie. Even in death, Jumbo was a hit. Six years later, on April 7, 1891, Barnum himself made his final exit. Barnum did not invent the circus, but he invested it with a high level of excitement that audiences have come to expect.[39]

There were other notable circus

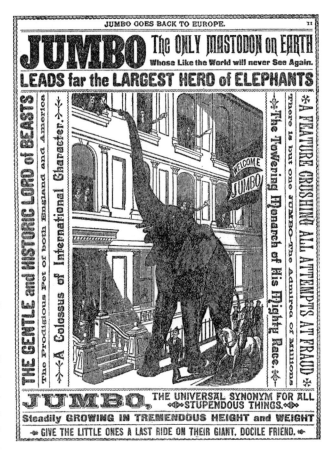

A circus pamphlet trumpets the name of Jumbo.

companies, such as Sells-Floto and John Robinson's Big Ten Shows, but only the Ringling Brothers matched Barnum for flair and innovation. Inspired by a Mississippi River showboat, the five Ringling brothers started with a variety show in Baraboo, Wisconsin, in 1882. The Ringlings prided themselves on a show that was both refined and funny. Designed to appeal to rich, poor, young, and old, the show had comedy routines, dramatic sketches, juggling, and instrument solos. For years, the brothers struggled with small ticket receipts, bad weather, and other obstacles, but they learned their trade. By 1887, the Ringling Brothers circus had sixty horses, custom-made wagons and chariots, and a menagerie. Two years later, their show took up eighteen railroad cars.[40]

Technical Improvements

The transcontinental railroad was completed in 1869. That accomplishment enabled large companies of performers, animals, and equipment to tour the west coast. Circus people were among the first to use the railroads extensively. By 1885, more than fifty circuses were on the rails. Medicine, vaudeville, and wild west shows soon followed suit.[41]

Medicine shows and other tent entertainments also benefited from improvements in lighting systems pioneered by the circus. The combination of the internal combustion engine and gas lighting resulted in a gas vapor lamp that was used by Barnum and Bailey and many other companies.[42]

Wild West Shows

Another traveling entertainment full of pageantry and livestock was the wild west show, invented by William F. (Buffalo Bill) Cody in 1883. Like Astley's circus a century earlier, Cody's exhibitions relied on spectacular feats of horsemanship and took place in roofless canvas enclosures. (Roofed enclosures would have been shredded by gunfire.)

Although there were similarities between Astley's and Cody's inventions, the wild west show was something that could only have sprung from American soil. Russell Nye writes, "The origins of the Wild West Show, completely and uniquely an American product, had nothing to do with the circus. It began and ended with one man, William F. 'Buffalo Bill' Cody, who dominated it while it existed."[43]

Although Native Americans had been put on display in east coast cities as early as 1820, credit for the germination of a wild west show goes to Barnum. In 1843, four decades before Cody's debut, Barnum brought a herd of buffalo to Hoboken, New Jersey, and billed the event as "The Grand Buffalo Hunt, Free of Charge." The herd, a bunch of scrawny calves, was to be roped and shot by a great buffalo hunter. The marksman in question was the buffaloes' former owner, a man named Fitzhugh, who was billed inexplicably as "Mr. C.D. French." At the first rifle shot, the herd panicked and scattered into the New Jersey swamp, to the great amusement of the crowd. According to Barnum, the spectators went home happy, having had a good laugh free of charge.[44]

Barnum contemplated producing a

Buffalo Bill Cody.

more extravagant wild west show, noting that anyone who did would make a "sure fortune." His concept was to hire a hundred Native American families and display them around the United States and Europe: "In all the glory of paint and feathers, beads and bright blankets, riding on their ponies, followed by tame buffaloes, elks and antelopes; then an exhibition on a lot large enough to admit of a display of all the Indian games and dances, their methods of hunting, their style of cooking, living, etc."[45]

That Barnum never acted on his vision was probably due to his hostility toward Native Americans. Barnum made his peace with immigrants and African Americans, but he never warmed to Native Americans, even though there were at least a hundred of them in his employ at the American Museum. Barnum had hired them to demonstrate war dances and other customs of Indian life. "Damn Indians *anyhow*," Barnum wrote. "They are a lazy, shiftless set of brutes — though they will *draw*. The lazy devils want to be *lying down* all the time," Barnum fumed, "and as it looks so bad for them to be lying about the Museum, I have them stretched out in the workshop all day, some of them occasionally strolling about the Museum."[46] When a western delegation of Native Americans traveled to Washington to visit "the great white father," Barnum invited them to New York to appear at the museum. Putting a paternal arm around Chief Yellow Bear's shoulder, Barnum introduced him to the crowd as "the meanest, black-hearted rascal that lives in the West," and as a "lying, thieving, treacherous, murderous monster," who would kill him if he knew what was being said. The translator

eventually told the chief, and the offended delegation departed for home.[47]

It was left to Cody, many years later, to realize the wild west show as a full-blown production. Cody came along at the right time; by 1880, the cattle business had changed. Cowboys no longer took herds on long drives. Ranch land was fenced, and work was seasonal. Cowboys, who had previously held contests of skill at the end of long drives, were eager to continue the custom in exchange for a paycheck. For a cowboy, work on horseback beat anything on foot.[48] Furthermore, in a culture where most people still rode horses and owned guns, trick riding and shooting were certain to be popular. Cody was the man to get things organized.

Cody, a natural showman, was also a real western hero. An army scout and Pony Express rider, he also had a decade of theatrical experience before he turned to producing. He got his start in a play called *Scouts of the Prairie*, a show that included "a temperance lecture, a lasso exhibition, a prairie fire, a lovely Indian princess (played by an Italian girl from Chicago), and a knife fight with ten Indians."[49] The play and Cody were a huge success.

In the early summer of 1882, he went home to North Platte, Nebraska. Outraged that there were no plans for a Fourth of July celebration, he complained to the city fathers, who "volunteered" him on the spot. He was hired to coordinate the cowboy attractions for the "Old Glory Blowout" for the summer of 1883. Immediately, Cody began to manifest his impressive managerial ability.[50] For the better part of a year, he accumulated personnel and livestock.

Cody was a stickler for authenticity. The team of mules that pulled the Deadwood coach in the first dress rehearsal was wild and inexperienced. At the opening war whoop and gunshot, the mules bolted around the track, causing great discomfort to the passengers — the mayor and councilmen of Colville, Nebraska. After that, Cody agreed to less authenticity and more illusion.[51] On May 17, 1883, the "Wild West, Rocky Mountain and Prairie Exhibition" opened to enthusiastic crowds. The events included roping, riding, and bronco breaking. Over 1,000 contestants competed for prizes. The event marked the beginning of both the wild west show and the rodeo.[52]

Thousands of spectators were drawn to North Platte. Cody, always alert to a business opportunity, saw the potential for his new entertainment. He took the show on tour, traveling eastward and always performing in the afternoon to make use of daylight.[53] The troupe was a great success wherever they played. The show, which eventually made its way to Coney Island, featured a shoot-out between scouts and Indians, an attack on a mail coach, rodeo competitions, and trick shooting.[54] Russell Nye says of Cody and his creation:

> The Wild West show was an instant national mania. Cody's show, which combined elements of the parade, the circus, the stage spectacular, the carnival and the melodrama, coincided exactly with current popular interest in the romantic West, and could hardly have been better qualified to appeal to the great American public. Nor was it a fake. Cody hired real cowboys, real Indians, and real marksmen. For that matter, he had been a Pony Express rider at thirteen, stagecoach driver, buffalo hunter, prospector, Union Army soldier, scout for Crook, Sheridan, Custer and Miles, and he also held the Congressional Medal of Honor. Buffalo Bill was the genuine article.[55]

Cody was a gentleman who treated his human and animal performers with respect and fairness. A complaint of animal cruelty against Cody was investigated by Henry Bergh, founder of the American Society for the Prevention of Cruelty to Animals (ASPCA). Bergh was not only delighted by the show, he was also impressed with the good condition of the animals. Cody knew it made good business sense to care for his livestock: An unhealthy horse not only detracts from the spectacle but can't perform properly.[56]

Cody's show grew to enormous proportions, both in size and stature. One Chicago performance drew 41,448 spectators — a sizable crowd in any year.[57] He was a sensation in Europe, where his Deadwood coach carried no less than the kings of Denmark, Greece, Belgium, and Saxony, and the Prince of Wales. The prince, an experienced poker player, remarked, "Colonel, you never held four kings like these before."

"I've held four kings," Cody answered, "but four kings and the Prince of Wales makes a royal flush, such as no man has ever held before."[58]

His show also included a native dignitary: Sitting Bull toured with Cody's show in the summer of 1885. Some people in the crowd threw money at the chief, while others shouted "Custer Killer!"[59]

A number of performers made their mark in Cody's show. Captain Adam H.

Bogardus, the "Champion Pigeon Shot of America," has the distinction of eliminating the use of real pigeons in shooting exhibitions. Passenger pigeons were lured to a trap by another bird tethered to a stool — the stool pigeon. Bogardus deplored killing real birds and popularized the use of clay pigeons; but not, unfortunately, before the passenger pigeon was shot into extinction.

The most famous of Cody's performers was the legendary Annie Oakley. "Little Sure Shot," as she was called by her friend Chief Sitting Bull, started her career shooting game for a Cincinnati hotel. When marksman Frank Butler arrived and issued his usual challenge for a shooting contest, Annie took him up on it — and won. Frank and Annie married, created an act, and applied to Cody for a job. When Cody saw Annie shoot, he hired her instantly. Frank happily took a supporting role as her manager. Audiences adored Annie. Press agent Dexter Fellows describes her appeal:

> She was a consummate actress, with a personality that made itself felt as soon as she entered the arena. ... Her entrance was always a very pretty one. She never walked. She tripped in, bowing, waving and wafting kisses. Her first few shots brought forth a few screams from the women, but they were soon lost in round after round of applause. It was she who set the audience at ease and prepared for the continuous crack of firearms which followed.[60]

Annie Oakley, more familiarly known as "LITTLE SURE SHOT"

Annie Oakley.

Annie shot different makes of guns in different calibers. She shot from horseback, on foot, and while riding a bicycle. Her success was not without obstacles, however. She said, "When I began shooting, it was considered almost shameful for a woman to shoot. That was a man's work, you see. It was uphill work, for when I began there was a prejudice to live down." Live it down she did. Annie's expertise both brought people to the box office and symbolized women's equality with men.[61]

Buffalo Bill's friend Wild Bill Hickok also performed in the show. Hickok had proved his *bona fides* as "a bad man to fool with," and he had the business sense to enlarge and promote his own image. "Wild Bill helped create his own legend by combining a certain amount of pose with a sense of his own mission."[62]

Cody had many imitators, but no equals. The western movies took up where he left off, but he originated the romantic vision of the west that has become a part of our national consciousness and cultural memory. Before Cody, cowboys were thought to be little more than criminals on horseback. In 1881, President Chester A. Arthur referred to cowboys as "armed desperadoes," who were a "menace to the peace." Cody turned cowboys into heroes in the popular imagination. No one was more influential in creating the modern image of the western frontier.[63] Cody also invented the notion of *cowboys and Indians*. The Jacksonian image of the brave frontiersman fighting Indians on foot had lost its appeal. The image of fighting Indians on horseback, on the other hand, has endured for more than a century.[64] The folklore of the wild west surfaced in medicine shows, movies, and popular fiction. Buffalo Bill Cody, "with flowing white hair, fringed buckskin jacket, and broadbrimmed hat held aloft," personified the myth.[65] Old and in poor health, he put on his last performance in 1916.

Indian Medicine Shows

Buffalo Bill's wild west exhibitions paved the way for the success of Native American medicine shows. In the 1880s, white Americans were fascinated by indigenous North Americans. As the industrial age dawned, there was a heightened regard (in the abstract, if not in actual practice) for the people who had come to symbolize unity with nature. Native American cures had already been adopted by white folks, and books of herbal recipes abounded. There were *The Indian Doctor's Dispensatory* and *The Indian Guide to Health*, to name only two. Dime museums frequently provided safe, sanitized exhibitions of native life and customs. Self-appointed healers, such as herbalist John Derringer (known as Indian John), advertised healings according to Indian methods.[66] Sincere health practitioners as well as hucksters used the repute of Native Americans to drum up business. Enter John Healy and Charles Bigelow, owners of the most successful Indian medicine shows ever produced.

John Healy was at different times a Union army drummer boy, minstrel, and salesman of a cure-all called King of Pain. In the fall of 1879 he met an Indian-style medicine salesman named Charles Bigelow. Bigelow was a country boy from Bee County, Texas, who had traded farm life for medicine hustling. He grew his hair to shoulder length, donned a sombrero, learned some Indian lore, and renamed himself "Texas Charlie." For several months in 1873 Bigelow sold herbs on the streets of Baltimore and shared a two-room flat with seven other pitchmen. In 1879 Healy hired Bigelow to sell liver pads, which proved to be an advantageous pairing for both of them — the two men were born to be partners. Two years later, in a

Philadelphia hotel, Healy had the idea to create and market Kickapoo Indian Oil.[67] Healy had no connection to the Kickapoo tribe, but was so amused by the name that he adopted it for his own use. Nevada Ned Oliver, a colleague of Healy's, said that "his plan was to hire a few Indians, rent a storeroom and have the medicine simmering like a witches' brew in a great iron pot inside a tepee. The brew of roots, herbs and barks, refined from a formula handed down through the generations, was to be ladled out to the public, who would provide their own bottles."[68]

The idea was rejected as impractical, and ultimately it was decided that they would present themselves as agents for the Kickapoo tribe, sell prebottled medicine, and have the vat and a few Indians in the background for effect. Their secret remedies were standard patent-medicine fare prepared by an established drug firm, but embellished by Healy and Bigelow with names like Kickapoo Buffalo Salve, Kickapoo Indian Worm Killer, and Sagwa. The best-selling Sagwa (the name was made up) was promoted as a cure for dyspepsia and rheumatism, though in reality it functioned as a laxative.[69] The formulas were always shrouded in mystery — supposedly only Kickapoo medicine men knew the ingredients. According to the company literature, these noble medicine men deigned to leave the reservation only for the benefit of suffering mankind. The formulas were said to contain an ingredient so magical that it defied chemical analysis. (Although an unhappy competitor claimed that the principal ingredients of Indian Sagwa were stale beer and aloes.)[70]

Healy and Bigelow started the Kickapoo business in a Providence hotel storeroom and then moved to Boston, where they pitched a tent in front of the train station and put on a show. They operated out of their Boston tent from 1881 to 1884. When they moved to New York in 1885, they took the show indoors, and their popularity grew. In 1887 they moved to New Haven, Connecticut, and created their headquarters, or "principal wigwam."[71]

The New Haven warehouse, or "Main Winter Quarters of the Kickapoo Indians" was "part factory, part dormitory, part dime museum, and part craft shop."[72] In addition to serving as the company's business headquarters, it was a showplace in which "the uncultured sons of the plain" displayed themselves for a fee. Tents were pitched inside the building in a bizarre attempt to re-create Native American life on the prairie. A company pamphlet stated without a trace of self-consciousness that "if one will but shut one's eyes to the fact that there is a roof between himself and heaven, there is little or nothing left to the imagination."[73] Apparently poor housekeeping stood in for real anthropological detail:

> The clothing and food supplies of the band are scattered about with that unstudied elegance of disorder which, as the initiated are well aware, forms a great attraction to the free and easy red and pale faces, constituting the grandest charm of life away from the trammels of civilization.[74]

Indian knickknacks were for sale in the gift shop, and visitors were also allowed a glimpse of Healy and Bigelow's private offices, which were festooned with animal skins and Indian artifacts — each one certified authentic by the proprietors.[75]

Healy and Bigelow were masters of image and promotion. As devotees of the great Barnum, they followed many of his practices, such as decorating every inch of the building and adopting a mascot. Unlike Jumbo, the Kickapoo mascot required no upkeep — she was fictional. Her name was Little Bright Eyes, an Indian princess who appeared in the company's literature. Healy and Bigelow played the exotica card for all it was worth, publishing countless ads, pamphlets, and magazines built around the romantic Indian who was in perfect harmony with the environment, never got an illness he couldn't cure, and was the physical and spiritual superior of the white man.

The Kickapoo advertising department churned out such titles as *The Indian Illustrated Magazine, Life and Scenes Among the Kickapoo Indians*, and *The Kickapoo Indian Dream Book*. Medicine pamphlets had been in circulation since the 1840s, but Kickapoo booklets cost little or nothing. Healy and Bigelow possessed an innate understanding of the reciprocity rule: Recipients of giveaways feel that a debt has been incurred that must be repaid. Free samples not only introduce potential customers to a product but generate purchases based on the unconscious desire to repay the debt.[76] The publications contained a mix of medical advice, stories, jokes, general information, and of course, ads for Kickapoo products. Kickapoo "literature" was designed to appeal to Victorian sensibilities; temperance and moderation were promoted with verses like these:

I am Chief of the Kickapoo Indian tribe
And I am strong as a brave can be,
Not brandy, nor whiskey do I imbibe,
Nor the Chinaman's poisonous tea.

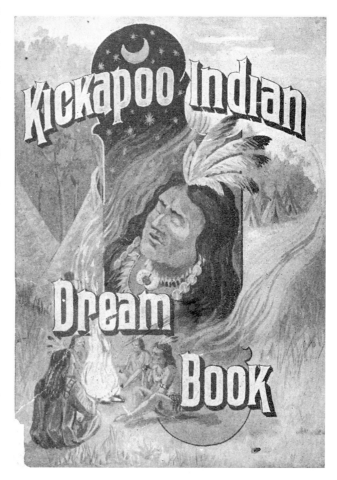

Kickapoo Dream Book.

But Indian Sagwa do I take,
For it's good for man at least.
It cures the body of many an ache,
And stomach for many a feast.[77]

Most publications were meant to be seen by every member of the family. However, in order not to offend the head of the house or alarm the children, women could send for a special pamphlet about women's complaints prepared by Little Bright Eyes herself. The prose in the Kickapoo pamphlets was decidedly purple: "Horrible to behold, dreadful to relate!" Many of the original pieces were written by Nevada Ned Oliver, author of such adventure tales such as *Mexican Bill, the Cowboy Detective* and *King of Gold: The Mystery of the Lost Mine.* Healy and Bigelow even got Buffalo Bill to endorse their products. He was quoted in ads as saying "An Indian would as soon be without his horse, gun, or blanket as without Sagwa." (Not one to let a business opportunity pass, Buffalo Bill "partnerized" with one of his drinking buddies, Dr. David Franklin Powell, a.k.a. White Beaver. They marketed their own nostrum, Cough Cream, from their firm in La Crosse, Wisconsin. Powell parlayed his retail success into four terms as the mayor of Racine.)[78]

Healy and Bigelow's public relations *tour de force* was the invention of the Sagwa legend, a fiction that was repeated endlessly and turned Charles Bigelow into a western hero. The tale describes how Texas Charlie, then a government scout, fell ill in the wilderness, lay at death's door, and was saved by the kind intervention of an Indian chief who just happened to have some Indian Sagwa. This "snatched from the jaws of death" theme was used ad infinitum.[79]

The first shows were primitive interactive affairs in which spectators could wander around an Indian encampment and get a close look at the noble savages in their natural setting — or as natural as you could get in a warehouse or vacant lot. The events were promoted as living history books, and spectators were entertained with the sight of Indians mixing medicine (supposedly the kind that was for sale) and meandering about the camp in a picturesque way.

Healy and Bigelow's operation grew rapidly, and soon there were many show units. At one point, they had 800 Native Americans in their employ. Performers were hired from the Iroquois tribe or recruited with the help of a Bureau of Indian Affairs agent, who supplied 200 men at a time, right off the reservation. Gordon Lillie, whose stage name was "Pawnee Bill," had worked with Buffalo Bill Cody and hired away a troupe of Native Americans from Cody for Healy and Bigelow. In a pinch, white men in makeup stood in for Indians; at least two Irishmen were known to have impersonated Indians in the Kickapoo shows. It was advertised that the company's white "medicine men" were real Indian fighters, perhaps a subtle hint that the hordes of natives on view could be kept under control.

As time went on, the shows became more presentational. Texas Charlie directed a unit that billed "Indian Medicine Men, Indian War Dancing, Indian Marriage Ceremonies, Indians Making Medicine, Indian Scenery, Indian Songs, Indian Curiosities," and even an "Indian Lecture." One scene depicted blood thirsty natives attacking a wagon train

⊕ 967. Take : WHITE : BEAVER'S : COUGH : CREAM.

DO YOU COUGH?   **DON'T DELAY!**

TAKE

White Beaver's

COUGH ✢ CREAM,

THE BEST COUGH CURE.

It will cure your COUGHS and COLDS. It will cure SORE THROAT and TICKLING IN THE THROAT. It will cure PAINS IN THE CHEST. It will cure INFLUENZA and BRONCHITIS, and all deseases pertaining to the LUNGS.

YOU WILL SEE THE EXCELLENT EFFECT, AFTER TAKING THE FIRST DOSE.

LARGE BOTTLES 50 CENTS.

MACHIAS, ME., Oct. 19, '90.

T. H. SPENCE, La Crosse, Wis.

DEAR SIR :—Yours received. I will send to Portland hereafter for White Beaver's Cough Cream. I consider it the Best Cough Medicine in the Country, and cannot praise it enough for what it has done for me. I consider it my duty to tell people about it whenever opportunity offers. You may sign my name to any testimonial you may see fit to print.

Respectfully yours,

W. G. SMITH.

———

N. F. WETMORE, M. D., of North Freedom, Wis., says, in a letter to White Beaver : "Your Cough Cream gives excellent satisfaction".

- SOLD BY -

and slaughtering all the white settlers; another showed the same warriors concocting medicine for the benefit of mankind. The theatrical dichotomy reflected white Americans' ambivalence toward indigenous people. Ultimately, however, it was all taken as good clean fun.[80]

Nevada Ned Oliver (who never set foot in Nevada) directed a unit consisting of six Indians and some vaudeville performers who did everything to promote, set up, and tear down the show. Nevada Ned started his show with his six Indians seated in a semicircle. He said,

Top and left: Card advertising White Beaver's Cough Cream.

The show customarily began with the introduction of each of the Indians by name, together with some personal history. The stage setting was simple — an open platform with an Indian panorama in oils as a backdrop. Five of the six would grunt acknowledgments; the sixth would make an impassioned speech in Kickapoo, interpreted by me; all made authentic by my scout habiliments and air of dignity.... It was a most edifying oration as I translated it. What the brave actually said, I never knew, but I had reason to fear it was not the noble discourse of my translation, for even the poker faces of his fellow savages were sometimes convulsed.[81]

After the introductions, the Native Americans whooped, the musicians played, and Nevada Ned sold medicine. Then came the vaudeville acts, with interruptions for more medicine sales.[82] At one point, he had a show with twenty-five Indians, two brass bands and 110 carnival workers. To leave no exotic stone unturned, he also had two Syrians impersonate Hindu priests.

Nevada Ned Oliver was a natural in the business, with his long hair and fringed jacket studded with paste diamonds. With his well-honed instinct for promotion, he was a show all by himself. He said,

In 1886, I had added ten-dollar gold pieces as buttons on my velvet and corduroy jacket, five-dollar gold coins as buttons on my fancy vests, three-dollar gold pieces as cufflinks. Around my neck, I wore 3,000 dollars worth of real diamonds and two gold-mounted mother-of-pearl .44s. My moustache was long and prettily waxed to points, my clothes foppish in the extreme. In such fashion I liked to stroll up Broadway or through the markets in Washington and Fulton Streets, followed by boot-blacks, newsboys and messengers, who could not decide whether to hoot or cheer.[83]

Healy and Bigelow let him alone to run his unit. Ned understood the appeal of the show very well, writing in 1929, "Now that the redskin no longer stood in the white man's way, he became a figure of romance. Fiction discovered him anew, added the cowboy, the gold camp and the desert, and the stage was set for the showmen."[84] Nevada Ned specialized in a catarrh remedy that contained menthol, sugar, milk, and cocaine. He sampled the merchandise too many times and became an addict, but his creativity never failed him. Whenever he was unable to run a Kickapoo unit, he wrote crime fiction.

More units added vaudeville turns, and before long, the Healy and Bigelow shows were a mixture of soft shoe, chalk talks, Irish and blackface comedy, acrobatics, and afterpieces. For extended runs in one place, the fare was changed nightly, and the town was papered with flyers advertising each evening's bill. Some of the acts that were known to play the Healy and Bigelow shows were "Professor Harry M. Parker and his New Mastadon [sic] Dog Circus," "The Skatorial Songsters," and "Doris' Interocean Circus." Balloon ascensions and fireworks filled out the program.[85] No one seemed to mind the lack of thematic consistency, least of all Healy and Bigelow, who sold up to $4,000 worth of Sagwa and Kickapoo Oil every week.[86]

A small Kickapoo unit consisted of a wagon, an agent, three Indian performers, and three vaudevillians. The very smallest played from the back of a wagon, a tabletop, or even a pile of cardboard boxes.[87] The large troupes traveled by train, and the sight of dozens of Indians disembarking and filing down Main Street was often all the promotion they needed.[88] Large companies had raised platforms with canvas siding and curtains stretched across a wire. Some units carried a roofed tent that could accommodate as many as 500 spectators. Gasoline torches or calcium lighting illuminated the show. The show area might be enclosed by a roofless tent or just a rope. Spectators stood or sat on the ground or on plank benches when available.[89] A standard-sized company had ten to twenty Indians and six tepees. The manager had a separate tent labeled "Indian Agent," and there was always the consultation tent, where "examinations" were conducted and large quantities of Kickapoo products prescribed. Performers were required to be in at least two acts and the afterpiece and to double as stagehands and handbill distributors.[90] One Wisconsin resident recalls his naive wonder at the sight of a dozen or more roustabouts who set up tents by day, vanished at night, and Indians who were visible at night and gone during the day.[91] In the winter, units performed in local opera houses or meeting halls.[92] The shows did very well for at least a dozen years. By 1888, there were thirty-one Healy and Bigelow units working out of Chicago and probably a hundred more in the rest of the United States and Canada.[93] Some units even toured Europe. Show-business insiders called them "the Kicks."[94] Everywhere they went, the Kicks stayed at least a week and behaved like model citizens to counteract medicine shows' ne'er-do-well image.

The peripatetic Healy tired of the business and sold his share in the 1890s. He had his eye on a new frontier that was wide open for a hustle — Australia. Texas Charlie stayed with the business until 1912. In that year he sold it to a buyer who shut down the tours two years later. The medicine they purveyed was later parodied in Al Capp's popular comic strip, *L'il Abner*, which made frequent reference to "Kickapoo Joy Juice."[95]

Accept No Substitutes

Many pitchmen copied Healy and Bigelow's style, but no one ever equaled their success. Some competitors had the nerve to call their show Kickapoo, and others used names like "Agawa" or "Sagwah" to capitalize on the success of Sagwa. The real Kickapoo units provided good entertainment and mostly harmless remedies (when used in moderation). Imitators sold their own mixtures and often had no talent for performing. The fake Kickapoos "burned the lot" by the time they were through, meaning they dared not show their faces again in a town they had swindled. Healy and Bigelow had to do a lot of advertising to thwart impostors. In promotional literature with the headline "Caution to the Public," readers were warned about low-quality preparations made by "Parties Without Principle or Honor."[96]

The imitators used all the same production elements as Healy and Bigelow, but not as artfully. Countless small-time operators donned buckskin jackets or fake diamonds in the manner of Nevada Ned. One Indian-show pitchman had his geography confused. He

Promotional cookbook for Dr. Morse's Indian Root Pills.

entered as Dr. Punja, the Hindoo, to pitch his version of Sagwa among his cast of ersatz Native Americans.[97] A pitchman who called himself Captain Jim lifted the Sagwa legend, substituted his own name for Texas Charlie, and used a different name for Kickapoo. He was hardly alone. The basic Sagwa legend was constantly in use.[98]

A minor variation on the theme was used by a Doc Porter in his unauthorized Kickapoo Medicine Show. One of his performers, William D. Naylor, recalls that part of the spiel was recounting that Doc's great-great-grandfather was rewarded by a chief with the "secret" healing recipe:

When my great-great grandfather saved the life of the Chief Medicine Man of the Kickapoo tribe, the "Bounding Cougar," that great Chief showed his gratitude by giving my noble pioneer ancestor their marvelous formulas and he bade them go forth and give his White Brethren the blessings the Great Manitou had bestowed upon his Red Children.[99]

Doc's description of the symptoms his remedies were supposed to cure "were enough to make anybody shiver." Naylor continues:

Why, I used to listen to Doc's horror stories of diseases till I'd get to feeling the symptoms myself! Doc was a foxy old bird and I guess he wasn't too far off base when he said, "Most diseases people get are just imagination, anyhow!" Doc was sincere in believing that the stuff he mixed up out of wild cherry bark, senna leaves, slippery elm bark, sassafras roots, and other "Indian herbs"—which he fortified with about sixty percent of good raw whiskey—were genuinely beneficial medicines and that he was a human benefactor. He used to say, "It ain't what anybody knows, but what they *think* they know for certain that counts, and if people buy Kickapoo Indian Medicine and think it'll cure them, it's darn near sure to cure them. And so they haven't been cheated!"[100]

Doc Porter wore a "Prince Albert coat, silk hat and double-breasted watch chain with a buck-eye set in gold bands … he looked and could act like a combination Bishop, Senator and Supreme Court judge all rolled into one. The natives in those small backwoods towns never had a chance with him."[101]

Naylor joined Doc Porter's show when he was nineteen and always performed in blackface, singing such songs as "Mourner, You Shall Be Free," and "After the Ball." The show traveled in wagons that doubled as open-air stages. Illumination was provided by flickering gasoline torches. Wandering through the backwoods of New York, New Jersey, Pennsylvania, and Virginia, the troupe made a practice of visiting towns that were too small for railroad depots. They provided the only entertainment some people had from year to year. Naylor reminisces, "One thing I'm sure of is that our old Medicine Show gave a lot of people who otherwise didn't have very much entertainment, a chance to see and hear something different and be amused."[102]

Arizona Bill was an Indian medicine showman whose Welsh origins and British accent did nothing to damage his credibility. Billing himself as "The Benefactor of Mankind," he wore fringed buckskins and long hair in the manner of an Indian scout. He told a story about being stolen by Indians as an infant and raised in their midst, all the while learning their miraculous herbal cures. His specialty was Rattlesnake Oil, a liniment that when rubbed on sore muscles would enable the most decrepit Indian warrior to keep on fighting. His show was in two parts, with pitches in the intermission; all the actors doubled as musicians. It was standard fare: bird imitations played on a violin, songs like "I'll Be with You When the Roses Bloom Again" and "Break the News to Mother." A husband-and-wife team ended the first act with a parody of a bullfight. At the selling point of Arizona Bill's pitch, the actors circulated throughout the crowd with bottles, shouting, "Sold out again, Doctor!"[103]

There was a Dr. Lamereaux, whose show combined Indians and minstrels. He always staged a parade with the Indians riding down Main Street and the minstrels following. While the doc shouted his pitch, the minstrels sang, and the Indians pounded on drums. They made buying a bottle of medicine seem like a religious ritual, and the "limited" number of bottles always sold out.[104]

The popular "sold-out" tactic was very effective for boosting sales. Medicine show actors typically bustled through the crowd, carrying only a bottle or two at a time, making it necessary to rush to the stage constantly for more. Like the old European mountebanks, clever North American pitchmen triggered a conditioned response in their audiences based on the perception of limited supply.

The Oregon
Medicine Company

There were many Indian-style medicine shows. One of the larger non–Kickapoo outfits was the Oregon Indian Medicine Company, the brainchild of Colonel T.A. Edwards. Before his foray into medicine shows, Edwards had a checkered career as a circus manager and Union Army spy. After the Civil War, he joined forces with a half-white, half–Native American trader and trapper named Donald McKay. McKay had distinguished himself as a real Indian fighter in the Modoc war, and even though he was unreliable, Edwards saw tremendous promotional value in him. McKay had difficulty pitching to a small crowd because he couldn't "lie to people when they get close to me." In a tent, however, he could "tell more lise [sic] than patch hell a mile."[105]

Edwards created a cure-all, Ka-Ton-Ka, that was supposedly prepared in the Oregon woods by McKay and the Indians of the Umatilla Reservation. It was actually manufactured by a drug firm in Pennsylvania and shipped west. Edwards was one of the first retailers to offer a money-back guarantee. The procedure for obtaining a refund required no less than a notary's signature with three witnesses; three months' use of the products, strictly according to directions; and the prepaid shipment of the empty bottles. Very few customers attempted the process.

The business was profitable for a time, but Edwards and McKay forgot to consider the Northwest rainfall. In an age without paved roads, a traveling unit was stuck in the mud before you could say "Ka-Ton-Ka," and salaries had to be paid, show or no. Edwards quickly realized that the way to continue his business was to farm it out to independent contractors. He supplied willing pitchmen with the medicine and all the promotional handbills and literature they could haul. He advertised for "managers and doctors" in *Billboard*, running pictures of McKay in a picturesque Indian-fighting costume. Pricing was suggested and it was hinted that "Lady Canvassers" could make as much as forty dollars a week selling door to door. It was an early form of franchising that would have made McDonald's proud. Edwards expanded the product line, adding Wasco Cough Drops, Quillaia Soap, Mox-i-tong, and Woman's Friend. When asked whether he partook of his merchandise, he replied, "That ain't to take, it's to sell."[106]

Doc McDonald

There were countless Indian medicine shows in the late 1880s, but eventually audiences grew tired of them. By the 1930s, there were only a few Indian shows left, among them the Blackhawk Medicine Company and the Pawnee Indian Remedy Company. They were among the last of a dying form.[107]

One performer who managed to hang on after the fad had peaked was

Doc McDonald, who was an anomaly in the business because he actually *was* a Native American. Doc McDonald's Indian Medicine Show was a family affair. He and his brother, Happy Mann, and his family toured every summer through the small hill towns of Oklahoma, east Texas, and Arkansas. Unlike many outfits, they were always welcomed back to the little villages they played. McDonald's nephew, Cliff Mann, was eight years old when he started working with the show in 1928. He acted in plays, helped the women mix medicine, and ran through the audience to sell it. He has this recollection:

> Medicine show coming! Boy, how the kids and dogs would run out to see us. We'd come tearing down those dirt roads in a cloud of dust, driving big old white cars all painted up, rigged fancy with steer horns on the radiators. The farm women would run out too; they knew now there'd be a little color in their lives for a few nights. We were entertainment coming where they didn't see entertainment from one year to the next. Because we played in little towns where they didn't have a movie theater, a drugstore, a doctor — or a sheriff. My dad was one-quarter Cherokee Indian, but my uncle by marriage was the real Indian of the group. A Choctaw, he had long, coal-black hair, wore feathers for the image…. Uncle Jude was a ham actor, just plain ham. During the day, all he lived for was performing in the show that night. Up on that stage he was in a world of his own. Jude had a talent for selling, and I guess back in those Depression days there wasn't an awful lot to sell. So he sold medicine — tonic, Magic Corn Salve, liniment.[108]

Mann goes on to say that his uncle really was an Indian medicine man. Whenever anyone in the family got sick,

his Uncle Jude had an effective cure. He knew which mold from a cave or creek bed would work as a poultice or which herbs should be eaten or ground into a salve.

For the public, the family made tonics of sugar, a familiar laxative called Black Draught, and moonshine. They'd add rainwater, which has a distinctive flavor, food coloring, and Epsom salts. They called their tonic McDonald's Compound and advertised it as a "pick me up." It delivered on its promise. As Mann said, "If you took a half bottle of that tonic, you'd *better* get perky. It would clean you all the way."[109] They also sold a special corn remover. This is the recipe: Melt cakes of Oxydol soap in pie pans, let cool, and cut into little chunks. Wrap in newspaper, resell as Magic Corn Salve. They told their customers to soak their corns in hot water and then rub them with Magic Corn Salve. It wasn't a swindle, according to Mann. Most of the farmers who bought the salve didn't have corns, they had "dirt calluses." If they hadn't been convinced they needed a corn remover, "they wouldn't have washed their feet any other way."[110]

McDonald and company would set up their show in a farmer's field at the edge of town, using a tent if they had one, and making do if they didn't. If they had a tent, they'd sometimes charge a dime admission, but even if the show was free, they knew they'd part the audience from their money during the medicine sale. They had a fold-up platform with canvas curtains and folding chairs for the audience. When times were good, they had a generator that powered five electric lightbulbs, which

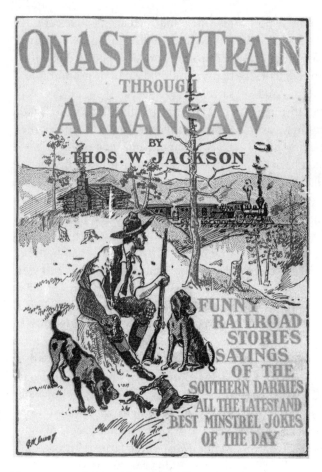

Front cover of *On a Slow Train through Arkansaw* (Chicago: Thomas W. Jackson Publishing Co., 1903). This type of publication supplied the jokes for Doc McDonald's troupe.

of the Lonesome Pine. Mann played the little boy in both plays. He was supposed to fall off a train trestle and have a death scene in *Trail of the Lonesome Pine.* Because the company's capacity for stagecraft was nil, the death occurred offstage. When the curtains parted, Mann would be seen lying under a pile of boards, or any other debris that had been collected nearby.[111]

In the middle of the play, just as things got interesting, they'd pause for a medicine pitch. Doc McDonald, making his first and only entrance of the evening, would come out front in full Indian regalia and pour on the hype: "There was this old lady on her deathbed, dying of dyspepsia, and she took my nature-brewed tonic, and she was up eating fried sweet potato the very next day!" If the farmers didn't have a dime for the tonic, Doc would barter, saying, "You there! I can see you're wanting this good tonic. You got a dime? No? Well, you take this bottle of McDonald's Compound and bring me back a half dozen eggs tomorrow!" Or, "I'll swap you all this medicine for a tow sack of potatoes!"[112] The farmers always came back the next day with the goods.

The country folk that McDonald and his family encountered couldn't get enough entertainment. Many times the family was invited to a party or barn

were often the first some in their audience had ever seen. The show started with all the musicians onstage, playing fiddle, guitar, mandolin, and banjo. Cliff says that his dad, Happy, was a truly talented guitar picker. Then came the dancing—a buck and wing, which is a comical tap dance in clown shoes. Next, they'd go into comedy routines, using skits out of a book they had ordered from Chicago. The main part of the show was a play. Mann's family did two of the hoarier ones, certainly by that time: *Ten Nights in a Barroom* and *Trail* dance. Local people gave them their hospitality, and in return, the medicine show people played music all night. Mann was proud of his show and thought of himself as a show business pioneer, bringing good laxatives and entertainment to the hinterland.[113]

Doc McDonald's Indian Medicine Show struggled to stay solvent. They didn't starve, but neither did they prosper. In 1931, the Great Depression dried up the business for good. Doc had nothing to sell, and hill country farmers had nothing to spend. Doc McDonald's Medicine Show and many others like it came to the end of the road.

5

Blackface and Slapstick

By the time medicine shows were in their heyday — the 1880s and 90s — they had absorbed elements of dime museums, circuses, and wild west shows. Another strand in that aesthetic fabric was the minstrel show, the most popular entertainment in the nineteenth century. Minstrel shows, another truly American phenomenon, dominated show business from the 1840s to the late 1870s. Medicine-show content was frequently based on minstrel songs and sketches, and thus medicine shows extended the life of a form that had lost its viability in the marketplace.[1]

High and Lowbrows

The War of 1812 was the second war America had fought and won against Britain in a forty-year period. By that time, Americans were thoroughly fed up with the old country, and a new feeling of nationalism was in the land. Thomas Low Nichols said of the period that

We were taught every day and in every way that ours was the freest, the happiest, and soon to be the greatest and most powerful country in the world.... We read it in our books and newspapers, heard it in sermons, speeches, and orations, thanked God for it in our prayers, and devoutly believed it always.[2]

It was not enough that Americans had their own holidays; they wanted their own culture, too. Wealthy Americans continued to patronize European opera and literary drama, but middle- and lower-class people disdained it. Actually, anything that smacked of aristocracy was liable to prompt violence.

Theater riots had occurred in America since 1825, when the well-known English actor Edmund Kean remarked on a Boston stage that Americans did not take the theater seriously. The enraged audience nearly stoned Kean to death before he was able to exit into the wings. In 1849, anti-aristocratic sentiment boiled over in the infamous Astor Place Riot. The conflict was sparked by a feud between English actor William Macready and his American rival, Edwin Forrest. Macready had been pelted with eggs and vegetables during a performance and resolved to board the next ship to England. However, a group of prominent New Yorkers, including Washington Irving and Herman Melville, persuaded him to finish the run of the play. The following night a mob of angry demonstrators descended on Astor Place. When the police arrested some of the protesters, pandemonium broke loose both in and outside the theater. The Astor Place Theater, originally constructed for grand opera, was filled instead with the sound of cracking skulls. Irish working class men, called The B'howery B'hoys, joined the fray in deadly earnest. The melee was so vicious that the militia was called in to stop it. Soldiers were given the order to fire into the crowd; when the smoke cleared, 31 people were dead and 150 were wounded.[3] The B'hoys, it was noted with horror in the newspapers, had not merely rioted against Macready, the Englishman. Their rage was also directed against the upper class of their own city. "There is now in our country, in New York City, what every good patriot has hitherto considered it his duty to deny — a high class and a low class," mourned the *Philadelphia Ledger*.[4]

The Astor Place Riot made the class divisions in American society all too obvious. In particular, it was apparent that there was a growing demand for popular entertainment, as opposed to European high culture. Not until the middle of the century, however, did supply and demand coincide. Up to and during the 1830s, all social classes attended the same

theater performances because there were not enough people to support separate venues. A typical night at the theater in the early 1800s was a hodgepodge of scripted plays, jugglers, acrobats, and animal acts.[5] A Shakespeare play, for example, might be interrupted by a pantomime or equestrian exhibition. Attempts to satisfy all tastes at once usually left at least one segment of the audience feeling cheated at any given time. Theater managers tried to solve the problem by showing a serious play one night and a troupe of jugglers the next, but that was not a workable scheme. Theater degenerated into a social event: Audiences focused not on the activity onstage but rather on the goings-on in the house. Wealthy patrons in the orchestra seats gossiped and showed off their finery; attendees in the cheap seats amused themselves by heckling performers, pelting them with vegetables, spitting tobacco juice, and even running onto the stage.[6] American stage shows in the first three decades of the nineteenth century were not in a tenable state. Even if class relations had not been tense, theater was destined to fragment along class lines, or, put another way, into "serious" and "popular" theater. The upper and upper-middle classes wanted high culture. Middle- and lower-class people wanted popular entertainment that related to their lives.

In the first few decades of the nineteenth century the working class took the matter into their own hands. Callithumpian bands, consisting of men with smudged faces and inside-out clothing, made rackets with pots and pans in the streets of New York, Philadelphia, and Boston. Their blackened faces, reminiscent of chimney sweeps and coal miners, were a precursor to the blackface minstrel clown and further suggested that class, not race, was the operative factor in American society. (Although some would equate class with race.) Callithumpians pelted houses and people with flour and lime, demanded food and liquor, and created havoc for the sheer anarchic joy of it.[7] They came as close to rioting as they could without actually provoking the police.

Callithumpians were in the tradition of medieval European carnivals. Carnivals were opportunities to upend the social order, if only for a day. Feudal "Lords of Misrule" presided over festivities in which peasants could say and do pretty much as they pleased, including lampooning their masters. Nobles not only permitted these occasions, they participated in them and suffered taunts and insults with good humor. These rituals of inversion were safety valves that let peasants vent their frustration and enabled nobles to hear and solve grievances before they festered.

In America, *carnival* is synonymous with Mardi Gras, another annual event in which the social order is overturned. By 1826, African-American Mardi Gras kings were at the head of the parade:

> Every thing is license and revelry. Some hundreds of Negroes, male and female, follow the king ... who is conspicuous for his youth, size, the whiteness of his eyes, and the blackness of his visage. For a crown he has a series of oblong, gilt-paper boxes on his head, tapering upwards, like a pyramid. From the ends of these boxes hang two huge tassels, like those on epaulets. He wags his head and makes grimaces. By his thousand mountebank tricks, and contortions of coun-

tenance and form, he produces an irresistible effect upon the multitude. All the characters that follow him, of leading estimation, have their own peculiar dress, and their own contortions. They dance, and their streamers fly, and the bells that they have hung about them tinkle.[8]

Minstrel clowns, like callithumpians, Lords of Misrule, and Mardi Gras kings, were "demons of disorder." Blackface minstrels actually had two functions: They were markers that helped one locate one's own position in society, and necessary fools who enabled the disenfranchised to challenge the social order in a sanctioned way. According to the traditional view, the minstrel character was invented by white men who performed in blackface makeup to show white audiences what they wanted to believe about Negroes. However, it is also reasonable to see minstrels as safety valves for class tensions. The minstrel character gave white working people someone to look down on, while simultaneously satirizing those higher up the social scale. It is no accident that audiences for the earliest minstrel shows consisted largely of young, rowdy, lower-class males — probably the very same men who participated in callithumpian bands (or theater riots, for that matter).[9] A third function is almost too obvious too mention, but neither should it be omitted: Minstrels were simply fun, with or without explanation.

Culture Schlock

The minstrel clown also bore a resemblance to Mose the B'howery B'hoy, a fictional New York City fireman. Mose

was the urban counterpart of back-
woodsmen Mike Fink and Davy Crockett, with one important theatrical advantage: In a theater, it's easier to create
structural fires and city streets than the
imaginary wilderness exploits of Crockett and Fink. Tall tales worked well in
print, but an attempt to stage them
would have been ludicrous. Backwoods-
men, for that reason, were generally not
the subjects of plays. (*The Gamecock of
the Wilderness* is a notable exception.)
Mose, however, could easily strut up and
down a stage re-creation of lower Broadway and boast about his exploits in an
offstage fire. Like Crockett, Mose was
pugnacious, boastful, sentimental, and
irresistible to women. Recalling a mother
whose baby he had saved, Mose said,
"[She] fell down on her knees and
blessed me. Ever since dat time I've had
a great partiality for little babies. The
fire-boys may be a little rough outside,
but they're alright there. (Touches
breast.)"[10]

The minstrel clown thus bears a resemblance to Brother Jonathan, Mose
the B'howery B'hoy, and even Davey
Crockett and Mike Fink.[11] He was the
irrepressible common man, ever opti-
mistic and undaunted. His role was
more complex than Brother Jonathan or
Mike Fink, however. As Gary D. Engle
notes,

> Among a nation of people devoted to
> social mobility there is a constant de-
> mand for a scapegoat, a fool who ex-
> aggerates the contrast between what a
> person is and what he wishes or pre-
> tends to be until that contrast becomes
> humorously grotesque.... During the
> nineteenth century, the minstrel was
> America's favorite fool.... When the
> blackface clown adopted any kind of

highbrow pose, he not only made a
fool of himself but somehow managed
to taint the adopted pose as well.[12]

The very notion of social mobility
set this young nation apart from the rest
of the world and motivated thousands
to emigrate to American cities. Trans-
planted farmers had to learn to live by
clocks, not the sun; immigrants had to
learn a new language and customs. Both
groups found themselves in a setting
that disregarded the songs, jokes, and
dances that were their common cultural
expressions back home. Ordinary nineteenth-century Americans studied man-
ners assiduously, turning to almanacs
and etiquette books for guidance in
shedding inelegance.[13] But information
wasn't enough to assuage a lack of confidence — people needed to laugh. Minstrelsy relieved the tremendous anxiety
that ordinary people experienced as the
world quickly changed around them.
White working-class audiences were relieved to know that as long as the black
clown was in their midst, there was
someone even more gauche than they. At
the same time, the clown acted out hostility toward authority that audiences
perhaps felt, but were not sufficiently
emboldened to display.[14] The minstrel
clown, like Jonathan and Mose, safely
pointed to the pretensions of those with
education and money.

In the 1840s, population explosions
radically changed urban demographics.
Rural folk and European immigrants
flocked to the cities and became ticket
buyers. By the 1850s, major cities were
sufficiently populated to support a variety of entertainment, from symphonies
to minstrels. The distinction between

high- and lowbrow culture was established.[15]

P.T. Barnum, the king of lowbrow
entertainment, demonstrated that the
key to success is volume: Sell lots of low-
cost tickets to lots of people, and vary
the program so audiences will come back
again and again. Minstrel-show entrepreneurs were eager to replicate Barnum's success, and audiences were happy
to oblige them. Adopting Barnum's
groundbreaking theory that entertainment was a commodity for mass consumption, minstrel-show producers
happily put his promotional methods
into practice. (Barnum's response to the
competition was to add minstrels to his
museum attractions.[16]) They staged parades, free band concerts, and what
would now be called "media events."
Nineteenth-century audiences were accustomed to parades, but minstrels made
them distinctive with colorful Prince Albert coats, silk banners and gold-headed
canes.[17] Minstrelsy met the need of the
great mass of working people to have
cultural events they could enjoy and understand.[18]

Jim Crow

Historically, the comic Negro pre-
dates the founding of the United States.
He appeared in English entr'actes and
afterpieces in the early eighteenth century. Lewis Hallam performed a "drunken
darky" act on the American stage in
1769.[19] Thomas "Daddy" Rice, a prop
man turned actor, put a song called "Jim
Crow" into a play called *The Rifle* in
1829. The story is perhaps apocryphal,
but tradition has it that Rice observed a
crippled African American stablehand
singing and dancing. The man's awk-
ward movements sparked Rice's imagination, and he invented the Jim Crow
character. A verse of the signature song
went,

> First on de heel tap, den on de toe,
> Eberty time I wheel about I jump Jim
>   Crow.
> Wheel about and turn about and
>   jump jis so,
> And eberty time I wheel about, I
>   jump Jim Crow.

Rice's Jim Crow was instantly popular and became the minstrel prototype.
The character's song was adopted by social and political satirists of varying
creeds. A death-row prisoner in Cincinnati, for example, wrote up to forty
satirical verses a day and sent them to
Rice to perform.[20] As the following
anonymously penned verse shows, Jim
Crow was elected to speak for Jacksonian Democrats:

> But Jackson he's de President,
> As ebry body knows;
> He always goes de hole Hog,
> An puts on de wee-toes [vetos].
> Old hick'ry, never mind de boys,
> But hold up your head;
> For people never turn to clay
> 'Till arter dey be dead.

Some Jim Crow verses went so far
as to advocate the abolition of slavery:

> Should dey get to fighting,
> Perhaps de blacks will rise,
> For deir wish for freedom,
> Is shining in deir eyes.
> And if de blacks should get free,
> I guess dey'll fee [see?] some bigger,
> An I shall concider it,
> A bold stroke for de niggar.
> I'm for freedom,
> An for Union altogether,

Aldough I'm a black man,
De white is call'd my broder.[21]

The tune to Jim Crow was minimal—"antimusic"; or, as Dale Cockrell suggests, "noise." The movements of the dance that Rice performed to the tune were jerky and bizarre—Jim Crow was decidedly a demon of disorder. Cockrell goes on to say,

> There was no character like Jim Crow for that time. The only remote equivalent was Col. David Crockett, roarer, braggart, fighter, dancer, fiddler, frontiersman, orator, politician, part myth, part man…. In league [Crockett and Crow] jumped and whooped, lied and satirized, exaggerated and trivialized, and loved and fought, thus blurring the boundaries between the real and the representational. Between them they gave joint definition to some of the central mythical beliefs of common people, white and black, of the East and West, North and South, all caught up together in an epoch of change out of their control.[22]

It was natural that the Jim Crow character should have his own show, and in 1843, Rice staged an *Ethiopian Opera* at the Bowery Theater. In the same year at the same theater, Dan Emmett and three other performers playing violin, banjo, tambourine, and bones staged the first all-minstrel show, which they named *The Virginia Minstrels*. Emmett and his cohorts, Billy Whitlock, Frank Brower, and Dick Pelham, were solo performers who banded together because the 1842–43 theater season was a disaster. Out of economic desperation, they inadvertently created theatrical history.[23] The show was a hit and started a minstrel fad that swept the nation. Professional and amateur groups sprang up all across North America. By 1855, San Francisco alone had five professional troupes.[24]

The Shows

In 1846, Edwin P. Christy standardized the minstrel show. Christy put his performers in a semicircle of chairs and invented the end men, called Tambo and Bones, for their instruments—the tambourine and bones. An "interlocutor" without make-up functioned as master of ceremonies at center stage.[25] He was the "straight man," and his job was to string out the comments in a loud booming voice so that even the most thick-headed audience member would get the jokes. He was both the announcer and the "feeder" of straight lines to the end men. The end men were clowns in the Jim Crow mold, and their function was to banter with the interlocutor and deflate his pretensions.

The first act consisted of a procession called the walkaround. It concluded with the interlocutor's command, "Gentlemen, be seated!" Then came funny and sentimental songs and dances (often modeled on Scottish reels), comic dialogue, and instrumental numbers. The second act, or "olio," was a mixture of skits and specialty numbers such as clog dances and steamboat imitations, performed before the drop curtain.[26] A common feature was a comic monologue that parodied the oratorical style of the period:

> When Joan of Ark and his broder Noah's Ark crossed de Rubicund in search of Decamoran's horn, and meeting dat solitary horseman by de

way, dey anapulated in de clarion tones of de clamurous rooster ... does it not prove dat where gold is up to a discount of two cups of coffee on de dollar, ... derefore at once and exclusively proving de fact dat de aforementioned accounts for de milk in de cocoa-nut![27]

Olio content was dictated by the talents of the cast. Over time, olios became very diverse, and any attempt at a unifying theme was discarded.[28] The third act was sketches, parodies, or possibly a plantation scene.[29] (Minstrel shows purported to "delineate" Negro plantation life, but were actually glossy fantasies for public amusement.) Within this general framework, each company developed its own program.

Minstrel shows were the primary delivery system of popular music to the masses. Everyone knew "Polly Wolly Doodle," "The Old Folks at Home," "In the Evening by the Moonlight," and "Buffalo Girls" from the minstrels.[30] Only occasionally was authentic Negro folk music used. Original minstrel songs were written by whites, even though northern composers like Stephen Foster had no acquaintance with plantation life at all. For that matter, most minstrel performers were from the Northeast and had no firsthand experience with the South or black folks. Rice, for example, was a New Yorker born and bred.[31]

In time, minstrel shows appealed to all classes of society. In the middle of the nineteenth century, as slavery became more controversial, northerners became very curious about blacks. Minstrel shows enabled northern whites to see blacks as worthy of sympathy, but much too different to engender true empathy. Minstrels' Negro caricature distanced white people from the sorrowful reality of slavery. Southern minstrels portrayed a compliant, happy field worker; northerners limned a shiftless, preening dandy. In either case, white audiences walked away feeling that the black man was at the bottom of the heap for good reason. Robert C. Toll, in his excellent history of minstrelsy, writes,

An unknown figure from a minstrel show.

From the outset, minstrelsy unequivocally branded Negroes as inferiors. Although it offered its audiences no heroic white characters, it provided even more certain assurances of white common people's identity by emphasizing Negroes' "peculiarities" and inferiority. Even sympathetic black characters were cast as inferiors. Minstrels used heavy dialect to portray Negroes as foolish, stupid, and compulsively musical. Minstrel blacks did not have hair, they had "wool"; they were "bleating black sheep," and their children were "darky cubs." They had bulging eyeballs, flat, wide noses, gaping mouths with long, dangling lower lips, and gigantic feet with elongated, flapping heels…. Besides picturing blacks as physically different and inferior, minstrels set them off culturally. Minstrel blacks would rather eat possum and coon than anything else…. In every way, minstrels emphasized, blacks fell far short of white standards.[32]

A modern audience would be horrified (one assumes), but in context, that view of the black man was not malicious.[33] It was ignorant, certainly, but it wasn't deliberately mean-spirited. For a time, minstrels portrayed various aspects of Negro life, but as the slavery issue became more contentious, characterizations became more simplistic. Antebellum minstrels did their best to preserve the fictional status quo of placid plantation workers and unhappy free men. Northern audiences might have been against slavery in theory, but neither did they want blacks as neighbors or competitors for jobs and land. Northern minstrels had no doubts about how to play the Negro: He was a buffoon. Southerners were equally complacent about their portrayal of the laughing, happy fieldhand, who could sing and dance all night after a day of picking cotton. As Toll notes, "[minstrelsy] provided a nonthreatening way for white Americans to cope with questions about the nature and proper place of black people in America."[34]

The form was popularized by whites, but after the Civil War, black performers had their own troupes. Minstrel companies were always segregated; oddly, even the black minstrels used blackface makeup and wigs.[35] When theatrical makeup was not available, burnt cork sufficed. Black companies added women and such characters as the warm-hearted old uncle and mammy, which possibly validated existing stereotypes.[36]

Minstrelsy reached its peak in the 1860s and declined steadily afterward. There were several reasons for its decline: After the Civil War, too many people had seen the suffering of blacks at close hand to be entertained by so extreme a fiction; the financial panic of 1873 put several companies out of business; many troupes never broke out of the format established by Christy, and others reinvented the show to such an extent that its original charm was lost; and a profusion of amateur groups diluted the form's appeal.[37] "Minstrelsy … died in the amateur productions of church organizations, young businessmen's clubs, Rotarians, and firemen's protective leagues."[38] Furthermore, a wave of immigration after the Civil War created audiences with a taste for entertainment with a European orientation. In the 1860s, there were 100 minstrel companies. By the 1880s there were only thirty, and by 1896 there were ten.[39]

Professional minstrel shows enjoyed a final burst of popularity in the late 1870s, thanks to the abilities of manager-producer J.H. Haverly, who observed that minstrel revues had not kept pace with the times: Other popular entertainments, such as opera and variety revues, were delighting audiences with their immense size and scale. In the show business climate of the 1880s, more was thought to be better, and Haverly rose to the challenge. He assembled a minstrel troupe from the best talent available and toured it throughout the country. The show was profitable, and Haverly set out to build an entertainment empire. By 1881, he owned several theaters, several minstrel shows, four musical comedy groups, and mining and milling interests. Like many aggressive businessmen of his day, Haverly became wildly overextended. Refusing to declare bankruptcy, he consolidated his minstrel troupes into one show:

> FORTY — 40 — COUNT 'EM — FORTY — HAVERLY'S UNITED MASTODON MINSTRELS, trumpeted his posters, playbills, and newspaper ads. "Forty is a magical number," one ad explained. "In the time of Noah it rained forty days and forty nights. The children of Israel wandered forty years in the wilderness. Haverly's famous forty are just as important."[40]

The "bigger equals better" strategy was both Haverly's and minstrelsy's undoing. By the 1890s, professional shows had become too large to sustain their own economic weight. Fifty- and seventy-five-cent admissions could no longer meet the payroll; scaling down the shows to decrease operating expenses only made the shows less appealing to audiences.[41] Slick extravagance was a quality better suited to vaudeville and musical comedy, into which the best minstrels were absorbed. Also, unlike musical comedy and vaudeville, which provided ample portions of sex appeal, all-male minstrel casts could not provide an enticing glimpse of female leg.[42] Minstrel shows at the end of the nineteenth century were no longer competitive. The only venues left for the blackface comedian were street fairs, carnivals — and medicine shows.[43]

Jake, Tambo, and Bones on the Medicine Show Platform

Minstrelsy was easily incorporated into medicine shows. Blackface comedy dominated most medicine shows even after minstrel companies per se were in decline. The bright, upbeat shows were the sort of simple, nontechnical fare that Main Street loved, and the producer could insert a medicine pitch at any point. In the Midwest, a few medicine shows had a white interlocutor-professor and a "colored quartette." The interlocutor, typically called Jake, was often the producer. Jake was responsible for the smooth running and pace of the show.[44] A typical medicine-minstrel show might have begun with the tried-and-true fake stabbing to draw the crowd. Then a banjo solo and a big musical number with the whole cast might follow. Jake and one of the end men would exchange some comedy bits, and then a sale would ensue. After that, there were the specialty bits like magic, mind-reading, or ventriloquism. Soap, an inexpensive item that loosened the audience's purse strings, would be sold after that. Then came more songs and specialties and the second lecture of the evening, followed by a candy sale or more specialty bits. The afterpiece was often a well-known skit, such as "Pete in the Well" or "The Three O'Clock Train." The skits were never actually scripted, but were handed around and rehearsed in the *commedia dell'arte* tradition. When the skits were written, they were full of general descriptions like "funny business follows." Rehearsals were brief and more like discussions than runthroughs: "Do you do the echo bit? Yes? Okay, all set."[45]

Vaudeville

The years from 1875 to 1925 belonged to vaudeville. Vaudeville, a fancy name for variety revue, was the most important source of medicine show material next to minstrelsy. It can be argued that the first presentation of unrelated acts for an audience's amusement — it might have taken place in a cave, for all we know — was the first vaudeville show. In America, vaudeville's origins are not much easier to trace. One thing vaudeville probably was not was French vaudeville, a farce interspersed with popular tunes. However, vaudeville-type entertainment was on American shores as early as 1769, when a group of Philadelphia comedians toured the East Coast. In 1824, John Robinson, a traveling circus manager, farmed out his cast to taverns so they could have winter employment. He was the first known American variety act booking agent. Early American circus troupes gave "circus concerts" after the main show for an extra fee. A popular act was living statuary — tableaux on a revolving platform consisting of white-wigged men and women painted with white fluid.[46, 47]

The vaudeville format — alternating skits, comedy routines, songs, and dances — was influenced by the minstrel revue. As previously mentioned, vaudeville absorbed blackface comedy and many of the top minstrel-show performers.[48] Dime museum shows — "the lowest rung on the ladder of theatrical entertainment" — were certainly an early form of vaudeville. A typical work shift in a dime museum was twelve hours, and performers sometimes did as many as twenty shows a day. By comparison, the rigors of vaudeville were nearly a vacation.[49]

"Blue laws" also contributed to the development of vaudeville. In northeastern cities like Boston and Brooklyn, singing on Sunday was fine, but comic makeup, animal acts, women in tights — indeed anything that did not "reflect upon the sanctity of the day of rest" was forbidden. Nevertheless, churchgoers wanted amusement on Sunday afternoons, and they flocked to parks that sprang up, typically at the ends of trolley lines. Restaurant and fairground owners offered their patrons a wide variety of entertainment, from singing waiters to ballerinas (presumably clad in nontraditional dance wear).[50]

Another theory of vaudeville's origin holds that it's simply the American version of British music hall. Both music hall and vaudeville were variety shows that ran continuously throughout the day, underwent a transformation from risqué to respectable, and eventually crossed class lines. British music hall ran heavily to singing, while its American counterpart relied more on broad comedy and dance. This has much to do with the influence of one very astute businesswoman: Lydia Thompson, an English dancer and comedienne, who brought a troupe of pulchritudinous showgirls to New York in 1868. "The British Blondes" presented for the first time on American soil what became known as a "leg show."[51] Red-blooded (heterosexual) American males have yet to lose interest in the form.

Like early music hall, early vaudeville took place in saloons. If the public suspected that theater actresses were immoral, there was no doubt about the status of women who performed in honkytonks. Dancing, serving drinks, and soliciting were all part of the same job.[52] Saloon shows often lasted until dawn. Chorines were given a break by jugglers, acrobats, and "buskers"—young male street entertainers who passed the hat after a clog dance or other variety act. As the evening wore on, the jokes got dirtier, the mostly male clientele got drunker, and miraculously, the girls got prettier. Saloon shows often concluded with a risqué sketch involving the entire cast. One popular pantomime had to do with sex behind a haystack, indicated by much smirking and rumpling of clothes.[53]

By the 1860s, even the smallest towns had bawdy saloon revues. These venues did not charge admission, but relied on the sale of food, watered-down liquor, and gambling for revenue. They became known as "free concert saloons," or "free and easies." Upstanding citizens

were horrified by the profusion of such sleazy places. In response to the public outcry against them, saloon owners took to calling their bars "concert rooms," "concert gardens," or "music halls," and gave them names like The Melodeon and The Alhambra. The Vauxhall Garden, in New York City, opened by William Valentine around 1849, was called a "variety theater" and brought that term into vogue. Valentine served alcohol to his mostly male audience, but his program was decorous. A trend toward propriety was in motion.[54]

Vaudeville's transformation from raunchy to respectable did not happen overnight, although one man, Tony Pastor, usually receives the credit. Pastor (who hated the term *vaudeville* and insisted on *variety* instead) elevated the shows' content. On October 24, 1881, he opened his revue in Tammany Hall on 14th Street and played to a "double audience" of both men and women. He prided himself on presenting the kind of show to which "a child could take his parents."[55] Middle-class audiences attended Pastor's wholesome programs in large numbers. The material was inoffensive and uncomplicated. "Vaudeville's early humor was mainly physical, its comedy low. But it was rich, robust, unbuttoned, having little truck with subtlety or sly sophistication."[56] Vaudeville was a reflection of the national mood. Americans, who were poised on the brink of what would be called "the American Century," wanted their entertainment as energetic and brash as their national character.[57] Blackface humor continued to please, even after the popularity of minstrel shows had faded. Many successful vaudevillians, such as

Bert Swor, Al Jolson, and Eddie Foy, adapted their minstrel show acts for the vaudeville stage.[58] Vaudeville was more even-handed than minstrelsy in its racial stereotyping, using every immigrant group as fodder for jokes. Ethnic humor, a response to a tidal wave of European immigration at the turn of the century, was extremely popular. Irish acts predominated, but Italian, Dutch, and German caricatures were also common.[59] Women were in for it, too: Old maids, suffragettes, and nasty mothers-in-law got their comeuppance on the vaudeville stage. All kinds of humor — tramp comics, husband-and-wife teams — were presented, but brief, punchy jokes and one-liners worked best. Most vaudeville acts were typically short and to the point. A comedy act that did not elicit big laughs in the first minute was doomed.

The Keith-Albee houses set the pattern for most vaudeville shows. The bill consisted of eight to ten acts, sequenced to give each act maximum impact and the show a cohesiveness over all.[60] One's order in the program dictated one's salary. Opening acts were paid the least, and next to closing paid the most. Acts tended to get pigeonholed by order — an opening act often remained an opening act. Small-time circuits had a lower pay scale than bigger ones.[61]

Touring

The primary goal of any professional vaudevillian was New York's

Vaudeville program featuring Eva Tanguay, one of the most popular headliners of her day.

Palace Theater, run by E.F. Albee, and variously dubbed the "Taj Mahal of vaudeville," "Mecca," "the home plate of show business," and "the *magna cum laude* degree in show business." Every other booking fell short of the mark.[62] There were indeed, many other vaudeville theaters in New York alone, but if one failed to secure employment at the Palace, it was time to hit the road. Big-time circuits were managed by Albee, B.F. Keith, Martin Beck, F.F. Proctor, and Alexander Pantages. Small-time circuits, notorious for mean-spirited managers, low pay, and lousy accommodations,

The B.F. Keith Palace, Cleveland, Ohio.

the night for split-week bookings. Dressing rooms were cramped and dirty, boardinghouse beds were full of lice, and disputes over billing were frequent. Performers also had to adapt their acts to their audiences. Urban audiences did not hesitate to heckle and boo a bad act. Rural audiences were more polite, but harder to please. An act that was "boffo" in New York might not have "played in Peoria."[64] Traveling vaudevillians often had to perform in makeshift theaters set up in barns, stores, and churches.

Touring the South was often difficult for northerners and always hard for African Americans. Boardinghouse and hotel conditions tended to be awful. Locals harbored animosity toward Yankees and outright hatred of blacks. Harpo Marx recalls that when he complained about some bug-infested train station food, the vendor replied that if his food was "good enough for white folks, it was good enough for New York Jews."[65] Such prejudice was usually, if not always, overcome with diplomacy and a good show. Still, most northerners couldn't wait to head for cooler climes. "I'm just saving up enough dough for an operation on

were called "The Death Trail," and "The Aching Heart" by those not fortunate enough to be higher on the show business ladder.[63]

Touring brought with it a host of difficulties. Performers constantly had to adapt to new conductors, orchestras, and theater managers. Train connections often had to be made in the middle of

Opposite: Vaudeville program.

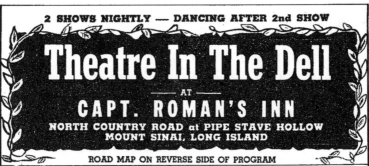

ROAD MAP ON REVERSE SIDE OF PROGRAM

1st SHOW 7:25 — GENERAL ADMISSION and RESERVED SEATS
2nd SHOW 9:25 — RESERVED SEATS ONLY

1st SHOW—General Admission 90c • Orchestra Circle $1.40 • Orchestra $1.90
2nd SHOW — Orchestra Circle $1.40 • Orchestra $1.90
Federal Tax Included • Children Half Price When Accompanied By Parent

JUNE 30th—JULY 4th

——— 1st Show on June 30th ———
Benefit of St. Charles Hospital—Port Jefferson, Long Island
FRANK KEENAN, *Master of Ceremonies*

VAUDEVILLE

IN ORDER OF APPEARANCE

——— OVERTURE ———

MARTELL BROTHERS
"Celebrated Comedy Cycling Comedians"

CATHY HARRIS
"The Girl With The Steel Toes"

FRANCISCO
"International Juggling Trickster"

RUTH & TOM RAFFERTY
"Popular Dance Satirists"

VIRGINIA SELLERS
"Dynamic Singing Star"

FRANK KEENAN
"Irish Ambassador of Wit and Comedy"

THE FOUR CARTERS
"America's Greatest Skating Family"

EARL CARPENTER and His Orchestra

PRODUCED and STAGED By KIRK & FAY

PROGRAM SUBJECT TO CHANGE WITHOUT NOTICE

MAKE EVERY FRIDAY, SATURDAY and SUNDAY
A VAUDEVILLE WEEKEND
AT THE THEATRE IN THE DELL

FRIDAY - SATURDAY - SUNDAY, JULY 7 - 8 - 9

HAROLD BARRY

Direct from N.B.C. Television
Prior To His Hollywood M.G.M. Engagement

my stomach once I get back up north," was a familiar vaudeville saying.[66]

There was a lot of resistance to vaudevillians in the hinterland, even in the twentieth century. They were lower on the social scale than "legitimate" actors. Groucho Marx says of his vaudeville days:

> [An] actor's position in society was somewhere between that of a gypsy fortune teller and a pickpocket. When [he] arrived in a small town, families would lock up their young daughters, put up the shutters and hide the silverware.... Theatrically, we were at the bottom of the social ladder. Five performances a day in a ten-cent vaudeville theater was about as low as you could get. The only things below us were the carnival shows, one-ring circuses and the crooked medicine hustlers.[67]

Vaudeville on the Medicine Show Platform

Variety acts worked very well in medicine shows. Some scholars assert that vaudeville was essentially an urban phenomenon, but its straightforward character made it equally appealing to rural people. In the remotest towns, where the vaudeville tours did not venture, intrepid medicine men parked their wagons. With the advent of vaudeville as a genre, vaudeville dominated medicine-show content, albeit without the emphasis on foreign atmosphere and costuming.[68] Furthermore, medicine shows took vaudeville and created a subgenre based on all the other forms that had gone before. Medicine-show workers, in particular, "crossed over" into carnivals and dime museums. They took

their work histories with them; and medicine shows, even more than vaudeville itself, contained a wide variety of acts.[69]

Mind-reading acts worked especially well in medicine shows, which relied on an aura of mystery to make the sale. The second half of the nineteenth century was a fertile period for all things spooky. Interest in spiritualism, table tipping, mesmerism, and séances ranged from parlor game amusement to religious conversion. Violet McNeal and her common-law husband, Will, were two of many show folk who capitalized on the fad. They had a simple, effective mind-reading act known as "the alphabet code." Leading a blindfolded Violet onto the platform, Will would orate a magnificent introduction before they went into their act: "To an infinitesimal number of persons in a generation is granted the rare power of probing the thoughts of others. I will show you how this little lady, blinded and immobile, can strip away bone and flesh, which separate her mind from yours. To her the innermost thought processes of each and every one of you are as clear as the pages of a book."[70] Violet had simply memorized a list of items and would name them when Will pointed them out to the crowd. Item A might be a hat, item B a pair of spectacles, and so on. They later worked out a more complicated code, but the idea was essentially the same.[71]

Harry Houdini, who eventually headlined in vaudeville, worked a mind-reading act early in his career. For a time, he was a cast member in Dr. Hill's California Concert Company, a midwestern medicine show.[72] It was a typical Indian medicine show that used the usual "medicine from nature's children" approach. Dr. Hill was a biblical-looking character with a flowing white beard. His actors spiced the pitch with variety acts and melodramas. In addition to their escapes and tricks, Houdini and his wife were required to act in *Ten Nights in a Barroom*. Dr. Hill got wind of a spirit medium in the area who was drawing big crowds and approached Houdini about doing a similar routine. Houdini, who had seen several spiritualists in New York, was convinced that they were all frauds whose acts could be easily duplicated. He was happy to contact the hereafter for the sake of the show. The crowd in Galena, Kansas, had already seen Houdini escape leg irons and handcuffs. They flocked to the local opera house to receive messages from their dearly departed. Houdini did not disappoint. Before the show, he went to the local cemetery and memorized the names of the recently deceased. A few discreet conversations with townsfolk also yielded useful information. That night, after escaping from the ropes that held him in his upstage chair, he crossed to downstage center:

> When the applause died down, Houdini talked about the spirit world. He said he could feel strange presences on

Harry Houdini.

the stage. He trembled. His eyes closed, then opened. Messages, he gasped, were coming through. He named names, gave dates, told family secrets, sent tremors down the spines of those for whom he had communications from the departed. Dr. Hill was in a merry mood as he totaled the receipts for the night. Henceforth, Sunday séances would be staged in every town.[73]

Houdini was an especially talented performer, but even ordinary medicine-show actors had to be versatile. A regular vaudevillian could work for years with seventeen good minutes, but medicine show actors had to change the bill every night for up to two weeks. Most medicine show performers had a large store of material. Many could sing, dance, act, do sketch comedy, perform magic, and do other specialties of their own. There was even a professional leaper, Frank Lexington, who jumped over piles of furniture. Anything that held a crowd would find its way into the show.

Vaudeville medicine shows were a wonderful training ground. Many radio and film stars, such as Gracie Allen, Al Jolson, and Red Skelton, originally learned their craft on the medicine platform. The shows "steeled the comedian and enabled him to judge audiences and to adapt himself to any group and adjust himself to meet assorted conditions."[74] Some of the best loved country and western stars polished their skills while working in medicine shows. Stars like Roy Acuff, Hank Williams, and Jimmie Rodgers "got their chops together" on the medicine show circuit.[75] Jimmie Rodgers joined his first show when he was thirteen, working in blackface. He gained confidence, experience and a strong desire to become a star.[76]

Although many performers did the exact same act on the medicine platform as on the vaudeville stage, there was a caste system among performers. One tent theater manager said that "stock company actors felt superior to tent repertoire; musical tab and repertoire actors looked down on each other and both felt superior to carnival people, who felt superior to medicine show people."[77] Medicine-show actors were disdained because they were required to do manual labor. Aside from pitching and striking their tents, they mixed, bottled, and sold medicine. Medicine-show folk often made a better, more steady living than other traveling artists, however. Many chose to stay with medicine shows for just that reason.[78]

What minstrel and vaudeville medicine shows lacked in artistic merit or intellectual stimulation, they made up for in fun. The medicine wagon brought the people what they needed — pure recreation. It was popular theater in the best sense of the term. Until movies and radio were available to the majority of rural Americans, the medicine show was synonymous with entertainment.

6

That Old-Time Religion

At the turn of the twentieth century, pitchmen, patent medicine, and religion were entwined in an odd yet profitable relationship. Theater attendance had gained acceptance in the last few decades of the nineteenth century, but many medicine show operators still faced opposition from townspeople on moral grounds. Crooked street corner pitchmen tainted the entire genre and caused difficulty for honest medicine showmen who needed permission from local authorities to perform. In order to overcome prejudice, some medicine show entrepreneurs put on scripted plays with highly moral messages to demonstrate their integrity and Christian orientation.

Melodramas were perfectly suited to nineteenth-century popular taste and worked especially well in medicine shows. The plays were not great literature; however, they dramatized a conventional set of values that gave credence to the appellation "moral lecture" and thus put theater-shy audiences at their ease. In the world of melodrama, morals like chastity, patriotism, honesty, and self-control are their own reward. Melodramas have sensational, action-filled plots and conflicts between virtuous heroines and dastardly villains. A typical melodrama begins with a presentation of an idealized family scene. The tranquil status quo is threatened by the machinations of an evil villain, who is eventually vanquished by the hero. This formula was not American in origin; stock characters, intensified emotions, and situations that were not necessarily governed by cause and effect had been elements of European drama since the sixteenth century. By the mid-nineteenth century, the genre of melodrama was well established in both Europe and America.[1] Melodramas thrilled audiences with improbable stories full of exaggerated dangers, while simultaneously extolling the virtues of middle-class domesticity.

Medicine-show producers assumed a greater risk with melodramas than variety shows because medicine-show actors had an inconvenient habit of disappearing. It's easier to fill a hole in a variety program than to replace an actor in a scripted play. Generally, family medicine shows did better with plays because casts were less prone to split up. Melodramas were not as peppy as variety shows, but could be made to work with lots of olios and afterpieces.[2] Some melodramas, such as *Ten Nights in a Barroom*, became perennial medicine-show favorites.

Temperance Plays

As noted previously, hard drinking had been habitual in America since Colonial times. Taverns were local meeting places, spirits were inexpensive, and drinking water was often impure. Furthermore, drinking was seen as an essentially American activity — everyone was equal in front of a bottle. Drinking was an act of volition and autonomy, and what could be more American than that? One who refused a drink was thought to be both rude and snobbish.

In the nineteenth century, America was still awash in liquor. Adults drank, on average, a fifth of hard liquor and a gallon of cider a week. Politicians "treated" voters with drinks on election days, workers drank on the job, and known alcoholics were in positions of public trust.[3]

By the 1820s, however, it was clear that rampant alcohol consumption was detrimental to family life, productivity, and public health. A movement for reform was afoot, largely promoted from the pulpit. Evangelical sects inveighed against the evils of drink, as did Presbyterian and Congregational churches. Sobriety, according to a large segment of the clergy, was the path to God, and God was the path to sobriety. Reformers viewed drinking in a way that now seems simplistic: People are naturally virtuous, but can be corrupted by an external factor such as liquor. (At the time, factors like family dynamics, social pressures, and hereditary predisposition were not taken into account.) Alcohol was scorned because it controlled those who consumed it, and the most dire consequence of the loss of control was thought to be the loss of prosperity. Early reformers incorrectly assumed that everyone was a natural-born winner — only a negative element like alcohol could damage a person's God-given chance of success. It was a view that coincided with the simplicity of melodramas, populated as they were with heroes, victims, and villains.

By the 1830s, there were 5,000 temperance societies in the United States and territories, with half a million members. Societies published pamphlets, held camp meetings, and sponsored lectures. There were pledges to sign, essay contests, and even temperance hotels in which no liquor was served. As the temperance movement gained followers, however, it began to fragment along certain questions of policy: Should the goal be total abstinence from alcohol, or merely moderation? Should drinking be regulated by legislation or religious conversion? Prohibitions were legislated in some states. Some laws were enforced, and some were not. Whether to drink (and if so, how much) was an unsettled issue in real life.[4] In the theater, however, alcohol itself was a melodramatic villain. Temperance plays were unequivocal in their attitude toward ardent spirits, but it took some time before temperance reformers accepted plays as an instrument of their work.

The temperance movement was influenced by a Christian revival movement in the early 1800s. The Second Great Awakening, as it was called, with its tents, stages, and florid testimonials, was a highly theatrical phenomenon. Nevertheless, most antebellum temperance advocates considered theater attendance to be on a moral par with drinking. Reformers were not favorably impressed with temperance dramas and did not see them as helpful to their cause. An 1843 production called *Moral Exhibition of the Reformed Drunkard* elicited this scathing review from the *Journal of the American Temperance Union*:

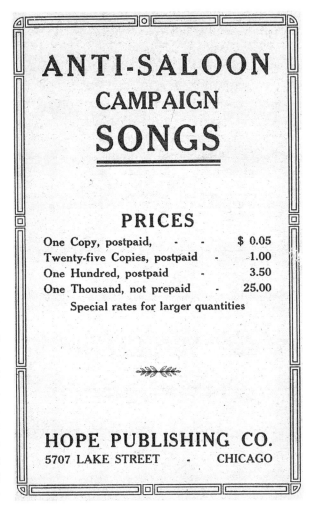

Front cover of a temperance song book dating from around 1910.

This is the right way to prevent our cause from ever enlisting the serious, enlightened and reflecting portion of the community. It is a great cause of God and humanity, and needs not the aid of buffoonery, mountebanks, and theatrical exhibitions, which are, after all, money-making affairs.[5]

One year later, temperance advocates dramatically changed their attitude toward temperance plays. An 1844 statistic demonstrated that Americans had greatly reduced their alcohol consumption, leading many reformers to believe they had won their crusade. Membership in temperance societies was no longer a radical act, but a conventional one, and societies passed into the control of middle-class nonsectarians. Nineteenth-century melodramas that dramatized the evils of drink now brought into the theater audiences that would not have attended under any other circumstance. Temperance societies embraced two plays in particular: *The Drunkard*, by William H. Smith, and *Ten Nights in a Barroom*, by William W. Pratt.

William Smith was a playwright, stage manager, and actor. *The Drunkard: Or the Fallen Saved*, which he wrote in 1844, was the first successful temperance drama. Smith countered objections to the theater's artificiality by claiming that *The Drunkard* was drawn from his own experience. The play emphasized moral suasion as the solution to drunkenness. Its initial run was a record-breaking 100 performances. Between 1844 and 1878, there were 450 productions on the boards; as late as 1953, a twenty-year run of the play closed in Los Angeles.[6] *The Drunkard* was a typical melodrama, with a destitute widow, her virtuous daughter, a conniving lawyer bent on throwing them out of their home, and of course, the title character. Some actors specialized in the title role. C.W. Clarke played the role for so many years that he was known as "Drunkard" Clarke. The Drunkard provided the leading actor with a plum delirium tremens scene:

> Here, here, friend, take it off, will you — these snakes, how they coil round me. Oh! How strong they are — there, don't kill it, no, no, don't kill it, give it brandy, poison it with rum, that would be a judicious punishment, that would be justice, ha ha! justice, ha ha![7]

Edward, the title character, has a religious awakening and stops drinking as suddenly as he started. On the brink of suicide, he is saved by the intervention of a Good Samaritan named Rencelaw:

EDWARD: 'Tis a sin to steal liquor — But no crime to purloin sleep from a druggist's store — none — none. Now for the univer-sal antidote — the powerful conqueror of all earthly care — death. (*About to drink, Rencelaw seizes phial and casts it from him.*) Ha! Who are you man? What would you?

RENCELAW: Nay, friend, take not your life, but mend it.

EDWARD: Friend, you know me not. I am a fiend, the ruin of those who loved me, leave me.

RENCELAW: I came not to upbraid, or to insult you. I am aware of all your danger, and come to save you. You have been drinking.

EDWARD: That you may well know. I am dying now for liquor — and — will you give me brandy. Who are you that takes interest in an unhappy vagabond — neither my father nor my brother? … Who and what are you?

RENCELAW: I am one of those whose life and labors are passed in rescuing their fellow men from the abyss into which you have fallen. I administer the pledge of sobriety to those who would once more become an ornament to society and a blessing to ourselves and to those around them…. Come with me, we will restore you to society. Reject not my prayers; strength will be given you, the Father of purity smiles upon honest endeavors. Come, my brother, enroll your name among the free, the disenthralled, and be a man again.[8]

The play ends with a tableau, that, according to the stage directions, depicts "everything denoting domestic peace and tranquil happiness." Edward's wife Mary is at her sewing table, and his daughter Julia is seated at his feet while he plays "Home, Sweet Home" on the piano. A Bible is conspicuously laid on a table, and sunshine streams in through the open window.

William Pratt's *Ten Nights in a Barroom and What I Saw There*, published in 1854, was an imitation of *The Drunkard*, and was no less successful than its prototype. Its anti-alcohol message implied that the best course of action was to outlaw taverns outright, a political rather than a religious approach to the problem. The play's first production coincided with the enactment of a Maine law prohibiting the sale of liquor, a synergistic event that promoted ticket sales. Pratt used the same rationale for his play as Smith — the narrative was supposedly reportage, not fiction. Pratt claimed that much of his dialogue was actual conversation that he had overheard in taverns. (Ostensibly, he frequented saloons solely for the purpose of research.) By modern standards, the play is as subtle as an elephant in the parlor — everything is spelled out for the audience in terms even an inebriate can comprehend. (The opening line of the play is, "After a long and tedious ride in a stage-coach, here I am in the quiet village of Cedarville."[9] The rest of the dialogue is similarly expository.) The play tells the story of a miller turned tavern owner who, under the influence of demon rum, beans an innocent girl with a beer stein, causing her death. The victim wouldn't have been near the tavern in the first place if she hadn't been trying to get her habitually intoxicated father, Joe Morgan, out of the bar. The girl's death, and a delirium tremens snake (a direct steal from *The Drunkard*), cause Joe to see the light and give up drinking. In contrast, the tavern owner sinks further into his alcohol addiction and dies. Joe laments, "Ten years ago there was a kind-hearted miller in Cedarville, liked by everyone, and as harmless as a little child; now his bloated corpse lies in a lonely room in a house that he himself has made wretched."[10] All is well when the town fathers enact a statute outlawing the sale of liquor.

Audiences loved *The Drunkard* and *Ten Nights in a Barroom*. Medicine-show producers loved the plays, too, because they enabled them to have it both ways: By staging temperance plays, they got "respectable" patrons into the tent, and then sold them alcoholic nostrums in between the acts. Alcohol, when used for medicinal purposes, was perfectly acceptable, even to temperance reformers.

Uncle Tom's Cabin

No melodrama had a greater impact on the public than *Uncle Tom's Cabin*. Dramatizations of Harriet Beecher Stowe's novel ("the big book that started the big war," as Lincoln remarked) were a theatrical fixture for decades. Mrs. Stowe's anti-slavery tale of Tom, Little Eva, Topsy, and cruel Simon Legree was a national bestseller at 300,000 copies in its first year. It's difficult to overstate the impact of the book on the public. Despite its inaccuracies and oversimplifications, readers accepted its picture of slavery as gospel, and the characters became embedded in the American zeitgeist.

Two theater companies immediately produced unsuccessful stage adaptations in 1852, the year of the book's publication. In September of the same year, a young actor named George Aiken had better luck with his version in Troy, New York. Aiken's first production ran for 100 performances, and when he moved the show to New York City in 1853, it ran for 200 more consecutive performances. Toward the end of the run, the actors did the show eighteen times a week, taking their meal breaks

Frontispiece from an early edition of *Uncle Tom's Cabin*.

a special trade publication for Tom actors.[12] In the South, the story was often changed to make the white characters more sympathetic. In the North, audiences endorsed the story's righteous stand against slavery.

Over time, there were some ludicrous additions to the script: Prize fights, afterpieces, brass bands — anything was fine if it got an audience into the tent. The plot was changed many times, and characters were added. Some companies had funny skits in the middle, or used alligators for bloodhounds. Al Martin's Tom show had eighty actors and a drum and bugle corps. Some companies were so tiny that the actors doubled on parts, changing wigs in full view of the audience. There were Tom shows with steamboat races, equestrian acts, dancers, and minstrel shows.

The show had a tremendous impact on the American theater. It created a whole new ticket-buying group: Upstanding Christians who usually eschewed the theater (aside from the occasional temperance play) felt wonderfully pious attending this "moral, religious and instructive play." *Uncle Tom's Cabin*, like *The Drunkard* and *Ten Nights in a*

in costume. No one has been able to count the number of productions (even Barnum had his own version at the American Museum), but it has been estimated that the play was staged four times a week for the next seventy-five years.[11] In the 1890s, there were some 400 "Tom" companies on the road. One company would pass another on the way to the next booking. The show was such a crowd-pleaser that many actors made an entire career out of playing Simon Legree, Eva, and so on. There was even

Barroom, made theatergoing a Christian activity. While standing on firm moral ground, "Methodists, Presbyterians, and Congregationalists of the strait-laced school" could thrill to "whippings, bloodhounds and sexual over-tones" that were common melodramatic fare.[13] Sex and violence were never mentioned in the advertisements, which always played up the religious and educational value of the play. A flier read, "the most exacting Christian people never hesitate to visit this great Moral show."[14] One company added an extra feature for the edification of the audience: "First Presentation on any Stage of a Genuine Cotton Gin and Press in Full Operation."[15] *Uncle Tom's Cabin* was a near-perfect, adaptable vehicle for a medicine show, and was in fact a mainstay of the genre.

Mojo Working

In contrast to righteous melodrama, a decidedly non–Christian approach to the medicine-show game was favored by Southern pitchmen who specialized in the sale of tobies. These lucky charms, also known as mojo bags, mojo hands, or conjure bags, are in use even today. Tobies are integral to hoodoo, a body of folk magic that combines African, European, and Native American lore. Although the term *hoodoo* is frequently interchanged with *voodoo*, the two are not synonymous, nor is hoodoo another name for Santeria, the African-based folk religion of the Caribbean. Hoodoo is also known as "conjuration," which, like the term *mojo*, is another word for magic. A male hoodoo practitioner is a hoodoo man, a female is a hoodoo woman. Hoodoo is also used as a verb.[16]

Like many folk-magic traditions, hoodoo places a great deal of confidence in the mystical properties of certain roots, herbs, and minerals. Mojo hands typically contain a root called "High John the Conqueror," prized for its magical power. According to ethnographers, High John the Conqueror was either a real or fictional slave who always got the better of his masters. Like Br'er Rabbit, he continually outsmarted the authorities by playing dumb. His namesake, the plant *Ipomoea jalapa*, is a woody tuber of the morning glory family. Mojo hands containing High John the Conqueror root are believed to improve one's love life, break jinxes, attract money, bestow luck, stop evil conditions, keep a lover at home, compel another to do one's will, find and keep steady work, put an end to fearful thoughts, heal the guilty heart, break bad habits, win a court case, master dangerous situations, bless a new baby, and much more.[17]

J.C. Julian worked in the oil fields near Seminole, Oklahoma, during the Great Depression. To supplement his income, he pitched tobies on the side. He appeared to be sincere about the value of his product:

> A toby helps people to be lucky. If you want something real bad, you don't get what you want without some help. That's where my tobies come in. I guarantee my tobies. But don't never let nobody else touch your toby. If you do, the toby will lose its charm…. The last time I got careless and left my toby home, I damn near got myself killed. I ought to have had better sense than to go to a dance sober and without my toby. If I hadn't have been sober, I couldn't of got drunk. And if I

had had my toby with me, I wouldn't of got in that fight. And even if I couldn't of kept out of the fight, I wouldn't of been the one to get all cut up.[18]

A typical sing-song, hypnotic toby sales pitch was street theater:

Put up and built by the Seven Sisters at the Crackerjack Drug Store at New Orleans, Louisiana. My toby will bring you Honor, Riches, and Happiness. It will help you Win in All Games. It will bring you Health and Wealth. It will Protect you against Evil Spirits and Witchcraft. Thieves nor Enemies cannot bother you. Now listen, everything you turn your hand to Prospers you and makes you Money. You succeed in your Trade, Job or Business. You got Seven Wishes to make with each Lucky Bag. Hold the Bag in your Left hand, blow your hot breath on it three times, and Make your Wish, and see if it don't come to Pass before the Seventh day is gone. To hold your True Loved one. To get anyone you love. To Protect yourself against all Law. To Kill all Voodoo and Witchcraft. Buy a toby. Just one dollar. But it's worth fifty.[19]

Tobies were outlawed in many states (including Oklahoma), but with an irresistible offer like that, business continued apace. Julian sold his bags to all kinds of people, but his best customers were poor folks. "Let me tell you right now it's the dumb folks who don't buy tobies to help them. Understand that right off! Poor folks need more luck than rich folks. That's the reason they buy more tobies."[20]

Preaching for Dollars

Both medicine pitches and religious sermons promised a better day, the one via a medicine purchase, the other through surrender to Jesus. Both medicine-show professors and preachers used a theatrical speaking style and cultivated a reassuring, authoritative persona, often supplemented with costumes, lighting, and props. Brooks McNamara observed the religious dynamic in his reconstruction of a medicine show:

[The pitches] were structured in exactly the same way as the presentations of tent evangelists, assembled out of a powerful combination of oratory and music and repetitive sounds in such a way that the pitchman gained control over the spectator. For the first time I really understood what the old pitch doctor Milton Bartok — who actually billed himself as The Health Evangelist — meant when he told me, "when you were talking to a big crowd it was like fighting a big fish. You could feel that they were your people. You would get on your toes — literally — working. You would come down from there wringing wet. It was a feeling you got, a sort of vibration you got from the people.[21]

Bartok had nothing but contempt for the Bible-thumping pitchman whose speech was nothing but "the Good Book says, 'roots and berries.'" His pitch was an art form so powerful it defied earthly law. When pressed to show his license to work on the street, Bartok roused the rabble to stand up for the rights of the good "Health Evangelist."[22] He hypnotized his audiences by turning himself into a human pendulum, walking back and forth across the front of the platform as he spoke.

We return once more to P.T. Barnum, whose use of religion to promote his businesses was shameless. A banner (or herald, as it was known in the trade) for his circus read, "Look for it. It is coming." Vertical type on the sides of the poster read, "I Am Coming." Barnum was well aware of the power such apocalyptic language would have on potential customers. He knew that evangelical Christianity was influential and he used the precepts of the religion to his own advantage. It was no accident that his circus was named "The Greatest Show on Earth," nor that he called it a "crowning success." The audacity of drawing a parallel between himself and the Christian savior was effective in terms of ticket sales, but infuriated his critics. *The Nation*, Barnum's perennial foe, ran an editorial saying, "He is the personification of a certain type of humbug which, funny as it often appears, eats out the heart of religion."[23]

Brother Jonathan

Barnum was hardly alone in his use of such tactics. And while his intent was to entice, never to defraud, many other pitchmen used religion to swindle their customers, posing as clergymen or Quakers. Jonathan Maloney, whose stage name was "Brother Jonathan," was one such medicine pitchman who operated at the end of the nineteenth century. His homemade remedy, the "Giver of Life," was promoted as a cure-all, but was absolutely worthless. The formula was mostly water, flavored with Epsom salts, rhubarb, licorice powder, wintergreen, and sugar. Jonathan justified his watery formula by saying, "Water is the great healer. Three fourths of the earth's surface is water."[24] His drab, gray-clothed wife, whom he called "Storm and Strife,"

was in charge of washing and filling bottles.

Maloney had a long, drooping mustache. He wore a dark suit with a long coat and always had matching gloves and spats. His gold-headed walking stick was engraved with the inscription, "To the Giver of Life from the Children of Chicago." When introduced, he would say, "Call me Brother Jonathan," adding in a low voice, "the Giver of Life."[25] He carried a Bible, an anatomy book, and a leather-bound copy of some *materia medica*, and called them all his Bibles. A notorious miser, he was known to be one of the richest men in the medicine game. He was a habitual name-dropper, working John L. Sullivan and Grover Cleveland into every conversation he could.

Maloney was an alcoholic who weaseled out of his bar bills. He had an alcoholic doctor named Fitzmaurice on the payroll whom he paid in quarts of Old Kentucky bourbon. Dr. Fitzmaurice was employable only in medicine shows, having long since lost his license to actually practice medicine. Maloney sent many unsuspecting patients to the former doctor whose prescription — a bottle or two of Giver of Life — never varied.

Brother Jonathan's actors were strictly prohibited from "chasing"— women, that is — and were fined if they were caught. Performers could stay in a local hotel if they paid for the room themselves, or sleep in the show tent *gratis*. Jonathan never mingled with ordinary townspeople, but strolled down Main Street with his gold-tipped cane, introducing himself to the mayor, the sheriff, and the newspaper editor. Maloney usually persuaded the local druggist to stock many bottles of Giver of Life.

Brother Jonathan considered a show a necessary evil to draw the crowd. His was a good-sized show with several vaudeville entertainers. They usually set up in a vacant lot, most likely to avoid the rent on the local opera house. Jonathan learned to put his talk in the middle of the show in order to keep the crowd from walking out. He could quote the Bible chapter and verse and equated a medicine purchase with a religious conversion:

> You must fain remember that our Blessed Saviour honored physicians by choosing one of them as a disciple — the learned Saint Luke of healing memory.... I come before you as a friend, la–dees and gentlemen — as one who bears the balm of Gilead from out of Judea — the healer of hurt hearts and souls, of cold people huddling from the awful blasts of life. I am the bearer of phosphorescent and beautifully burning coals of life.... Blessed are the meek, for from them shall the burden of the world be lifted by the Giver of Life! Here it is ladies and gentlemen ... the Giver of Life — a small silver dollar, a small silver dollar — Doctor Maloney's great Life Giver![26]

His assistants worked the crowd, shouting and running to the stage for more bottles. They'd rush back again to make change, following the axiom that "Nothing so confuses people as counting money in public while others talk."[27]

Friends and Shakers

Jim Ferdon, of Litchfield, Illinois, invented the most blatant of the religious medicine show cons, the Quaker show. Ferdon served his apprenticeship with Nevada Ned Oliver in a Kickapoo show and went on to sell German Elec-

tric Belts. One day he had the bright idea to pass himself off as a member of the Society of Friends. He reasoned that because the sect was known for its probity and high standards, anyone could be persuaded to buy medicine from a Quaker. He teamed up with a Dr. J.L. Berry, a failed medical doctor who had nearly starved to death in general practice in California. Berry was an imposing man with a long black beard, Prince Albert coat, and tall silk hat. Before his partnership with Ferdon, he sold Dr. Berry's Mineral Salts up and down the Pacific Coast. The two formed the Quaker Medicine Company, donning fawn-colored clothing and wide-brimmed hats. Their trousers and vests were the "barn-door" type that buttoned up the side. While not entirely authentic, it was a passable imitation of Quaker dress.

Soon they were "theeing and thouing" all over the continental United States. Ferdon usually botched the Quaker language, saying things like, "Where's thou's baggage?" When questioned, he'd say, "I have lived so long among the world's people that I have had much of my orthodoxy wore off of me."[28] Ferdon's pious act kept the city leaders at bay. He often got away without having to pay a license fee. Timing his appearance just after the harvest, Ferdon caught farmers in a relatively unhurried and introspective mood. They were in a frame of mind to consider their aches and pains, real or imaginary, and spring for a liniment or tonic.[29]

Ferdon and Berry claimed that their special mineral water was discovered by prospectors in the Panamint mountains in Death Valley. One swig was the recommended dose for indigestion caused by a diet of sourdough and pork. A spoonful of the desert salts mixed with a gallon of spring water would replicate the water from their secret spring. Their so-called Quaker remedies were supposedly produced by a genius botanist in either Bucks County, Pennsylvania, or Cincinnati, depending on what came into Ferdon's head while he was lecturing. Quaker Botanical Herbs were to be mixed with eight ounces of whiskey or gin and a quart of water. The resulting mixture tasted awful, but never failed to clean out the user's intestinal tract in a frightening hurry.[30]

Ferdon's show was much more lively than a real Quaker meeting, but audiences didn't seem to mind the discrepancy. After years of Indian shows, they were charmed by the novelty. He toured the midwest with an African American quartet dressed in the latest fashion: bulldog yellow shoes, three-inch collars, and wide-brimmed fedoras for the men, leg o'mutton sleeves, wasp waists, and peek-a-boo hats for the women. Ferdon was one of the few medicine showmen who had a mixed-race troupe. They were quite a spectacle in a region that didn't see many African Americans—or Quakers, for that matter.[31] They carried their own stage, which consisted of a large platform surrounded by high canvas walls.

In the Northwest, Ferdon worked with a trio of Irish comics, Ed Young and Pat and Fanny Kelly. They did a street-corner pitch with minimal stagecraft. In Portland, they ballyhooed the show riding a dray down Main Street while playing a portable organ. Fanny sang, and Ed and Pat did what was called "monkey-face comedy." They always drew a good crowd. Ferdon's pitch was pure nonsense:

> The blood is the life of the flesh thereof. Without good blood, thee and thine can't have good health. But if you will take this wonderful blood purifier, which contains no mineral poisons whatsoever, it will clean and purify your blood and drive all the impurities out of your system.[32]

Ferdon and Berry traversed the United States and even made it to the Hawaiian Islands in 1898. The Quaker Medicine Company made them very wealthy men. Despite his personal fortune, Ferdon himself was a skinflint. He once advertised a Christmas basket giveaway as a promotion. The indigents who came hoping for a bit of poultry or cheese were instead feted with baskets of lettuce and other cheap vegetables. One of his actors asked if he might have a basket, since he had not been paid in weeks. Ferdon's reply was, "Certainly not. Those are for poor people."[33] Ferdon's Los Angeles home was a showplace in the twenties, but he wasn't content to stay there. By 1928, he was back on the road in Pennsylvania Dutch country, wowing the real Quakers as the Great Pizarro.[34]

Ferdon had numerous imitators, including one with an actual Quaker background, Asa T. Soule. Soule sold Hop Bitters, the Invalid's Godsend and Hope, Hop Cure for Coughs, and Hop Pad for Distressed Midriffs. By the time he had entered the business, he had joined a Presbyterian church, but he could still walk and talk like a Quaker. Having left the Friends behind, he regularly attended cockfights, owned a ball club called the Hop Bitters (rechristened the Rumbleguts by the newspapers), and turned Rochester, New York, into the third-largest center of nostrum manufacture. Rochester loved him for the color he brought to a dull environment and forgave him his excesses. As one vaudevillian put it, "Hail to Asa Soule! Rochester's fairest jool."[35]

Brother John, also from Litchfield, Illinois, had the curious notion not only to pass himself off as a Quaker, but to call himself "The Great Kamama." His entrance, in a chariot pulled by four horses, was a cross between Barnum and Cecil B. DeMille. As if that weren't audacious enough, he invented and killed an offstage relative to get the audience's sympathy. Producing a telegram, he'd announce that his great-grandfather, Brother Josiah Baker, would arrive the next day to impart his wisdom to the crowd and would they please come to see him? The next night, in tears and with a choking voice, he would say that the old man had been too frail to make it and was dying in a hospital as he spoke. "My friends," Brother John whispered, "I am overcome. I can say but a few words. You can show your sympathy for me and for this dear, aged man by buying this medicine without forcing me to tear my heart out with more words."[36] The yokels would flock to the stage, eager to buy and say a few words of comfort to the grieving great-grandson. Women who normally put the brakes on any im-

pulse purchase elbowed their husbands to reach into their pockets. Eventually, Brother John's perfidy was exposed from the stage by a disgruntled performer. The phony Quaker died broke in a state hospital.[37]

Lou Turner traded on the skill and reputation of another ascetic sect, the Shakers of Lebanon, Pennsylvania. The Shakers had an ethic of hard work, plain living, and celibacy. In addition to their prized furniture, they also made herbal remedies. Two Shaker physicians, Abiathar Babbitt and Andrew Houston, had an herb garden that produced the ingredients for Turner's Shaker Cough Remedy, Great Shaker Blood Cure, and other medicines. The Shakers supervised the manufacture of the products and kept a close eye on Turner's show. Turner did his best to comply with Shaker standards of piety and propriety, presenting a numbing program of hymns performed by singers in drab, Shaker-brown clothing. Theatrically speaking, the show was disastrous, so Turner later added some mild entertainment.[38] William Burt, an experienced medicine-show lecturer, joined a Shaker unit in the summer of 1893. Working against the dullness of the show, he said, tested his mettle.[39]

Religion was one of many "hooks" or "angles" used by medicine pitchmen. They were bound only by the limits of their own creativity and nerve.

7

Street Corners
and Big Tents

Medicine shows spanned a wide spectrum of sizes and production values. Producers with substantial financial resources put on extravaganzas with large casts and tents that seated thousands. At the other end of the scale, street corner pitchmen whose practices often tended toward petty larceny, favored simplicity for the sake of low overhead and a quick getaway. This chapter is an examination of the variety of medicine shows as personified by several street workers and tent show performers.

Street Workers

Tripes and Keister

Standard equipment for street pitchmen was a suitcase mounted on a tripod called a tripes and keister, and those who used them were called "T&K men." Another familiar set-up for street workers was a folding table and a gasoline torch on a pole. The torch and pole, which came apart for easy transport, facilitated evening shows where street lights were absent or inadequate.[1]

In medicine-show parlance, a tripes and keister placed on the ground was a "low pitch," and if it was on a truck bed or car tailgate, that was a "high pitch." High pitch operators thought themselves to be superior to low pitch men, and neither would be seen with carnival workers or circus performers. However, it was socially acceptable to associate with gambling house managers, saloon owners, bookies, and thieves.[2] Street-corner pitchmen, high and low, were looked down on by the big tent operators. Such was the logic of their professional and social order.

Prince Nanzetta

Street pitchmen were not always strictly honest, but usually made up for shoddy merchandise with high quality entertainment. As a rule, they reinvented themselves as colorful personalities with exotic backgrounds and sold remedies they prepared themselves. Prince Nanzetta, for example, was a Mexican boy from Los Angeles who claimed to be a Himalayan prince. He started pitching medicine on street corners sometime around the turn of the twentieth century, when he was only eighteen. Influenced by Healy and Bigelow, his pitch was a variation on the old "snatched from the jaws of death" theme. Tibetans are not known for war-like behavior, but Nanzetta claimed that his family was captured, tortured, and put to death by a tribe of hostile Himalayan yak herders. Nanzetta said that he was spared and made a slave to the High Priests at Lhasa. His captors, who were enamored of him, taught him their medical arts and made him a prince — an odd, homoerotic touch in an otherwise standard medicine pitch. Even though his captors hoped that he would become one of them, Nanzetta plotted his escape and eventually got away. He went to Los Angeles, where he determined to share his esoteric medical secrets with the good people of America. That was his story and he stuck to it, dressing himself in a long crimson robe with gold trim and tiny mirrors. At his side was a short sword in an ivory case — the royal sword of Tibet — and around his neck hung a medallion on a chain. This, he claimed, was the royal seal of Tibet.

Nanzetta was either a natural actor or a lunatic: He appeared to believe that he was what he claimed to be. He was so convincing in the role of foreign royalty that Mark Hanna, a well-known Indiana politician, once invited Nanzetta to sit with him on a campaign platform. Nanzetta accepted the invitation but made it clear that his presence on that occasion was an act of noblesse oblige. Nanzetta had an African American valet who followed him around bowing and scraping. The man's wages depended on how many times he called Nanzetta "Your Royal Highness" in public.[3]

Arthur Hammer

Muscle reading is the ability to detect the tiniest twitch or tension in another person's body. Arthur Hammer was a muscle reader and crafted his medicine-show act around his unusual talent. He set up an audience participation murder mystery on a public street that went like this: He gave a pocketknife to someone in the crowd who was to pretend to stab someone else and then plant the knife on a third person. Hammer asked the "murderer" to grab his wrist, and then Hammer ran through the crowd with the person in tow. Weaving in and out of the crowd, Hammer would first pretend not to know who held the knife, although the involuntary twitches of the "murderer's" hand told him who held the knife the moment they came close to that person. When Hammer felt the trick was at a dramatic peak, he revealed the holder of the knife. Hammer never faked his act — he was truly sensitive to involuntary signals.

Hammer had an even more dramatic

version of his muscle-reading act — he drove a horse-drawn buggy blindfolded. The stunt had to be approved by the municipal authorities, whose part in the act was to designate a route with several twists and turns. The act generated a blizzard of publicity and the route was always packed with spectators. With great ceremony, the officials blindfolded Hammer themselves and selected a passenger from among the town's most upstanding citizens. Hammer sat in the driver's seat, held the lines, and asked the volunteer to grasp his wrist. Then he'd set off at a brisk pace while the audience held its collective breath. Hammer explained that the nervous passenger would always unconsciously transmit signals via his grip. When asked about the danger, Hammer said, "Dangerous? Hell, no. That damned fool up on the seat with me doesn't want to get killed any more than I do. The faster we drive, the more muscle signals he gives me. If there was any real danger, he'd grab the lines." Hammer never paid a license fee to perform on the street. He made a deal with the authorities that he would pay only if there was an accident — and there never was. After his breathtaking stunt, Hammer sold lots of medicine. It's not known exactly what he sold or what it was supposed to cure, but audiences probably got their money's worth in entertainment.

Hammer always performed in a frock coat and silk hat. Like many pitchmen, he was an opium addict. He preferred to work cities where he had access to the drug.[4]

Assorted Characters

Los Angeles was a winter rallying point for pitchmen at the beginning of the twentieth century. They congregated on Fifth Street, an area now known for warehouses and homeless people. Among the usual characters who wintered in Los Angeles was Will Cooper, who sold a cure-all called Tanlac. The sartorial style for pitchmen was gold, and lots of it. Cooper buttoned his coat and vest with ten- and twenty-dollar gold pieces. Similarly, a pitchman named Phenomenal Kraus wore a watch chain made of gold nuggets embedded with diamonds. His pockets held a cache of unset stones. (For those like Kraus who were constantly one step ahead of the law, banks were impractical. Diamonds were easy to conceal, compact, lightweight, and fungible.)

Henry Gale sold a cure for corns, known in the business as "corn slum." The main ingredient was cellulose, which has no effect at all on corns. He conducted foot examinations from the platform. After cutting a man's corn he would conceal the specimen and instead display a piece of horse's hoof that he had previously palmed. The trick never failed to horrify and fascinate the crowd. He claimed that no one need submit to a surgeon's scalpel — a three-day application of his remedy would dissolve any corn. If he planned to be in town longer than three days, he'd add, "repeat as necessary in stubborn cases." Gale was good-looking, charismatic, and irresistible to women. Like modern day rock and roll groupies, women flocked around him. Gale usually took up with a woman for a week or two and didn't care if she was married or single. He eventually made two grave mistakes: The first was running off with a dentist's wife and taking her to Florida; and the second was returning to the woman's town, where her aggrieved husband killed him with a sawed-off shotgun.[5]

Ray Black was a kidney man whose pitches went on for hours. He reasoned that by the time his listeners had been standing for a long time, their lower backs would ache, and they'd be convinced they had kidney trouble. Black roamed as far as Australia, where he saw birds that live to be 500 years old, or so he was told. The birds lived by springs where crystals formed, and that gave him the hook for his pitch. Black repackaged ordinary Epsom salts and threw in a little flavoring. The salts, he claimed, were the special kidney-healing Australian crystals. Epsom salts cost pennies; Black resold them for a dollar a box. Black's pitches turned kidney disease into high drama:

> Kidney trouble sneaks up on you like a snake in the grass. Like a thief in the night. It spares neither rich nor poor. The Archbishop of Canterbury was descending the steps of that great English cathedral when he fell down like an ox smitten in the shambles, stone dead! They held an autopsy; there was nothing wrong with his stomach, heart, or lungs. But gentlemen, when they turned him over and looked at his kidneys—(pause, dramatic lowering of voice)—they looked just like a rotten tomato![6]

Black was illiterate, but he enjoyed pretending to read. Once while he was posing in a hotel lobby with a newspaper, someone said, "Mister, don't you know your paper is bottom side up?"

With a disdainful sneer, Black replied, "What of it? Any damned fool can read a paper right side up. Reading it this way exercises my eyes and my brain."[7]

Violet McNeal and Will

There were few women in the medicine game, but Violet McNeal distinguished herself among her colleagues both for her femininity and her salesmanship. She also wrote a book detailing her medicine-show life. In the late 1890s, she left her rural midwestern family at the age of sixteen to find work in the Twin Cities. She had been in St. Paul for only a day or two when she read and answered an ad for a doctor's assistant. At the doctor's office she met her husband-to-be, Will, whose real last name she never learned. Will had a magnetic personality, and she was immediately enthralled by him. A master con artist, Will was older than Violet and had been "on the grift" for years. His first gesture was to buy her clothes, and his second was to introduce her to opium. Within a short time, Violet was addicted.

Will took Violet to a phony minister and went through the motions of a wedding. It wasn't until ten years later, when she wanted to leave Will, that she found out her marriage hadn't been formalized. (An argument can be made that they were married under common law.) Will trained her in the art of medicine pitching. Their first season together, she did a mind reading act that preceded his lecture. If she made a mistake from the platform, he'd pinch her leg until it bruised. If she made a mistake off the platform, he'd break her nose. (She learned not to make mistakes.) In addition to the mind reading act, they played in *Ten Nights in a Barroom* and *Bibbs and Bibbs* for Arizona Bill, the Welsh Indian-style medicine man. McNeal proved to be a terrible actor in conventional drama, but was splendid playing characters of Will's invention.

Will was only eighteen when he became the first pitchman to use the Chinese angle. Observing a street corner pitchman, he saw how easy it was to make money selling medicine. The medicine game, he decided, was the way to support his opium habit. His friend and opium supplier, a Dr. Lop, suggested that he costume himself in a Chinese robe and call his medicine Chinese Headache Oil. Young Will hit the streets of Chicago and found his calling.

Years later, when he met Violet, he knew he had found his meal ticket. He prepared her to perform on her own, and when the time was right, he left her on a street corner and said, "Talk until I get back." Will spent the next two hours bar-hopping. Sweating and shaking, Violet lectured nonstop until his return. To her surprise, she netted fifty dollars, a grand sum even for an experienced professional.

At first he had her sell soap and wrote every word of her pitch. He made up a story about a fierce Indian tribe in a remote part of Mexico that cultivated special beans. Naturally, he had risked his life to bring these beans to Violet's listeners. When placed inside clothing, the beans killed moths and bugs and made luxuriant shampoo lather in the bargain. They were willing to part with his special bean soap for the very low price of twenty-five cents.[8]

As time went on, McNeal did all the performing, which enabled Will to retire to a life of reading, drinking, and smoking opium. He invented her most successful persona, Princess Lotus Blossom. Costumed in a mandarin coat, she sold Vital Sparks — aloe-coated "buck-shot" candy that was guaranteed to restore virility. It was supposedly made from rare Chinese turtles and saved the Chinese population (so the story went) from an epidemic of infertility. McNeal told the crowd that the discoverer of this magical remedy cried, "Pong Wook-ee!!" which, she explained with a straight face, is Chinese for "Eureka!" Vital Sparks was free with every purchase of Tiger Fat. Tiger Fat was actually petroleum jelly, paraffin, camphor, oil of eucalyptus, and wintergreen, heated and poured into tins. It cost seven cents per unit to make and retailed at a dollar. She later sold an herbal mixture of senna and cascara root, a surefire laxative. The one-dollar tin of herbs cost her ten cents, but she reasoned that it was a "darned good physic, and the natives got their money's worth."[9] McNeal preferred pitching in cities, where her listeners were mostly men. "If a man is convinced by the pitch," she explains, "he will reach down in his pocket and buy. A woman seemed to have to talk it over with her husband and the whole family."[10]

Whether buying herbs or worthless Tiger Fat and Vital Sparks, McNeal's audiences did indeed receive value for money tendered. She had a wonderful, captivating speaking voice which she cultivated for maximum effect. McNeal was a beautiful woman; under Will's tutelage, she created a striking image on the platform. Her good looks were undoubtedly a factor in her success; physically attractive people are more successful in changing their audience's opinions.[11] Her pitches were more than mere litanies of the product's qualities, however. As this excerpt indicates, they were story-telling sessions:

> In the faraway land which is my home there is a story which has come down to the present through the misty corridors of many decades. It is the story of peril, of overwhelming danger, of a dread and mysterious ailment which threatened to wipe from the face of the earth the greatest people of the Chinese nation. This nation, which had contributed so much to the world through its teachers, its philosophers, and its physicians, was losing its virility. To the horror of all who were aware of the impending tragedy, it seemed inevitable that this mighty race must perish. Its life force was gone. Its manhood no longer possessed the strength required for perpetuation of the strain which had existed throughout history.[12]

Violet liked to pitch on Skid Row.[13] Most of its habitués, she discovered, were courteous and surprisingly appreciative of poetry. She once recited a portion of the Rubáiyát to the Skid Row crowd in Seattle and was met with cheers. From then on, she included poetry in every presentation. Aside from the poetry lovers, however, there were the ever-present drunks, whose heckling could rattle the most seasoned performer. One surefire way to discourage drunks was to get them up to the edge of the platform and then "accidentally" step on their fingers.

Confidence was the key to McNeal's success as a pitchwoman. If one does not hesitate, she said, the audience will follow like sheep. Uncertainty spoils a presentation every time. McNeal was an proponent of the "single pitch rule." This meant fine-tuning a speech and repeating it, with little or no variation, for years at a time. One might pass the speech on to a fellow pitchman or train employees to speak it, but a successful pitch was not to be tampered with.

Violet had wads of cash, jewelry, and all the opium she could smoke, but her life with Will was filled with difficulty. As if drug addiction and physical abuse weren't bad enough, Will had relationships with other women and encouraged Violet to see other men — not for romance, but for money. Impressionable young Violet adopted Will's ethic: "No one but a sucker ever works."[14] Will had larceny in his heart and taught her how to grift. Pitching medicine, stealing silverware from a restaurant, or conning an old man out of his money were all in a day's work. Will told her, "You must be ready to take opportunity wherever you find it. If you happen to be passing a street-car which has just had a wreck, for example, lie down on the street and begin to scream. One way or another, there will be money in it."[15]

McNeal and Will had no compunction about bilking men out of their money. If Will spotted a rich old man, he set McNeal after him like a retriever after a duck. Her job was to make the mark fall in love with her and then get as much of his money as possible. Will had conning a lovesick sucker down to a science:

> Never try to trim a young handsome man; all the women will be running after him. Your best bet is a man over

forty, and the homelier, the better. Don't be vulgar or too talkative. If you listen, a person will always betray himself. Don't smoke. If a prospect asks you to have a drink, say yes, and then order lemonade or milk.... Never let a man paw you. He can get all that rough stuff in the red-light district. Never have physical relations with a prospect, no matter what he promises. A woman's body is the cheapest commodity on the market. Always use New Mown Hay perfume in the daytime and lilac at night.... It will merely remind him of his carefree youthful days on the farm, and he will feel more kindly toward you. Always go for money the first week. If the prospect doesn't come across, drop him. If he does, get hard-boiled when you've cleaned him. Never let him think circumstances have kept you apart. He might brood and kill you. Make him disgusted with you and ashamed of himself. Never feel sorry for a chump, even if he cries.[16]

McNeal quickly learned the nefarious ways of medicine-show life. A case taker (the private "consultant" for audience members) might hold out on fees, or a lecturer steal medicine and sell it as his own. She once discovered that a colleague of hers had rented a case-taking room down the hall from her own and was waylaying her clients before she could see them. One pitchman's wife ran away with another man, which was no great loss, excepting that she took their trained dog, whom he counted on for ballyhoo.[17]

McNeal was a good student and as Will's disciple she made and lost a fortune. By day, she trimmed the suckers on Skid Row, and by night she and Will patronized the best restaurants wearing the finest clothes. Like their friend Phenomenal Kraus, they often converted their earnings into diamonds, which they sewed into their coats. It was the quintessential "easy come, easy go" lifestyle. Years of spousal abuse and drug use took their toll, however: Eventually Violet's health as well as her "marriage" were in shambles. After a long struggle, she finally got rid of Will and her opium addiction and dropped out of the business for two years. When she returned to the platform, she had reinvented herself as Madame V. Pasteur, cashing in on a vague association with the famous scientist. Her autobiography, *Four White Horses and a Brass Band*, reads like a primer for con women. It's clear from her own terminology that she had nothing but contempt for her audiences, referring to them always as "suckers," "marks," or "chumps."

In many ways, McNeal personifies the American female con artist, fitting a profile of a criminal type who arises at certain points in history. The turn of the century was a time of great opportunity in America, especially if one happened to be white and male. Immigrant and African American women were in the labor force, but white, middle-class women were largely consigned to hearth and home.[18] "Respectable" females belonged to the "cult of true womanhood," which embraced women for their decorative value. Real "ladies" were expected to be fragile, idle, submissive, and housebound. The only respectable professions open to women not willing or able to find a male provider were teaching and nursing.[19] For many women who were not comfortable within those rigid societal constraints, an acceptable alternative was running a confidence game — an active rebellion against an unworkable ideal. Historically, periods in which the dichotomy between the ideal of womanhood and the reality of women's lives is particularly wide produce female con artists in force: So it was at the beginning of the twentieth century. Certainly some independent women expressed themselves by becoming writers, social and labor reformers, ranchers, and so on. However, some women craved adventure and became spies, soldiers, and medicine pitchwomen.[20] Violet McNeal's life is a casebook study of such an adventuress, whose conduct was not always strictly illegal, but usually unethical. Supremely self-confident, or at least projecting the appearance of self-confidence, she saw life as a game and dealt fearlessly with whatever confronted her. She sold remedies, but her real product was a carefully designed image of herself, which is, of course, the essence and method of the professional actress.

Owen Tully Stratton

Another medicine-show practitioner whose autobiography provides valuable insights into the life was Owen Tully Stratton. In the summer of 1897, Stratton was unemployed, broke, and unsure what to do next. He ran into his friend Jim Ferrell, who invited him to watch his electric belt pitch. That evening, Ferrell ballyhooed his act from a one-horse cab, promising the crowd they'd see a decapitation. Swinging a huge knife as he rode through the streets of Winona, Minnesota, he bellowed, "Hurry down to the park corner. You can see the biggest free show on earth — the great decapitation act, which has mystified millions and caused more hair to stand on end than all the three-ring circuses in the world."[21] At the park, Ferrell hung a gasoline torch from a pole and hooked it to the cab. He filled a bowl with silver coins, fanned a roll of bills on top of it, and then he went into his spiel. The crowd never saw the promised decapitation.

Back in the hotel room, after counting his take, Ferrell convinced Stratton to become a medicine man. "Where do you think you're going to get, working for three dollars a day?" Ferrell asked him. "Now this is virgin territory out here, and these rummies'll fall for anything. I've got an electric belt and a velvet suit old Dr. Sykes used to wear, and I'll stake you to them. Learn a spiel, get yourself a banjo plunker, and you can make some real money working water-tank towns around here. All you need's a little nerve."[22] Stratton, who didn't have a better idea, followed Ferrell's advice and got into the medicine-show game.

Stratton found a blackface comedian named Tom Murray and the two did their first show in Buckley, a few miles east of Tacoma, Washington. After picking a corner and lighting their torch, Murray did his routine, and then it was Stratton's turn to pitch. Like most streetworkers, Stratton had no training, no experience, and no qualifications other than desperation. He struggled through a couple of pitches in Buckley, and barely made enough to keep from starving. Retreating to Portland, he fell in with J.L. Berry and did the Quaker pitch for a time. When business fell off, the ersatz Quakers let him go and Stratton was on his own.

For the next few years, Stratton meandered around the Pacific Northwest with a series of partners. Stratton was a better gambler than a pitchman, and from time to time he supplemented his income with a poker game. Talent came and went; it was difficult to find good performers who didn't mind not getting paid. Stratton was a clever man, but the Pacific Northwest at the turn of the century was a frontier that abounded with schemers of every type. Stratton was an honest man at heart and was pained by the low life.

Stratton observed many experienced pitchmen and noted their techniques. These are the basics of medicine pitching according to Stratton:

- Venue — Street pitches are more effective than those done in a hall. Keep people standing up and a little uncomfortable. It makes them more attentive.
- Lighting — The platform must always be well lit. Spare no expense. Electric lights are better than gasoline torches.
- Height — Don't make the platform too high. The greater the distance, the less the persuasion. Always draw the crowd close.
- Personality — Perception is everything. The audience is more interested in a magnetic personality than in what the speaker has to say.
- Projection — Speaking outdoors is hard on the vocal cords. Distinct pronunciation of vowels will help the voice carry. A broad-brimmed hat will keep sound from dissipating.
- Content — There's a difference between oratory and selling. Don't be too flowery. (This point would have been disputed by many successful pitchmen.)
- Closing — Know when you've made the "joint" (the sale). Don't go for it too early or too late. It's possible to talk a customer out of buying. Watch the audience carefully. A good pitchman can see the shift happen.
- Repetition — Say the selling points over and over.
- Flexibility — Cultivate the ability to ad lib (a contradiction of McNeal's single-pitch rule.)
- Crowd control — Hire a policeman to keep the crowd from getting rowdy.
- Stall — Constantly change the running order of the show and put in a pitch at unexpected times.
- Propriety — Keep it clean. Men have the money, but women tell them when to spend it. Don't offend the wives.
- Status — Brandish fake medical diplomas.[23]

Stratton pitched medicine for a number of years. Medicine-show life took him from Kalispell, Montana, to Fairbanks, Alaska. He got an education of a sort and had some adventures, but he wasn't cut out for the life. Finally, he had to admit to himself that he was "sick to death of living like a nomad and having no home but a hotel room and being about as popular as a polecat with the home guards and having no friends and knowing that the medicine racket had no real future."[24] In 1905, he enrolled in Barnes Medical College in St. Louis, and he spent the rest of his working life as a practicing physician.[25]

Hamlin's Wizard Oil

For many midwesterners, medicine shows were synonymous with Hamlin's Wizard Oil. In the early 1870s, John Hamlin was an unemployed magician who needed a way to revitalize his career. A medicine peddler gave him a liniment, which Hamlin incorporated into his act. Hamlin professed that the liniment, which he dubbed Wizard Oil, would enable the purchaser to duplicate his feats of legerdemain. The claim was nonsense, of course, and Hamlin left a trail of disgruntled buyers. When a customer claimed that Wizard Oil cured his rheumatism, Hamlin took it from there.[26]

Hamlin reinvented his act as a standard medicine pitch, went into business with his brother Lysander, and the Hamlin Wizard Oil Company was born. The Hamlin brothers claimed that in addition to rheumatism, Wizard Oil would also cure pneumonia, cancer, and hydrophobia. The formula for their liniment was unremarkable as patent medicines went, but it was sure to produce an unmistakable sensation when massaged into the user's skin: Camphor, ammonia, chloroform, sassafras, cloves, turpentine, and up to 70 percent alcohol must have created quite a tingle. In certain cases, the user was directed to take Wizard Oil internally; one shudders to think of the effects of ingesting ammonia, chloroform, and turpentine. Nevertheless, Wizard Oil was held in high regard by the public.

The company operated out of

Chicago, and performing units were set up primarily as advertising crews whose purpose was to convince local druggists to stock Hamlin blood and liver pills. The Hamlins were one of the first — if not the very first — nostrum sellers to advertise on a large scale with live performers.

Wizard Oil units were small and rigidly standardized, consisting of a driver, a lecturer, and a vocal quartet that also played brass band instruments. Hamlin performers were welcome visitors in small midwestern towns, and often stayed up to six weeks in one location. They traveled and performed in a horse-drawn wagon that was a marvel of compact efficiency: The stage was self-contained, the sides of the wagon were emblazoned with advertising, and special compartments held the products. There was no room for luggage, however. Performers could carry small bags, but trunks had to be shipped. Occasionally, a Hamlin unit would play indoors at the local opera house, but most performances were outdoors on the company wagon. It was a company practice to cultivate good will by volunteering at church fairs and bazaars. Many small town choirs were bolstered for a time by the loud if not necessarily melodious tones of a Hamlin quartet.

The Hamlin Wizard Oil company personified rectitude and wholesomeness. Its employees were contractually bound to wear identical Prince Albert coats with gray dress vests, striped trousers, spats, and high silk shoes. Their style of dress was a Hamlin trademark. William P. Burt, the baritone in a Hamlin quartet, was once fined two dollars for appearing in public in a roll collar,

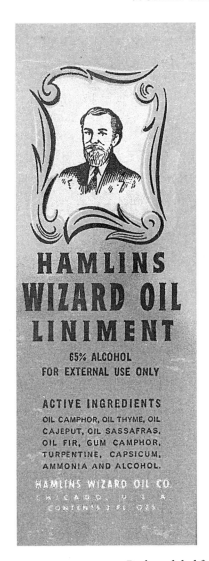
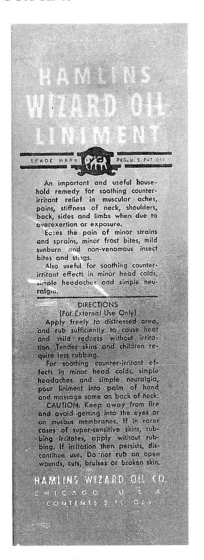

Package label for Hamlin's Wizard Oil.

instead of a more gentlemanly wing collar. Hamlin performers were, according to Burt, "the last word in class, dignity, and social distinction."[27]

Burt's quartet, the Lyceum Four, worked for Hamlin in the northern states in the warm months, and, like a flock of migrating birds, headed south in the winter. After the quartet broke up, Burt found work with another medicine show headed by a former surgeon who had suffered a nervous breakdown. This hapless fellow generated one of the best known anecdotes in medicine show lore: The doctor, who had degrees from several respected institutions, hoped to recover his sanity by working as a medicine pitchman — an ill-advised strategy. His liniment was for rheumatism and he employed the trick of massaging a patron so that the symptoms abated temporarily. One customer was incensed that his symptoms returned and went after the doctor with malice aforethought:

> The Doctor, forewarned and advised that the man was really dangerous, decided to get out of town, instructing the quartet to pack up and meet him at La Salle. There was no train scheduled until late that night, so the badly frightened man set out afoot and avoided the traveled highways. It was about midnight when the Doctor heard the barking of dogs coming in his direction. He pictured a posse, led by bloodhounds. He pictured lynchers led by bloodhounds and he remembered the killer with the gun. Just ahead was an apple tree and up he went to await the worst. And it came — a rabbit being chased by a pair of rabbit-hounds passed directly under the tree. As they continued on in their nocturnal rambling, he dropped to the ground and sought lodging at a small town a mile or so up the road.[28]

The poor doctor, his nerves shot for good, went into a rapid decline. He couldn't make a speech without hesitating and stumbling. His medicine sales fell to nothing and soon the show closed in Joplin, Missouri.[29]

A most effective promotional gimmick was the Hamlin Wizard Oil song books, which were available in every midwestern drugstore for a nominal cost or by mail for a penny stamp. The books were titled *Hamlin's Wizard Oil New Book of Songs* and *The Book of Songs as Sung by the Wizard Oil Concert Troupes.* They were distributed at the shows so the audience could participate in sing-alongs and they contained the lyrics to the popular tunes of the day: "The Old Red Cradle," "Listen to My Tale of Woe," "The Agricultural Irish Girl," and "Grandfather's Brown Pants."[30] In addi-

tion, they contained testimonials that touted Hamlin products as efficacious for cholera, diphtheria, deafness, and headache. One booklet contained a page-long testimonial from a doctor in Portland, Oregon, who claimed to have cured his wife's breast cancer with five bottles of Wizard Oil.[31]

Hamlin Imitators

Like Healy and Bigelow, the Hamlin troupe had many imitators. Harlow Hoyt, a resident of Beaver Dam, Wisconsin, recalls a man who claimed to be Hamlin himself. He was the only medicine man permitted to use the local opera house, and he performed there year after year. He was a small, dapper man who, like the real Hamlin, was a professional magician. His sidekick was a Mr. Mack, who played the piano, did Irish and blackface comedy, and helped sell the Hamlin products.[32] The duo performed a sketch called "The Load of Wood," and sang "Pat Malone Forgot That He Was Dead," "Swim Out, O'Grady," and "Do, Do, My Huckleberry, Do." (This Hamlin might have been who he claimed to be, although no other authentic Hamlin unit varied from the one lecturer/four singer configuration. The pair sold Hamlin products, but their song books and labels may have been counterfeit.)

Doc C.M. Townsend was a Hamlin imitator who traveled around Ohio and Indiana selling plain Wizard Oil — no mention of Hamlin. Like a Hamlin unit, his show was contained in a single wagon and featured a band. He timed his arrival in a town just as school let out. Hordes of noisy children would follow him to the center of town, where he would distribute handbills that advertised the upstanding nature of his show. The Hoosier poet James Whitcomb Riley banged a drum in Townsend's band in his youth. At first ashamed of his new trade and cringing at the sight of his friends and relations, Riley later waxed enthusiastic about the pleasures of roaming the countryside:

> I am having first rate times considering the boys I am with. They, you know, are hardly my kind, but they are pleasant and agreeable and with Doctor Townsend for sensible talk occasionally, I have a really happy time. We sing along the road when we tire of talking, and when we tire of that and the scenery, we lay ourselves along the seats and dream the happy hours away as blissfully as the time honored baby in the sugar trough.[33]

Riley wasn't much of a musician; his true talents were writing and drawing. He made himself useful by setting up a chalkboard and doing impromptu illustrations while the doctor spoke. He'd draw a fanciful skeleton with the caption "Can't Come In," or Shakespeare's head with the couplet, "Why let pain your pleasure spoil, For want of Townsend's Magic Oil?" "Oh!" says Riley, "I'm stared at like the fat woman on a side show banner.... When the moon rose to blend her light with the decorations and costumes, I was transported to the land of Arabian Nights. It was an Aladdin show."[34] For Riley and dozens of midwestern boys like him, medicine show life was all romance and adventure.

Tent Shows

Ton-Ko-Ko

Malcolm Webber was the strong man in the big Ton-Ko-Ko show. Before he signed on with the show, he gave lectures on phrenology and palpated his listeners' heads for a dime. He was also in a down-at-the-heels Tom show that employed only four actors. Everyone but Uncle Tom had to play four parts. Little Eva was an offstage voice and the bloodhounds were a couple of setter pups that Webber had to drag around by the scruff of the neck.[35]

Eventually, he joined the Ton-Ko-Ko Medicine Company, which traveled by rail and performed in a large tent. The company, according to Webber, included some very talented performers; everyone played both band and orchestra instruments and had at least one specialty act.[36] They could play many styles of songs and never needed sheet music. Two canvasmen ballyhooed the show with a banner in the parade that was held in every new town. A pretty female dancer did a solo turn, and a married couple were a song and dance team. Everyone acted in the usual sketches: "Pete in the Well," "Razor Jim," "Shadow," and "Mr. and Mrs. Brown."

The boss of the operation was a man called Doc Wellington. His brother, Henry, was the company's advance man and treasurer. In addition, there were a cook and an occasional stranded performer who signed on until he could get back on his feet.[37]

The Ton-Ko-Ko Company was a two-railcar show. Because the Ton-Ko-Ko cars were dilapidated, railroad lines refused to hook them to fast-moving trains, so they were tugged around the country by slow freight engines. The first car contained Wellington's office suite: a reception room, two private offices, Wellington's sleeping area, and an operating room.

The second car was a converted day coach that contained the kitchen and dining area, bunks for the canvasmen, and the tent. The rest of the car was divided into tiny rooms for the cast. Doc Wellington did not have a privilege car, which is a car used as a lounge, usually containing a snack bar and tables for cards and dominoes. He made up for that with plenty of well-cooked, wholesome food for his cast and crew. Doc Wellington paid his people small salaries, but the pay was regular. Jobs in his company were in demand.[38]

Wellington was not a licensed medical doctor, but that didn't stop him from performing surgeries. Many of his patients were women seeking an abortion. At a time when abortions were strictly illegal, medicine show doctors were among the few providers of that service. With nowhere else to turn, some women were willing to go under a knife wielded by someone who, like Wellington, either had no medical credentials at all, or had lost them. Abortions accounted for a significant part of Wellington's income.[39]

The show followed the usual formula. The band played outside the tent as the audience filed in. After a few numbers, Doc Wellington made a pitch. At just the right moment, a basket of medicine bottles appeared onstage. The cast circulated throughout the tent, shouting, "More medicine, Doctor,"

making it seem as if supplies were short. Ton-Ko-Ko herbs were made by a firm in Kansas City. To Webber's knowledge, they never harmed anyone.[40]

Webber reports that "it was mob hypnotism, of course. A voo-doo witch doctor couldn't have handled it better. Most of those who bought were hardly aware of their action till they found the stuff in their possession. Sometimes they went away and left it lying on the seat. Occasionally someone would come around afterward and want to sell it back."[41] Wellington viewed his audience as "a goose to be plucked. His motto was: 'From him who hath, it shall be taken away.'"[42] When the selling slowed, Wellington announced that he would sell no more that night, but everyone who made a purchase could come by his office the next day. He lavished praise on his performers and left the stage. The audience was then entertained with specialty numbers and the ever popular "Pete in the Well." The entire cast assembled onstage for a rousing finale, and the curtain came down.[43]

Although the acts in the Ton-Ko-Ko show were the sort of thing one could see in any medicine show, Webber says that the versatile cast performed them exceptionally well. Les Williams sang and accompanied himself as an Italian or Gypsy with a guitar or in blackface with a banjo. He also played violin, cornet, cello, and several novelty instruments, all with a high degree of proficiency. A man named Moody did a clog dance on a metal plate and a soft shoe on sand. Jack Clough was the most accomplished member of the company. He played tuba in the band and bass viol in the orchestra; he also played solos on the piano, mandolin, banjo, and guitar. Webber thought him to be the company's best blackface and dialect comedian. In addition, he was an excellent sleight-of-hand magician who manipulated cards and coins.[44] In his spare time, he sequestered himself in his bunk to practice pen-and-ink drawing. No one was ever allowed to see his work. Webber later discovered that Clough was a counterfeiter whose pen and ink drawings were actually hand-rendered one-hundred-dollar bills. Clough passed them successfully for a number of years, until the day two U.S. Treasury agents dragged him off the train and took him away in handcuffs.[45]

Webber did an "iron man" act, billing himself as "Ajax, Man of Muscle." Most strong man acts are faked, Webber explains, but his was somewhat authentic. His specialty was a circus trick of pulling against a team of horses. Webber's unique spin was to attach the ropes to a steel comb in his hair. Several men did the trick with their teeth, but to Webber's knowledge, he was the only one who used his scalp. (He doesn't recommend it.) He also did the spike bending trick: After letting the front row inspect an iron spike to see that it had not been treated in any way, he wrapped it in a towel, supposedly to protect his hands. In reality, the towel was used to switch the straight spike with a bent one. He also bent an iron bar and broke rocks. There wasn't any sleight of hand to those tricks, just hard work. Webber explains that the faked acts were more sensational, especially when performed by women. According to Webber, there were lots of strong-man acts that didn't require a ounce of strength.[46]

For additional ballyhoo, male audience members were challenged to match Webber in feats of strength or wrestling. The challenge was worded in such a way that few accepted it. A notable exception was Johnnie Lang, a sweet-natured college football player from Greenville, Oklahoma. Webber knew he was outmatched and was terrified to get in the ring with Lang. Wagering on the match was furious. The contest started with the spike-bending contest and Webber won with his usual cheat. To cut the contest short and protect Webber from grievous bodily harm, Wellington declared him the winner, but the crowd wasn't having any of that. They were set on seeing a wrestling match and were going to riot if they didn't get what they came for. Webber was sure he was going to be sacrificed for the good of the Ton-Ko-Ko company, but his compatriots had a plan: They solved the problem by oiling Webber from head to toe, and no matter how good a hold Lang got, Webber slipped out of it. Soon Lang was covered with oil himself and the show people accused *him* of cheating. Gentleman that he was, Lang just shook Webber's hand and walked out of the tent. After the show, Webber was remorseful and wanted to give the winnings back, but his co-conspirators cited the dictum: "Never give a sucker an even break."[47]

The Ton-Ko-Ko Company played the Oklahoma oil fields. Natural-gas lines criss-crossed the ground in every direction. To illuminate the tent, one need only make a series of nicks in the lines and set them on fire. When it rained, the tent was surrounded by a moat of muddy water. Planks had to be laid to gain entrance. The tent was full on rainy nights because it was one of the few warm, dry places around. If a gusher came in away from the rail lines, the show moved to that location by means of mules and trucks. Webber recalls one night when the show was canceled because an oil well had caught fire. Every able-bodied person in the area was busy fighting the blaze.[48]

In Tulsa, a twister destroyed the tent in a matter of seconds. Oil-field workers came running to see if anyone was injured, and Wellington, ever alert to a promotional opportunity, declared that the show would go on that very night at the opera house. He failed to mention that he hadn't actually rented the opera house, but fortunately it was available. That memorable evening, Webber recalls, the performers gave their best show ever to their most appreciative audience.[49]

The oil towns that Ton-Ko-Ko played were hotbeds of delinquency. There was no running water, sewage, or law enforcement. Alcohol consumption was out of control, as were prostitution, gambling, and every other vice, all fueled by a feverish longing for easy money. Audiences were volatile, but at least they were lively. Wellington preferred to play small county seats. Big towns were "too wise" for them, but county seats had just the right balance of population and naïveté.[50]

Webber's favorite town was Pawnee, Oklahoma. It was there that they encountered a county fair, to the mutual benefit of both organizations. The Ton-Ko-Ko crowd spent their money at the fair, and the fair workers bought medicine. The medicine show cast finally had a chance to have some recreation and en-

tertainment themselves. They started their show just as the fair closed and did good business from local people who were set on seeing everything.

The Ton-Ko-Ko show had lots of trailers — pickpockets, beggars, and petty thieves who tagged along with any traveling group that drew a crowd. Circuses had canvasmen and roughnecks who worked hard, but on a medicine show, a trailer could pick up a day's salary for pitching the tent, then hang around all week, eating and creating mischief. Another kind of trailer was a concessionaire who took advantage of the crowd drawn by a medicine show. He sold the shoddiest merchandise available and never hesitated to short-change a customer.

Some trailers were stranded performers desperate to get back on their feet. Out of kindness, the Ton-Ko-Ko show let a stranded family circus join them for a time. It seemed like a good deal; at the time, only the males in a family act drew a salary. In this case, the stranded performers turned out to be not only ravenously hungry but also untalented. Until they were gotten rid of, they ate up all the profits and discouraged sales. They were so bad, they inspired some egg-throwing. Untalented they may have been, but they were proud, nonetheless. At the height of the pelting, one of them yelled, "Hey, Rube!" — a provocation akin to waving a red cape at a bull. Soon the audience and the medicine-show company were engaged in a "clem," a brawl that broke up the set, the tent and a few heads.[51]

Doc Wellington, apparently not one to learn from his mistakes, made an even worse error in judgment with the Haley

Circus troupe. The Ton-Ko-Ko troupe met the penniless and hungry circus people in Bartlesville, Oklahoma. Their assets had been seized by creditors and they were reduced to shining shoes, cleaning spittoons, and washing clothes for food and shelter. All of the sideshow freaks had been let go to fend for themselves, except for Lolly, a true anatomical hermaphrodite, who exhibited her/himself in doctors' offices for pennies. The troupe was in a truly miserable state.[52] When the Ton-Ko-Ko company showed up, it was as if the cavalry had arrived. Haley's people moved in as a custom of the road and ate everything in sight. That would have been tolerable had they refrained from giving constant direction to the Ton-Ko-Ko cast. Being on the receiving end of unsolicited advice from a failed company was more than anyone could stand. Wellington's only choice was to cut his losses, buy train tickets for what was left of the Haley Circus, and escort them to the depot.[53]

Webber worked in the Ton-Ko-Ko company for a time, but, like Stratton, performing was never really his calling. One of his fellow performers made an assessment which could be applied to any misguided show business hopeful — past, present, or future:

> Now don't get me wrong. You're as good as any of the others and better than most. The trouble is, you lack that something that's hard to put a name to. They call it personality, showmanship, color, but none of these fit. They can often be acquired. I'd say it's a kind of fire; when it burns nothing can stop you from going to the top. Sometimes it goes out. Never does bring any happiness to those who have it. Just hunger and craving for something that can't quite be reached. Be glad it's passed you up — but get out of this damn business, or you'll be troupin' in the sticks till you've got white whiskers down to your navel, and don't you forget it.[54]

After that conversation, Webber's interest in the show waned. Not long after that, the Ton-Ko-Ko cars were in a terrible, fiery train wreck. Doc Wellington perished in the blaze, and that was the end of the show.[55]

Doc Bartok

Doc Bartok and his Bardex Minstrels toured with a tent that seated 4,000. With Bojangles Robinson, Redd Foxx, Bessie Smith and her sister, Walking Mary, among his performers, Bartok wowed rural audiences in the 1930s and 40s. Starting in Florida in April, the tour followed the strawberry, bean, and tomato crops northward. By August, the troupe was in Pennsylvania, ready to head south and play to the Carolina and Georgia tobacco and cotton farmers.

Bartok said, "My secret was keeping everything local and dealing with people right there on their own level." Following the proverb, "When in Rome…," Bartok got the "skinny" on local restaurants, stores, prices, accents, and allegiances at each stop along the route. Gathering intelligence that would put the CIA to shame, he always knew whether the show should be racially mixed or segregated, sophisticated or lowbrow. "You name it, we had the book on it. Up in Pennsylvania you got your Amish and your Mennonites. They'd come in droves in their little black buggies and bonnets, and they loved a good show. But it had to be clean. No dirt, none."

Medicine shows were usually no competition for movies, but Bartok's show was so good, theater operators closed their doors until it left town.

> We'd be playing a town of maybe 200, and along about the first dark, here they'd come. They'd be coming down the railroad tracks carrying their shoes tied around their necks.... And they'd be bringing us iced tea and fresh flowers and pies and cakes. And if we were near an apron factory or an overalls mill, they'd be bringing some of that, too. I tell you we were *all* they had. They treated us like *kings* and *queens*.[56]

Thomas P. Kelley

Thomas P. Kelley, known as the Fabulous Kelley, was a medicine show producer and performer from roughly 1885 to 1930. He ran the Big Free Fun Show, which played Illinois, Ohio, Michigan, and eastern Canada. Kelley's remedies, which he obtained from drug firms, were called Banyan, Shamrock Healing Oil, East India Tiger Fat, Miracle Corn Salve, New Oriental Discovery, and Passion Flower Tablets. "The secret of a successful sales pitch," he said, "is a smash opening, a crash finish — and keep them close together." Following his own advice, he made over two million dollars during his career.

Kelley bristled at the image of the medicine man as small-time hustler, a portrayal he felt was "ninety-nine point nine percent wrong."[57] There was a world of difference, in his view, between street workers and honest theatrical entrepreneurs like himself. He hedged his position by saying, "As for my stretching the truth, is there a merchant or a business man today who has not exaggerated at one time or other when lauding the merits of his wares? Of course not. They do it, I do it, and the occasional minor deception is just good business. You expect it. It does no harm if not carried to extremes and I have yet to claim to raise the dead."[58] One may well ask what is meant by "minor deception," "harm," and "extremes." His business philosophy was *caveat emptor*; but in fairness, he operated before the enactment of modern regulations.

Kelley had no use for opera houses; his playhouse was a tent that seated no fewer than 6,000 people. He was a calculating businessman who said:

> An audience isn't worth a tinker's damn to a medicine man with heavy expenses unless he has at least two thousand people before him. It all boils down to percentages and the number of people who will buy.... Out of an audience of a thousand, three hundred are bound to be noisy kids who have no money and are only there to see the show. Then allow another three hundred for the love in bloom group: young girls and fellows who are only interested in each other... So what does that leave you? It leaves you with just half your crowd, exactly five hundred people to work on and sell to. And always remember, that in any audience, just as sure as there's corn in Kansas, you are going to find that ten per cent are honorary members of the W.S.A.D.C. club — the "Won't Spend a Damn Cent" group who wouldn't give a nickel to see Lady Godiva ride a bicycle.[59]

The platform in Kelley's tent was eighteen square feet, five feet high, and illuminated first by gasoline torches, and later by electric lights. He also had a consultation tent for more medicine sales. The show was usually situated in a park or fairground. He employed first-rate vaudeville talent, many of whom went on to careers in radio and television. Kelley's hour-long lecture was sandwiched between the songs and skits. Typical material was used, including skits called, "The Book Agent," "Dollar for a Kiss," "Ma, Look at Him," and "Widow Bedot." After the last act, Kelley pitched more medicine or electric belts.

Kelley pioneered promotional events that featured audience participation: an enormous wedding for a local couple that was attended by 12,000 people; the Strong Man contest; and the Most Popular Baby contest. The audience's favorite contest was Amateur Night. Show business hopefuls poured out of the Canadian woods and midwestern fields for the chance to strut their stuff on Kelley's platform, often to hilarious effect. Store clerks did comedy, housewives sang sad songs, policemen did the soft shoe, and spinsters did bird calls. One man kicked his dog when it failed to perform and was chased off the stage by the snarling mutt; a girl dancing-duo got mad and came to blows; a homing pigeon decided it was time to go home and flew off in the middle of a presentation; and an oversized woman in Nova Scotia emerged from a trunk in a pirate outfit complete with mustache. Raising a hand to silence the tittering crowd, she said, "My father was Captain Kidd, I was his only child." That was as far as she got before she was heckled off the platform. It was great fun for everyone — except

the irate pirate maiden, who dashed offstage in search of someone to keelhaul.[60]

Kelley's first foray into show business in the early 1880s was a desultory stint as a high-wire walker in a circus. Dissatisfied with the experience, but not at all soured on show business, Kelley went home to ponder his next move.[61] He created an act with legendary pitchman Bigfoot Wallace, and, for a time, had fun getting in and out of trouble with his notorious partner. Wallace was a lovable scoundrel who made lots of friends and not a few enemies. Rounding out the troupe was a broken-down Shakespearean actor named Wellington who delivered monologues and scenes. One of his specialties was the graveyard scene from Hamlet. Wellington played all the characters, pausing to identify them and to explain the action to bewildered rural audiences.

With his usual grandiosity, Wallace dubbed their trio the Royal Players. Kelley reprised his high wire act and Wallace presented an animal act: Brutus, the wrestling bear. Anyone who could pin Brutus would win fifty dollars. It seemed a safe bet until someone actually pinned the bruin. Not only did the Royal Players lack the fifty dollar prize, but their audience of burly backwoods mountain men did not take kindly to a swindle. Undaunted, Wallace rose to the occasion. Shaking a finger at the man who was disentangling himself from the bear, Wallace bellowed, "I saw you. I saw when you did it. You deliberately kicked that poor bear in the kidneys and I'm going to have you arrested for cruelty to animals."[62] The bear had already been treated cruelly at the hands of the Royal

Players, who didn't have the wherewithal to feed the beast. The poor creature was weak with hunger. The mountain man, however, was a well-known ruffian who had been in trouble for drunkenness and brawling. He leaped up and ran out of the opera house. Wallace's quick thinking and facile tongue saved them all from being tarred and feathered, Brutus included.

The Royal Players left the hamlet and regrouped. They retreated to the southern boardinghouse of a widow named Zilpah, who carried an inextinguishable torch for Wallace. After sponging off her for a while, they worked the village into a frenzy of anticipation by posting signs that read "The Great Guzamba Is Coming." During their highly touted performance, carefully timed to coincide with an outbound train, they slipped out the back of the opera house, ran for the depot and left a sign that read, "The Great Gu-zamba Is Gone." So were the Royal Players, with the box-office receipts and several days' worth of unpaid boardinghouse bills. Brutus got the best of it; Zilpah adopted him and gave him plenty of food.[63]

Kelley formed his own medicine company on his twenty-first birthday — April 14, 1886. Although he was a fairly good wire walker, he knew he would never be the best. He wanted to excel at something and had a hunch that the medicine show business was his true métier. At the time, he lacked funding, information, and experience, but he had loads of desire and went on to enjoy great success. He called his show the Shamrock Concert Company.[64]

His first hire was a vaudeville comedian named Jock McCulla, a dour

man offstage who could fracture his audiences with physical bits and dialects. This was a typical routine:

> He comes on with a rush and the wild pratfall that sends his feet flying upward ... [which] lands him heavily on the seat of his well-padded trousers. With a howl of feigned pain he attempts to rise and crashes forward on his face; then with legs thrown over his head he regains his feet and comes to an upright position. [He] seems to have suddenly lost his left arm. He mugs alarm and horror, strikes his empty sleeve in his right hand and it whirls around. Now he is running all over the stage in a frantic search for the missing arm. He is looking behind the wings and backdrop, then in his pockets, his hat, between his legs and even pulling out the wide waistband of his baggy trousers to peer downward. Finally he seems resigned that it has gone forever, and brings out the bandanna from his pocket that conceals a well-filled sponge, applies it to his eyes while he shakes with sobs, and out pours the miniature deluge of water that brings howls from the audience.[65]

McCulla was in show business for the money. When he wasn't performing, he stayed to himself. After he had accumulated a nest egg, he disappeared without the customary two weeks' notice or even a word. According to Kelley, he retired to a Louisiana bayou, where he grew a long, white beard and fended off visitors with a shotgun.[66]

Kelley did very well his first year; he made five thousand dollars at a time when eight hundred dollars was a good salary. Nevertheless, he decided he wasn't ready to play big towns and resolved to play the backwoods for another season. The Shamrock company, with Jock McCulla and two other performers, played northern Ontario. It was a primitive region where wildlife abounded and actors were rare. Kelley reports that "the locals gaped at 'them actors' as though they were men from Mars."[67] There were no hotels, so the troupe had to rely on local villagers for food and lodging. Shipping was unreliable and often the remedies didn't arrive.

The locals were unsophisticated, to put it kindly. Few newspapers reached them and the ones that did were weeks out of date. Bathing was for sissies and even scraping manure off one's shoe was cause for suspicion. On the bright side, they were starved for entertainment and flocked to the show every night by horseback, wagon, and buggy. They bought plenty of medicine and Kelley turned a profit, which he wisely invested in Florida real estate. Subdivisions transformed his medicine-show earnings into a fortune.[68]

Kelley had his share of trouble with young women desperate to escape farm life. Girls who had performed in amateur contests thought themselves fit to join the company as professionals, even if they were underage or undertalented. Their constant propositions were taken in stride: "You've got to expect tart trouble in the med-game," one of Kelley's performers allowed.[69] An especially persistent young lady was Pearl Hart, who obtained the troupe's itinerary from one of Kelley's medicine suppliers. She saved her money for train fare and eventually presented herself at Kelley's office tent, insisting that she join the show. Hart, who did not have a career in show business, later attained notoriety as the only known woman to hold up a stage coach.[70]

Perhaps the constant importunings

of distaff show business hopefuls was the inspiration for Kelley's Lady Minstrels. The idea hit him with great force during a brainstorming session with Bigfoot Wallace. Kelley's theory of marketing boiled down to two simple points: Sell something unusual and create the perception that it's much better than it actually is. "A Greek army proved that three thousand years ago and won a mighty city by palming off a cheap wooden horse," Kelley said. "They fell for it as humanity has fallen for hokum ever since and will continue to fall for it if you just dish it up right and gift wrap it."[71] He envisioned a dream-like pageant in which girls in flower costumes bloomed onstage as other girls danced around them. Then a rain shower and a rainbow would appear. He planned an undersea tableau with mermaids and lighting that mimicked water. Other tableaux were along the same lines: The Bath of Venus, At the Court of the Queen Bee, The Death of Cleopatra, and for extra titillation, The Battle of the Amazons, and The Victims of Nero. Kelley was the Zeigfeld of the cornfields, who brought a fleshpot to the hinterland and advertised it in Barnum-like fashion: He blanketed his territory with billing paper and big, colorful billboards.[72]

Kelley's Lady Minstrels ran for five seasons. During that time, he assumed responsibility for the girls' protection. He had to fend off amorous men in the front row, backstage, at hotels, and train stations. Mill and steel towns were tough, but the worst of all were college towns. Boys mobbed the girls at the stage door and circled hotels like wolf packs. Kelley even had to give the bum's rush to notorious playboy and architect Stanford White.[73] He made a lot of money with his all-girl shows, but they wore him down:

> Yeah, the show made me plenty but it was also the damnedest heartache ever inflicted on any one man.... There were more catfights and hair-pulling contests than ants at a picnic. I have broken up some backstage brawls that for sheer savagery would have shamed those of Roman gladiators, while the obscenities screamed out during those melees might have caused hardened mule skinners to hang their heads. I had to guard them ... from the advances of young Casanovas as well as the old lechers in "bald-headed row."[74]

When Kelley closed his last all-girl minstrel show in 1899, nothing was more appealing than a stint in rugged Newfoundland, where he planned to get a "co-ed" show underway. The Kickapoos had been through the region a few years earlier, but Kelley gambled successfully that the audience was sick of the "medicine heap good" approach.[75] Newfoundlanders were a cautious, frugal, reticent lot. Doc Kelley knew the way to their pocketbooks was through their collective hypochondria. Many inhabitants were of Gaelic descent and had fearful superstitions about this life and the next. Kelley played on those fears through his powerful lectures. His remedies sold so well that one of his suppliers asked if he had been holding a gun to his customers' heads.[76] A harangue wouldn't have worked on its own, however. Kelley relied on the strengths of his performers, all of whom were able to "change strong for ten nights." Jim (Banjo) Gay played banjo, piccolo, bells,

bottles, and did character dances. Sal Salval did magic, comedy card skits, and mind-reading acts. George Grant did comedy juggling, baton twirling, and slack wire walking. The other cast members were equally versatile.

Newfoundlanders liked their comedy lowbrow and physical. Nothing was more hilarious than a pratfall, until Doc Kelley invented the pie-in-the-face bit. A pie in the face has been a comedy staple for decades, used by Buster Keaton, Charlie Chaplin, Soupy Sales, and countless others. Few people know that Kelley invented it. After watching some locals crack up when an angry cook threw a half-eaten piece of pie at a kitchen boy, Kelley decided to do an experiment: He bought a whole pie, gathered a crowd, staged a fight with Banjo Gay, and at the right moment, slammed the pie right into Banjo's kisser. The crowd was convulsed, and comedy history was made. Sal Salval says, "For my money there is no doubt as to the identity of the originator. The first time a pie was ever thrown into someone's face in view of an audience and for the sole purpose of entertainment was just before the turn of the century, behind the hotel in a Newfoundland town with fourteen spectators looking on while Doc Kelley, the King of the Medicine Men, threw a fresh baked pumpkin pie into the face of Banjo Gay. I was there, I saw it, and I know."[77]

Kelley died in 1931; by that time, the medicine show was a quaint and nearly extinct artifact of a bygone era. Although solo street workers and small family units like Doc McDonald's continued to work their respective territories, the big tent shows were almost gone. Kelley was nearly the last of his breed and was well aware that a great tradition was dying. That's why he continued to run his show for as long as he could. Voluble to the last, he talked three skeptics into buying a large quantity of medicine not more than thirty minutes before he died.[78]

8

Medicine — Show Life and Tricks of the Trade

Medicine showmen had a repertoire of angles and gambits for convincing their audiences to buy, and many tricks came from carnivals. Even though carnival workers were looked down upon by some medicine men, carnival midway tactics worked well on medicine platforms. For some performers, medicine shows, carnivals, and circuses were simply different names for the same thing: show business.

"Carnies"

Anna Mae Noell and her husband, Robert, had their own medicine show before they joined the carnival circuit. As latter-day pitchmen who worked during the 1930s, they typify small-time, not exactly honest medicine-show people who lived hand-to-mouth and were constantly on the move. Their son,

Bobby, also a carnival worker, has a vivid recollection of traveling with his folks' show:

Up until the time I was eight, my old man and lady ran all kinds of con games besides jam auctions — gaffed wheels, the razzle-dazzle, three-card monte, shell-game — anything to separate a mark from his dough. We traveled through the Deep South, Alabama, Georgia, Mississippi, Louisiana, all red-neck territory and oney [sic] in small towns or crossroads villages. I'd go to school maybe three, four months of the year, like November to February, and it was hard for me to get along with kids who'd grow'd up together and never went no place. But most of the time I di'nt go to school at all. We was always on the move, different town pretty near every day in the week includin' Sundays. I can remember goin' to sleep many a night in Alabama and wakin' up the next mornin' three hundred miles away some place, maybe Arkansas.

I got enough to eat — sometimes–

and sometimes I di'nt. But I di'nt say nothin'. It was the oney way to live I knew and I thought maybe that was the way all kids lived.[1]

Anna Mae's parents had also been in the medicine-show business, and Anna Mae was on the road as soon as she was born. Her father, who had an aversion to anything like a regular job, was a sleight-of-hand magician, juggler, ventriloquist, and piano player. Her mother played the Swiss zither. They put on a show that lasted an hour and a half and sold Pizarro's Soap, snake oil, or whatever they could get their hands on. (Snake oil was usually a combination of Vaseline and camphor, or similar ingredients.) Perpetually broke, they shipped their trunks by rail and walked the ties to the next town. Anna Mae was in the act before she was six years old, playing the ghost in "The Three O'Clock Train." It was her job to hit "the darkie" (her father in blackface), over the head with a jaw bone. The audience, according to Anna Mae, thought the gag was hilarious.

Anna Mae's family also staged *The Drunkard* and *Ten Nights in a Barroom*. Anna Mae's mother felt that her husband's preparation for the lead role was too realistic and the act split up. Anna Mae soon met her husband, Robert, who was a T&K man. Robert sold medicine, snake oil, can openers, spark plugs, or whatever he could get, and wasn't particular about the elevation of the pitch. The Noells worked circuses, carnivals, tent shows and medicine shows all through the Depression.[2]

Jam Auctions

The Noells conducted jam auctions, a dangerous process of defrauding consumers with overpriced junk. Jam auctioneers must have a prodigious gift of gab, a flair for street theater, steel nerves, and no conscience. It also helps to have a working automobile for a hasty exit before the crowd comes to. A jam auction can be run on a street corner, in a carnival tent, or from the trunk of a car. Arthur Lewis, who studied a jam auctioneer, says, "Unless you're on the 'inside' you can watch a good jam auctioneer at work for hours without having any more than the slightest idea of what he's doing. Furthermore, you'd better keep your hands in your pockets and make a conscious effort to resist hypnosis or you'll have an excellent chance of winding up as a 'successful' bidder."[3]

The auctioneer trades on the mark's belief that something can be had for nothing. Starting with simple giveaways like cheap fountain pens, or sewing machine needles, he fools the "tip" into thinking he's giving away hundreds of dollars worth of goods, when the actual value is pennies.[4]

Next, he conditions the crowd to spend by asking for pocket change as a sign of good faith. After all, hasn't he given them gifts? Aren't there more to come? The crowd is eyeing the expensive items—cameras and radios. The audience's own greed does the auctioneer's work for him. He hands out more freebies: factory-rejected toothbrushes, or "never fail" cigarette lighters. This goes back and forth for an hour or more, the cheap "presents" getting flashier and the requests for "good faith donations" going up. The crowd feels indebted to him, because no matter how small a favor may be, a person on the receiving end of one feels compelled to reciprocate. Once the jam auctioneer gets the crowd to agree that he's doing them a favor, they'll continue to behave as if that were true. People like to be consistent, even if it produces a foolish result. The dynamic is further reinforced by pitching to a crowd, rather than to individuals. Humans are herd animals and will follow their group, even if it's right off an economic cliff.[5]

At the right moment, when it seems like an honor to make a purchase, the auctioneer sells items that can be bought elsewhere for a tenth of his asking price. By the time he's finished, he's taken in hundreds more than he spent on his merchandise. One auctioneer said, "You know, sometimes when I see how the tip responds automatically to certain subconscious signals I send out, I think of Pavlov's dogs. If I told them to go to sleep, I'm sure most of them would…. I may confuse them from time to time. But I never con them. They get exactly what they pay for."[6]

Bobby Noell is less sanguine about his father's relationship with the audience: "I can remember as a kid when my father was operatin' a jam auction and takin' the marks for everything they had, we'd all be packed, ready to pull away in a hurry the minute the old man'd turn out the lights on the trailer platform."[7] Like the Noells, many jam auctioneers worked with their wives or women of the moment. A woman's presence reassured the crowd and allayed suspicion.[8]

One of the most notorious jam auctioneers was the aforementioned Big Foot Wallace, Thomas Kelley's friend and one-time partner. Born Frank White, Wallace took his stage name from an actual nineteenth-century Texas Ranger known for outrageous exploits. The latter-day Wallace, called a "natural born pitchman and genius" by *The Billboard*, was a street worker who employed a most artful hard-sell con. Waving a pistol at the audience, he swore he would shoot anyone who dared to sell fake medicine to one of his children (not that he had any) and if his medicine didn't work, one should prepare to die, because hope was lost.[9]

Many legitimate medicine pitchmen turned to jam auctioneering during lean times, but inveterate, unrepentant con artists like Wallace gave a bad name to street workers in general. Local merchants disliked them for undercutting prices — an easy thing to do with little overhead. "There was all the difference in the world between a medicine man and a pitchman, who carried his slum [worthless goods] in a satchel, ran like hell when he saw an approaching cop and rarely returned to the same place twice," Thomas Kelley remarked.[10] In fact, the distinction between pitchman and showman was seldom clear because so many careers spanned a wide spectrum of experience. In a country as big as the United States plus some of Canada, a pitchman down on his luck or reputation could always start over on a straight and narrow path. (On the other hand, it can also be said that life in a large, mobile society enables criminality.) Whatever else pitchmen might have been, they were independent. If one had a run of "mud-luck" he always found a way to keep going. Carnival worker Earl

Bowman said, "You don't see any genuine, old-time carnival birds working
the street for a dime or picking up
crumbs from a kitchen back door. If the
show goes flat, they'll raise tickets to the
next burg some way and they'll raise it
on the square, according to the ethics of
the profession: 'Give the suckers nothing
for their money, but when you give them
nothing, you give them *something*!'"[11]

Grifters and Grafters

Bobby Noell worked as a carnival
"grifter," someone with a "privilege" to
sell novelty items on the carnival lot. His
parents were "grafters," those who run
the often crooked games such as shell,
tivoli, monte, and spindles.[12]

Successful grifters are master im-
provisers and are proud of their skills.
For example, a certain Mr. Keith sold
blood testers at carnivals. The mechanism consisted of two glass balls connected with tubing and filled with pink
liquid. When grasped, the liquid bub-
bled. If it flowed quickly, Keith's speech
would go like this:

> Your blood is in excellent condition!
> The best test I have seen in weeks! You
> are in really wonderful shape!
>   WON-der-ful! But the important
> thing is to keep it that way. By having
> this perfectly regulated scientific in-
> strument on hand you can tell the
> minute your blood needs regulating.[13]

If the liquid moved slowly, he changed
the pitch:

> A slow, even flow of the secret chemi-
> cal distillation which is hermetically
> sealed in the specially blown, crystal
> glass bulb, denotes a perfect blood

condition... No feverish symptoms...
No uneven heart action.[14]

If two or more suckers were interested in the blood tester, Keith would
play one against the other, creating a
subtle competition to see who was the
real red-blooded he-man. He always
spoke slowly and deliberately, using the
"long con," that is, taking his time to
persuade. (A "short con" is a quick, aggressive hard sell. "Bull con" is intimi-
dation, using rapid-fire insistence and
some elbowing and shoving.[15]) The
"candy butchers" were grifters who sold
peanuts and candy. The name and type
of concession made its way from carnivals and tent girlie shows into burlesque
theaters.[16]

Until they were regulated out of
business, itinerant pitchmen never lacked
for second chances. Trade papers like
*Amusement Business, The Billboard, The
Spieler* or *The Money Maker's Manual*
carried a range of ads. Patent medicine
companies needed pitchmen. Carnivals
and circuses needed grifters and grafters. Opportunities abounded for those
who simply wanted a fresh start, or perhaps a new identity and another shot at
a big score.[17]

Tapeworms

One of the most popular medicine-
show gambits was the tapeworm scare. It
was used in big tent shows and street-
corner pitches alike and went something
like this:

> How many ... are there of you stand-
> ing before me who, unknown to your-
> selves, are harboring death within

your digestive organs in the form of a vile and slimy entity known to medical science as a *Taenia Solium*? Better known to you as a tapeworm. And if you do not remove the tapeworm, the tapeworm is going to remove you.[18]

A litany of symptoms ensued: sleeplessness, lethargy, ravenous appetite that produces more weakness. On and on went the list, while the listener grew ever more convinced that he was being eaten alive from within. Thomas Kelley, like many showmen, lined up jars of pickled tapeworms across the front of the stage. Enormous tapeworms for display purposes were available at local stockyards. Violet McNeal used to drape them around wires for maximum exposure in the jar.[19] At Kelley's show, each jar was labeled with the name and address of the creature's former host. The jars always drew the milling crowd up front for a look before they took their seats. At the time of the pitch, they were primed to buy Shamrock Tapeworm Remover, a pea soup–colored concoction that cost a whopping seven dollars.[20]

The tapeworm pitch was surefire because the symptoms of infestation mimicked many other ailments. Nostrum makers have included a tapeworm cure in their product lines ever since the reign of King George III (1760–1820). A shop handbill from the period shows His Majesty graciously accepting a box of Ching's Patent Worm Lozenges. Pitches were often dressed up with scientific names like "anthelmintics" and "vermifuges." Descriptions of tapeworm symptoms were in every nineteenth-century home remedy book. Many people thought they had one; many actually did, owing to poor sanitation and un-

clean meat supplies. The critters could be tiny or gigantic. An ad for Quaker Herb Extract announced, "Another Monster Parasite Over Sixty Feet Long."[21]

Immigrants, who often could not afford to be discriminating about their food sources, were particularly vulnerable to infestations of both worms and scam artists. It was an easy matter to fake a tapeworm "retrieval." For example, some showmen administered pills that contained balls of string. The pill dissolved and only the worm-like string emerged. The grateful, convinced patient became a loyal customer.[22] A more sophisticated version of the trick was the tapeworm trap, a piece of string inserted into a Murphy button — an old-fashioned surgical device made of two silver halves that snap together. Murphy buttons are not supposed to be swallowed, but if a sucker could be convinced to eat one in which a string had been planted, it seemed as if the button caught a worm on its way to the exit.[23] There was even a firm in Kansas City that made artificial tapeworms.[24]

Tapeworm specialists left nothing to chance. To make sure that a sucker had something to show for his money, some sellers planted artificial worms inside big gelatin capsules.[25] If a parasite failed to make an appearance, the pitchman claimed that the medicine had dissolved it.[26] On occasions when a preparation expelled a real tapeworm, the customer was fussed over in public and his former tenant was displayed from the platform. Extroverts were encouraged to give testimonials like this speech delivered at a Kickapoo show:

> I have been troubled for the past year and a half with a disease which baffled

the doctors, and not one of the many who treated me could bring relief. I finally bought and took one 25-cent box of Kickapoo Indian Worm Killer; and soon enough, to my great astonishment, I passed a worm of some size. It measured head and all, some fifty feet.[27, 28]

Electricity

Other big sellers along with tapeworm cures were liver pads and electric belts. John Healy sold them before he started the Kickapoo shows and they were a standard item in many street-corner pitches for years. Nineteenth-century people were obsessed with liver and kidney

Top and right: Card advertising Dr. Jayne's Tonic Vermifuge, a tapeworm cure.

"WORDS OF COMFORT,"

Is the significant title of our Fifteenth Card, illustrating a scene familiar to many homes in Christian lands, and is, we think, the best executed of our series. The reverent air and thoughtful countenance of each member of the group—the appropriate expression of each individual, so beautifully and carefully delineated, shows the sympathetic genius of the celebrated Scotch artist, Thomas Faed, at his very best. Our object in presenting this card is to ask you to remember that

WHEN YOUR OWN HEALTH Is in question, and such symptoms are apparent as low spirits, restlessness, sour stomach, sick headache, a variable appetite, rising of food after eating, oppression of the stomach, low fever, languor, and irregularity of the bowels, rest assured it is a form of Dyspepsia—a complaint tending to break down the general stamina, and thus open the way for many serious physical evils. The remedy needed is DR. JAYNE'S TONIC VERMIFUGE, not as a Vermifuge, but as a general Tonic. Two teaspoonfuls of this medicine, mixed with four tablespoonfuls of water, taken after each meal, keeping the bowels gently open when necessary with DR. JAYNE'S SANATIVE PILLS, will soon overcome the worst symptoms and remove this distressing disease.

WHEN YOUR CHILDREN'S HEALTH Is in question, and such symptoms are noticed as a variable appetite, with strange cravings, picking the nose, excessive thirst, low fever, bad breath, pale, sallow complexion, occasionally flushed cheeks, a wasting away, great nervousness, fitful sleep, grinding of the teeth, accompanied by weakness of the bowels—they indicate that the child is troubled with those dreadful pests, WORMS, which worry its delicate system, and are producing such irritation and debility as will surely break down the constitution, and, if the cause is not removed, may bring on St. Vitus' Dance or Convulsions, and render its after-life a burden. To save your child use DR. JAYNE'S TONIC VERMIFUGE, according to the directions, and you will not only destroy the Worms, but its Tonic properties will rebuild the general health,—no other Worm Medicine possessing such qualities. When Worms are not indicated, and a gentle Tonic is required, the VERMIFUGE may be given with excellent results after each meal, in much smaller doses than for Worms.

For **Coughs, Colds, Throat and Lung Troubles,** as everybody well knows, DR. JAYNE'S EXPECTORANT is the Standard Family Remedy.

PRESENTED BY

C. A. PATCHIN,
            Livonia, Livingston Co.,
                              New York.

THE MAJOR & KNAPP LITH CO N Y

The inside back cover of the Kickapoo Dream Book featured this ad for tapeworm remedy.

function and were easy to convince that those organs were in desperate need of treatment.[29] The answer, according to many pitchmen, was electricity. Electric belts usually consisted of a pad laced with glue and capsicum — red pepper. When applied to the bare midriff, it produced heat and a tingling sensation, "proof" that life-giving electricity was being transmitted to the liver. The belt produced nary a volt. Neither was there any scientific data to indicate that electricity was the correct protocol for liver trouble; but the belts sold as fast as lightning. Some pitchmen went so far as to attach wires and electrodes, while others stuffed their pads with sawdust to make them smell like drugstores.[30] More than one electric pad pitchman called himself "Electric Bill from Over the Hill," and bragged with this bit of doggerel, "I've Never Worked and I Never Will." It's impossible to say who was the original Electric Bill, but clearly the moniker caught on.

Jim Ferrell was a street worker who plied the Northwest, combining electric belts with a jam auction. After giving a mild shock to one of the rubes, he'd preach the virtues of his product:

It looks like a belt, and it is a belt. But beneath its trappings, there is a powerful galvanic battery. Worn next to your skin, it will generate a life-giving current, which will restore to your glandular system all the virility of youth! Not only that, but if you are afflicted by any departure from health, which you have not neglected for too long, the belt will produce a cure.[31]

Ferrell then took his audience through a confusing process of asking for deposits, then tossing bills and change back out into the crowd — the retail equivalent of throwing chum to sharks. He'd sell belts for one price, then another price, and then give some away. By the time his inventory was gone and

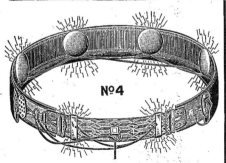
Electric belt ad.

he was ready for the blow-off, the suckers had no idea how much money had changed hands, or what had really happened. By the time they figured out that they'd been cheated, Ferrell was well down the road. The only problem with his strategy was that he "burned the lot" and could not return.[32]

Catarrh

Catarrh was another easily exploited ailment. An old-fashioned word for mucus, *catarrh* conjured up visions of tuberculosis and other truly dreadful diseases. Violet McNeal, a consummate pitchwoman, knew how to put fear into her audience:

> Write to any consumptive sanatorium and ask them what causes consumption and they will tell you nine hundred out of every thousand are there because of a neglected case of catarrh. Catarrh causes ringing and buzzing in the ears and even affects your eyesight. I claim catarrh is a germ that goes all through your body. Now this package I am holding contains twenty-seven different herbs. If you will take one fourth of a teaspoon … catarrh cannot live in your body.[33]

McNeal had a special catarrh-detecting gimmick. It was a glass graduate, a drinking tube, limewater, and vinegar. McNeal would drink some limewater, which was perfectly clear, to convince the tip that it was plain water. Next, she'd invite someone in the audience to step forward. "If you have catarrh, the water will turn milky when you blow into the tube," she'd instruct. Everyone who blew into the tube made the water milky because that's the effect carbon dioxide has on limewater. McNeal gave the unvarying diagnosis of "galloping catarrh." When she put a few drops of her vinegar remedy into the solution, the acid turned the water clear again. "You see, gentlemen," she'd say, "what happens to catarrh when it meets *scientific* attention?"[34]

Lefty LeClair, who borrowed McNeal's limewater trick, also cured deafness from the platform. Many rural people with hearing problems had nothing more serious than impacted wax. LeClair would invite a deaf person onstage, administer a few drops of his Nonpareil Rubbing Oil into the person's ear canals, rub vigorously, and presto! Hearing was restored and the crowd was converted.[35] Corns were treated with preparations consisting largely of gasoline. The medicine was so efficacious, said the pitchman, that you didn't even have to take off your shoes for it to work. Then he'd pour some tonic on a person's workboot, and warmth spread over the foot as the gasoline penetrated the leather.

Soap

"Talking soap" was a favorite pitch because overhead was low and soap was easily transported. Specialists in this item bought large cakes of commercially manufactured soap, cut them into small bars, and applied their own label. A two-cent piece of soap could be resold for ten cents or a quarter. Low overhead enabled a street worker to bounce back from a lean patch. For instance, Charlie White, who sold White's White Wonder Soap, found himself broke and stranded in

Omaha. All he had were his white broad-cloth suit, his hat, a gross of soap, and ten dollars. He didn't stay broke for long:

> I paid three dollars to get the suit cleaned and the hat blocked. I paid two dollars for a license. I hired a white horse, hitched to a cream colored buck-board, paying three dollars in advance. I drove to a street corner and gave a boy the last two dollars to get me a pitcher of water — and the "flash" of that two dollars for a simple errand sold over three gross of that soap, at twenty-five cents each, in two hours. That night I ordered another gross of soap, together with salve and liniment, and with the aid of a colored banjo player and singer, I averaged a little over $100 a day for the next four weeks in Omaha.[36]

Soap salesmen tended to engender less hostility in local druggists than did medicine men, whose pitches were seen as direct competition. Advertisements in trade papers extolled the versatility of pitching soap:

> They travel with all large Tent Shows, Carnivals, Midways, and Street Fairs. They are at Seaside Resorts and Watering Places wherever there are large gatherings. They show up, Shampoo Heads, Clean Teeth, Make Pyramids of Lather, Blow Soap Bubbles and Talk Soap.[37]

Perhaps the best-known soap talker was Silk Hat Harry, whose picture, in his trademark hat, adorned the wrapper. He emphasized the purity of his product, which contained "no poisons, acids, dead dogs, cats, or other dead animals." Card and rope tricks were his specialty, and for the final filip, he munched a cake of soap.[38]

Doc Ruckner lathered his hands before the pitch and let the soap dry on his skin. When it came time to demonstrate, his hand washing produced mountains of suds. A variation used by another "doc" was drying lather on a shaving brush. That trick was in frequent use, as was the wagon-wheel con: A very effective black tar soap looked like grease when it was rubbed on a wagon wheel before the show. While the pitchman talked, an assistant wiped a black smear from the wheel onto a white handkerchief and displayed it to the crowd. When washed, the "grease" disappeared, to the astonishment of the housewives.

Pitchmen tended to view their gimmicks in a proprietary way, certain that they, and no other, had thought of such clever means of parting a crowd from its money. Art (Doc) Miller said of the wagon-wheel trick, "I consider this … scheme the greatest I have ever known and never duplicated on any other show that I ever heard about."[39] Yet it was performed elsewhere and often. Medicine show culture was far too free and casual for any one person to have a monopoly on a pitch. As personnel went from one show to another, there was a fluid exchange of lore and material.

Mineral salts were another favorite item with pitchmen, because they were lightweight and easy to carry. A down-to-earth, populist approach with this product was a natural: The salts, when mixed in water, were just as good as the mineral spring water at resorts that were patronized by the wealthy. The salts were God's healing crystals from God's own laboratory, the ground itself. Mineral salts were supposedly good for rheumatism, malaria, chills, weak bladder, constipation, and anything else the pitchman could name.[40]

Dentistry al Fresco

Tooth-pulling was one of the most popular medicine-show attractions. In the nineteenth century, when dentistry was still in a painfully primitive state, people loved to watch a suffering soul undergo public torture. Free entertainment was a distraction from the business at hand, and many itinerant dentists enlivened their practices with medicine-show ballyhoo. One of the few women in the business, Madame de Bois (also known as Madame du Plat) and her husband, Dr. Andrew Dupre, were legends in their profession. He was a flamboyant character who dressed like a French cavalry officer in a horsehair helmet and used forceps that were attached to the hilt of his sword. Madame and the doctor employed a brass band to drown the screams of their victims.[41]

Madame was a role model for Violet McNeal, who, in the early stages of her career, yanked the teeth from Skid Row denizens for practice. Heaving and sweating, she'd work on a tooth until she held the bloody trophy in her pliers. McNeal also admired Hal the Healer, who "pulled the tooth with his right hand and choked off the chump's windpipe with his left. At Hal's signal the band would strike up a lively tune and if the chump did get out a gurgle or two, no one ever heard him. After it was all over the chump was so glad to be rid of his aching molar he never said a word."[42]

Diamond Kit, a street-corner dentist, used a variation on that trick. Attired in a coat adorned with rhinestone buttons, a zircon tie tack, and a diamond-encrusted pill box hat, he started his show with an impressive display of dental instruments. He claimed his proprietary painkiller was so effective, he'd do free extractions as a public service. Swabbing the patient's mouth and yanking the tooth with forceps (the only instrument he ever actually used), he'd stuff the bleeding mouth with a big wad of cotton. Flinging the tooth in the air, he'd turn to the patient and ask, "Did I hurt you?" Protestations were inaudible and Diamond Kit, never missing a beat, went on with his pitch.[43]

J.I. Lighthall, known as the Diamond King, dazzled Texas audiences in the 1880s. Lighthall's costume was covered with a bushel of diamonds. His remedies were mixed by his mother, who shipped them in barrels to his campsites. Lighthall combined an Indian-style medicine pitch with dentistry and boasted of pulling "fourteen teeth in nineteen seconds without pain." Hailing from Peoria, Lighthall told his audiences that his Illinois home, the finest in the state, had garden paths paved with teeth. His exploits were frequently described in newspapers. When he died of smallpox in 1885, a San Antonio reporter wrote, "Dispatches are wrong in asserting that Lighthall leaves a wife. The fact is that two wives left Lighthall."[44]

The Big Sensation Medicine Show employed a husband-and-wife team. He billed himself as "The King of Forceps." She, naturally, was his "Queen." They were hefty types, probably weighing 400 pounds between them. She did the holding while he did the pulling. Once, the show had to leave town without them. They had to stay behind to deal with a lawsuit: In the course of a tooth extraction, they had broken the customer's jaw.[45]

Malcolm Webber writes of the dentist who joined his troupe, a Dr. Jean St. Pierre. He offered free services to any member of the company, and while everyone was reluctant at first, soon he was doing a land-office business. Webber noticed that shortly after the good doctor's arrival, the show "went hammy. Performers began missing cues, singing off key, forgetting dance routines, and getting their 'bits' all balled up. There also seemed a sudden lack of initiative and cooperation."[46] Webber discovered the cause after Dr. St. Pierre extracted a molar and gave him some pain tablets. The "medication" turned out to be a processed form of opium. The entire company was under the influence. The doctor's own addiction stemmed from his experiments with anesthesia.[47]

The most famous performing dentist of them all was Painless Parker, a licensed dentist who practiced for many years. After earning his degree from a Philadelphia dental college in 1893, he traveled around the backwoods of Canada, billing himself as "the greatest all-around dentist in this world or the next."[48] When business was slow, Parker took to blowing a cornet to attract attention. For fifty-nine years, he practiced dentistry with medicine shows and even ran his own circus. He owned a chain of lucrative dental parlors which he promoted with Barnum-like flair. His building on Flatbush Avenue in Brooklyn sported a sign that read, "Painless Parker. I am positively IT in painless dentistry!" The "IT" was four stories high. Tight-rope walkers ballyhooed his services from cables strung between his building and the ones across the street. Unable to stay away from the public for

any length of time, Parker would leave his office and perform extractions on the sidewalk, to the accompaniment of the ever-popular brass band.

Aside from his dubious outdoor settings, Parker's dentistry was quite professional for its time. He was one of the first dentists to promote preventive practices at a time when dental hygiene was given little attention. Most of his contemporaries rendered their patients unconscious with ether, but Parker pioneered the use of hydrocain, a local anesthetic that predated novocain.[49]

He later moved to the west coast and started the Parker Dental Circus. In his employ were four dentists, four doctors, four optometrists, and a dozen nurses. Supporting them was a band that sat on a platform framed by a huge gaping mouth full of teeth, giving the impression that the band was about to be chewed. Parker typically made his entrance on an elephant, throwing coins to the crowd. The Parker crest was a gigantic molar with the doctor's picture in the middle.

Parker made plenty of money and even ingratiated himself with the upper crust of San Francisco society, but he loved the folks on the street. He was known to blow his cornet and pull teeth at the cable car turn-around at Powell and Market streets. The authorities became alarmed at the unsanitary conditions of street-corner dentistry and pulled his license from 1930 to 1935, but his friend and Bank of America president, A.P. Giannini, intervened with the governor and got it back. Legislation was passed outlawing medical advertising. Parker got around that restriction by legally changing his name to Painless, so

The School of Dentistry, University of Pennsylvania.

that his telephone directory listing was in effect an ad. As time went on, the medical community viewed him as an amusing and mostly harmless artifact of a bygone era. In 1952, shortly before his death, *Collier*'s ran an affectionate three-part series on him. The photo they ran showed him in his top hat and a necklace of 357 teeth that he had pulled in one day in 1905.[50]

The Consultation Room

The most lucrative medicine-show practice — the consultation room, or case-taking parlor — was actually an adjunct to the show. It was used both in big tent shows and by street workers. Violet McNeal would only do her street-corner pitch within sight of her room so she could show it to the suckers. She'd point out the location several times during her lecture and emphasize the phrase "free consultation." Like any good pitchman or carny worker, McNeal knew that the lure of getting something for nothing was irresistible. After her performance, she'd lead the crowd to the office herself, taking no chances that the office would not be found, or that anyone would be dissuaded by a skeptic. Those who bought her remedies on the street were entitled to a free medical consultation at the "office," a cheap hotel room that she had rented for the day. Once inside, the sucker was greeted by McNeal, who functioned as a code-worker. Engaging patients in casual conversation, she'd find out what was troubling them, while making surreptitious notes on a card. Then she'd say that she was going to the next room to see if the doctor was ready, but her real purpose was to hand off the card. With a quick glance at the card, her accomplice, the doctor, would dazzle the patient by listing his symptoms as soon as the unwitting fellow walked through the door. The treatment was always a case or two of whatever they were selling. A good code-worker/doctor team could con thousands of dollars from gullible victims. McNeal had two rules: Never doctor a genuinely sick man and never doctor a woman, sick or well. Women, said McNeal, are better at spotting scams.[51]

Owen Stratton believed that the true purpose of the medicine show was to promote office visits. Like McNeal, he and his partner included a coupon for a free examination with every purchase. Their come-on had the ring of a game show; if the doctor could not accurately name the symptoms, the bearer would be entitled to a free suit of clothes or a new dress. The doctor, usually a down-and-out type who had been barred from regular practice, would describe the patient's physical condition in terms so general they could be applied to anyone. Saying something like, "You experience tenderness in the abdominal region," he would "poke the patient with an index finger that had the rigidity of a billiard cue and could not fail to find tenderness."[52]

Another sure-fire method of separating a mark from his money was to suggest that he couldn't afford the treatment. Puffing himself up and asking the cost, the indignant customer would assure the doctor that he could afford it and more. Taking the customer at his word, extra charges were then added to the bill, which was always paid with a flourish. Stratton and his accomplice always collected big fees for their medicine sales in the office. The doctor would labor over the sum and come up with odd amounts like $72.50 or $112.60. To Stratton's credit, anyone whose complaints were completely at odds with the nostrums got a refund.[53]

Occasionally, local doctors sent informers to the consulation room to try to observe something illegal. Stratton and his partner had a sixth sense for spies, and subjected potential informers to rectal exams so embarrassing and painful that they were sure to keep quiet about the whole experience.

Some medicine-show operators took pride in actually diagnosing a customer's condition. One man who ran a case-taking tent alongside his show announced:

> Don't you say where the pain is! You be here tomorrow morning at ten o'clock. When it's your turn you will be ushered into the little blue tent in the back, that's my office. When you come there, I want your name, address and the kind of work you do. Then I'll do the talking. Don't even say where the misery, the pain, the ache is. We'll tell you.

He added, "We never missed!"[54]

It was an easy matter for a practiced pitchman to see the signs of an aching back, sour stomach, and many other common complaints. On the other hand, while he might have been able to spot obvious symptoms, his diagnoses were not subject to a second opinion. In any case, more than medicine, the office visits were an extension of the show: an opportunity to further dazzle the audience member, one-on-one, with the showman's artifice and expertise with language.

Trouble with the law always loomed for case takers, which is the reason they never did a consultation with a third person in the room. If they had to go to court, they wanted the testimony to be their word against the sucker's. Even having their own stooge in the room was dangerous; the opposing lawyer could suggest that there was a conspiracy afoot.[55] Office-tent doctors were always on the wrong side of the medical establishment and more than one was hauled into court for practicing without a license.[56]

Ballyhoo

Medicine shows varied in size and quality, but they all had some kind of promotion, or ballyhoo, to attract a crowd. From a parade with a brass band to a simple magic trick on a street corner, medicine-show ballyhoo was limited only by the imagination and resources of the performer. Every medicine man who thought of a stunt to promote his show owes a debt to Barnum, the king of ballyhoo.

Barnum's inventiveness is unequaled. In his way of thinking, it was natural for a businessman "to promise everything for next to nothing." His excellent humbug was not due to a lack of scruples, he insisted, but rather due to his superior ingenuity and drive. Barnum's promotional stunts were so audacious that newspaper editors and ordinary New Yorkers discussed them for weeks afterward, which is exactly what Barnum wanted.

Barnum could turn any situation into ballyhoo: During a slow period at the American Museum, a man came to Barnum looking for work. Barnum paid him $1.50 a day to place a brick at the corner of Broadway and Ann Street, another brick at Broadway and Vesey, another in front of the Astor House, and one more in front of St. Paul's Church. The man held a fifth brick that he exchanged for the one at each location as he made the rounds from brick to brick. Barnum instructed him to say nothing. Within a half-hour, the man had gathered a crowd of 500 people who followed him around the Bowery, shouting for an explanation of his odd behavior. In silence, the man led them to the door of the museum, presented a ticket, and walked in. The crowd, thinking that the answer to the mystery must surely be inside the building, bought tickets and followed him. The trick worked for several days, until the police complained to Barnum that the procession of curious onlookers was congesting traffic. But no matter — Barnum was never at loss for promotional gimmicks, and more important, he set the bar for future generations of hucksters and showmen.[57]

Violet McNeal knew that for her to make a sale, her audience had to be right next to the platform. Simply asking her listeners to come closer would only make them back off. She used a Gila monster named Gus to draw the tip close. After introducing Gus, she'd say, "Now I'm going to show you his teeth," and the tip would always move closer to see.[58] Gus died, but she kept him on ice and took him out of refrigeration for her performances, explaining that he was immobile because he was hibernating. This went on for ten days until another Gila monster was shipped from Texas.[59] Any kind of reptile would do; snakes were a favorite with pitchmen, as were trained monkeys.

Street performers, or "buskers," worked outside factories on payday, or hung around saloons, singing for small change. They were easily pressed into medicine-show service. Buskers used a lot of peculiar ballyhoo as well: Milton Bartok pretended to turn a blow torch on himself or to burn up a pile of money. Ray Black, whose lectures were known to go on for hours, started his performance by silently arranging and rearranging a rope, a human skull, and a Bible on the sidewalk. He'd glance sideways every now and then to see if the crowd was big enough. Once he started his talk, the props were never mentioned.[60] A Professor Balrod walked down Main Street after dark, covered in phosphorescent paint. Then he'd go to his platform where two men beat a kettle drum around a green fire. That was it. After a few minutes, they'd get up and leave. The crowd didn't know if Balrod was a magician or a barn painter, but they showed up the next night to find out.

One pitchman, for lack of better props, stared at the sky through a cardboard tube until people gathered around. McNeal and Will also employed an air of mystery. Costumed in Chinese robes, he'd lead her down the street blindfolded. By the time they reached the corner selected for the pitch, they'd drawn a curious crowd. The self-titled Diamond King sashayed around in a huge Mexican sombrero covered with diamonds, or something that sparkled, anyway. His coat and vest were also bejeweled. He never spoke, but let his assistants spread the word that the great Diamond King would have something to tell them the following evening. Before he started his talk, he showered the crowd with coins. Doc McDonald and his brother, Happy, staged fake fights in the center of town, either pulling their punches or swinging at each other with a "slapstick," a board rigged to make a loud, popping noise.[61]

Handbills were a method of advertising borrowed from the circus. Units that could afford them had advance men to paper a town before the show's arrival. Some troupes required their performers to do handbill distribution. Still others employed armies of local boys to distribute medicine samples. In Beaver Dam, Wisconsin, small burlap bags with samples and flyers left on the doorstep were a "harbinger of spring."[62]

Shills

Shills, or shillabers, added to the show's overhead, but were worth the expense. Shills were paid audience members who supported the pitchman's claims, either by helping in demonstrations or by being the first to buy. Such activities provided necessary "social proof." That is, a consumer is more likely to buy if he believes that others also think the product or service is a good one. That's why advertisers say "fastest growing" or "largest selling."[63] Medicine pitchmen knew this technique instinctively. It required excellent timing to make the switch from light entertainment to medicine sale. Pitchman and writer Charles S. Mundell says,

> The secret of the pitchman's art (and it is an art) is to make the "switch" so subtly, so imperceptibly, and so scientifically, that he holds his crowd and

carries them along with him…. The wise medicine man always provides for this contingency by arranging for three or four shills to be the first to step forward and buy. These shills may be hired from the ranks of the unemployed in any large city, at from two to three dollars per day.[64]

Shills were only useful in cities. Small-town dwellers knew each other too well to fall for the deception.

One catarrh-remedy pitchman had a shill who used to pack his nose with custard. He'd drag himself on stage, swallow some of the remedy, blow his nose, and produce a horrifying glob of phony mucus. Violet McNeal had a shill who walked with crutches, but was able to stagger a few feet on his own. He could be counted on for great dramatic effect. Swallowing a dose and throwing his crutches aside, he was living "proof" of the medicine's efficaciousness. After the sale, the shill would give the medicine back and get a buck or two for his trouble. One thing a pitchman could not do was use the shill to guide suckers to the consultation room. That was "steering" and was punishable by jail time.[65]

Contests

If a company got low on material during an extended stay, there were always the contests. Amateur Night and the Most Popular Girl were among the contests that brought the locals back night after night to vote for their favorites. Voting was a privilege that came with a medicine or soap purchase. The competitions built excitement among the populace until the final night (the blow-off) when the winner would get

her cheap set of fake china or silver-plated platter.[66]

Thomas Kelley started a Most Popular Baby Contest after hearing two Ohio townspeople arguing over whose baby was the cutest. Credit for the idea goes to Barnum, who invented baby contests for the American Museum. Although Barnum claimed the contests glorified motherhood, his critics were horrified that babies were put on display for public amusement. By the time Kelley came along, however, attitudes had changed. Motherhood was valued, but it was no longer the cult it had been in Barnum's day.

Kelley figured he could generate sales and promote his show by setting the town's parents against each other, in the most good-natured of ways, of course. The contest was simple; each purchase of Banyan, priced at a dollar, came with a ballot for one hundred votes to be deposited in a metal drum on the show lot. A fifty-cent purchase of Shamrock Healing Oil or Miracle Corn salve entitled the buyer to a fifty-vote ballot. Each night, the votes and names were written on a scoreboard and the numbers changed as the contest progressed. Sales and fistfights were brisk as factions formed for this infant or that. After the last show, some spectators were invited onstage for the final tally. The proud parents of the winning baby were given a gold locket with an inscription. Kelley was especially struck by one elderly man who had sired a son in his dotage. It was the old man's proudest moment to stand in front of his neighbors and acknowledge their applause, even if he did buy hundreds of dollars' worth of Banyan for the honor.[67]

Rules and Regulations

Medicine-show life was fraught with legal problems. In many towns, traveling shows were required to get a permit. Circuses usually had advance men who took care of legalities before the troupe's arrival, ensuring that the show would run smoothly in an advantageous venue. For medicine showmen, however, obtaining permission to perform was often a more informal task. Street workers often had to "fix" a town, that is, bribe the sheriff, or whoever had the authority to shut down the show. Gamblers and pickpockets also fixed with the police. Fixing meant first finding out whom to contact. Bartenders and local attorneys tended to know what went on behind the scenes.

Violet McNeal fixed for herself and Will. They relied on her good looks and charm to get a low fee, but at the same time, she often courted unwanted advances. She frequently had to time her exit from a town carefully, to avoid a more personal form of payment. Entering the local saloon through the ladies' entrance, McNeal would strike up a conversation with the bartender and find out whom to see. Corrupt officials often used an underling to handle that sort of graft. The go-between took a percentage of the fee in exchange for talking to the man in charge. Will taught her to eliminate the middle-man whenever possible and get to the real person in authority. This kept time and expense to a minimum. She'd pay a call on the appropriate town official and haggle with him. It was tricky business. She couldn't downplay the amount of money she expected to make, because these people

were very savvy. Conversely, she felt bad about exploiting someone's soft spot when she laid on a hard-luck story.[68] Neither could she walk right up to a chief of police, notorious as he might be for accepting graft, and instantly make a deal.

Relationships are as important in bribery as they are in any other business deal. It usually took two or three visits to win the trust of a crooked cop. One police chief showed her the picture of a murdered man and asked if she knew anything about him. When she replied, "You don't think I'd tell you if I did, do you?" the fix was in.[69] He knew she could be counted on to keep her mouth shut. Failure to fix a town meant that just before the sale, a cop would go through the crowd swinging his club to clear what he claimed was a traffic obstruction.[70]

Life in a wholesome midwestern town like Beaver Dam, Wisconsin, was regulated more by custom and status than statutes. Harlowe B. Hoyt's grandfather was the town physician and it was up to him to decide which traveling entertainers were worthy of using the opera house. His standards were changeable and arbitrary. If he gave thumbs down, there was no recourse or appeal. The only other choice, and the one used most often by medicine men, was to rent the fanciest hack in Beaver Dam, and do an open-air pitch on Front Street.[71]

Small-time operators, without the kind of capital raised by big medicine shows and circuses, needed to find creative ways around local ordinances. Some druggists were willing to make arrangements, allowing pitchmen to operate as their concessionaires. Other pitchmen simply raised a fuss with the authorities and brazened their way out of paying for a license.[72] In one northwestern town, Owen Stratton refused to pay a five-dollar-per-night fee and was arrested five days in a row. Stratton insisted on a jury trial — due process to which he was entitled, but one in which the locals had no interest in serving. The marshal caved in and never formally charged him. The two got to know each other so well over the course of the arrests that the marshal lent him his twelve-gauge shotgun for a hunting trip. Shady dealings went both ways: Stratton once rented a lot from a man who didn't own it and was presented with an enormous bill when the real owner showed up.[73]

As the twentieth century progressed, food and drug legislation constricted the activities of medicine men. Violet McNeal eventually had to have a lawyer on retainer to keep her apprised of changes in the law. She kept his correspondence on file should she ever have to prove that her intention was to comply. First, she had to eliminate the use of the word "cure." She was required to list on her labels all diseases for which the medicine was intended. A later law stipulated that her medicine had to be manufactured under sanitary conditions under the supervision of a licensed pharmacist. She got around that rule by hiring a drug store clerk to come to her hotel room and have a beer, while she mixed her potions in a Lysol-scrubbed bathtub. The label had to be carefully worded to avoid product liability, and an insurance policy was underwritten in case anyone was injured while listening to her street lectures.[74] From the point of view of the consumer, all this was right and proper. For McNeal and her colleagues, obeying the law was expensive and bothersome.

The Boozer

To conduct medical examinations, it was a legal necessity for medicine pitchmen to have a physician in tow. The only licensed doctors who were willing to put up with show life had drunk themselves out of a stable practice. In medicine-show parlance, the doctor was "the boozer." Most of the information about the boozers is anecdotal, because they were at the very margins of society — basically one performance away from the gutter. Boozers were easy to find. A showman in need of one generally had several from whom to choose, but care and feeding of the boozer was a constant travail. Owen Stratton tells of his difficulties in continually having to locate his partner, Dr. Park, whose alcohol addiction compelled him to be in perpetual search of a drink. Once found, he had to be sobered up for work, prevented from spending all his money on whiskey or running up bar bills, or conversely, made drunk enough to ward off *delirium tremens*.[75] It was time-consuming and irritating, but it had to be done. There was a constant turnover. Boozers would disappear and a new one had to be hired in time for the show. Boozers did have one good quality — they worked on the cheap. It was said of at least one doctor that "all he wants is his quart of liquor a day. Works better with it than without it."[76]

Drug and alcohol abuse pervaded medicine-show life. One painless dentist couldn't get through an extraction without having two or three drinks himself. Pretending that he'd heard a heckler in the crowd, he'd say, "I heard that. You say it is harmful—this wonderful painkiller. It is as harmless as mother's milk. I'll show you."[77] Then he'd take a long drink out of one of the bottles he had with him on the platform in response to the imaginary criticism. Another performer got so drunk he had to be pulled off stage with a hook. Backstage, he started a noisy fistfight with his wife.[78] One tapeworm specialist was known to get so desperate for a drink, he'd swallow the alcohol from a tapeworm jar. Many pitchmen "kicked the gong around" after the show. That is, they went to the local Chinatown to smoke opium. There are endless anecdotal examples of alcoholism and drug addiction in medicine-show lore. Narcotics of all sorts were easy to obtain at the turn of the century.

Medicine-show relationships were frequently unstable. Family troupes not only struggled with alcohol and drug addiction, but also contended with poverty and all of its attendant problems—illiteracy, poor nutrition, lack of hygiene, and so on. As Bobby Noell said, children of medicine show folk were rarely in one place long enough to get a decent education. When they did settle in one place for a time, they were looked down on by townspeople. Cliff Mann was regularly taunted by town kids, who called him "blanket ass," either as an aspersion on his Native American roots or his family's use of tents.[79] Men and women formed temporary liaisons on the road, but the life was not conducive to lasting relationships.

Life on the Road

Medicine-show people encountered the same prejudices as all traveling performers. It was often difficult to persuade a hotelier or boardinghouse owner to rent a room, and when they did, the accommodations compared unfavorably to the average jail cell. Rooms were dirty, dark, and infested with lice, and the food was inedible. Dining rooms were partitioned with drapes hung on wires to separate actors from respectable guests. Before a troupe's departure, a constable frequently appeared with a warrant to enforce payment.[80] Thomas Kelley said, "During the nineties and for at least ten years after the turn of the century, you had to have the bravery of a Spartan plus an iron stomach to survive in some of the small-town hotels I put up with."[81] An oft-repeated joke was that boardinghouse walls were so thin, "You could hear the fellow in the next room making up his mind." Medicine men had to pay in advance. Kelley once brandished a big roll of bills in front of a hotel manager. The illogical response was, "Well, since you've got it, I don't want it. But if you didn't have it, I'd want it right now."[82] The bright side of such inhospitable places was that "the inhabitants of the remote areas were show-hungry; they had never seen the like of it before, and flocked in every night by wagon, buggy, and horseback, eager to buy almost anything that was strange and new."[83]

Before the advent of automobiles and paved roads, traveling was a hardship. That's why medicine shows flourished in the first place; sensible folks stayed put and only actors were crazy enough to endure the privations of travel. Wagons got stuck in the mud, rivers had to be forded, and frequent stops were made to open and close farmers' gates to prevent the loss of livestock. If a bridge was too narrow, many extra miles were traversed to reach a destination. When mud was too thick on the unpaved rural roads, troupers trekked miles through the woods.[84] If they did make it to a destination, there was no guarantee they'd get out when it was time to leave.

In the 1930s, southern medicine showmen traveled and lived in cars with the bodies stripped off and houses built on top of the chassis. These "house cars" had small sleeping platforms and cookstoves. Cliff Mann and his family rolled down the road with smoke puffing from the metal chimney when there was flour enough for biscuits. If they had a tent, it followed along in a flatbed truck. The cars usually cost fifty dollars and were continually breaking down. Unpaved roads tore up tires, so patching and inflating flats was a regular activity. Dirt roads were preferable to gravel, because gravel ate up moving parts. Like most early automobile drivers, medicine men were self-taught mechanics. Instead of using jacks, they propped their show trunks under their cars.

Creeks were the Mann family's sleeping quarters, bathroom, laundry, and grocery stores. Dinner was fish, if there were any to be caught, and a "poke" of greens gathered from the creek bed. If they met with other travelers, perhaps a handyman or other medicine show family, food would be shared. But there was rarely enough to eat. Mann says,

> You see, there was no money in the medicine show business in those Depression Days. Oh, we did all right until about 1931, then more and more people were out of work, and they didn't have cash to spend on tonic and corn salve. So we just survived. If we could make enough money to buy gasoline and flour, sugar and coffee, that was about it. As a kid I was always hungry. You got used to it, and after a while, I didn't notice so much. To keep from being hungry I would pick up a little piece of tar off the railroad tracks, just to have something to chew on.[85]

When they were flush, a big meal was a ten-cent bowl of chili with lots of ketchup and crackers. Guns were indispensable for shooting game and the only bank account was a gold watch. Mann's main ambition was to have clothing other than overalls.[86]

Medicine-show memoirists tend to wax nostalgic, but to the modern observer the life seems harsh. Still, perhaps physical discomfort was an affordable trade for a life unfettered by conventional rules.

9

Yahoo, Hadacol!

The last big medicine show closed in the early 1960s, but the form had begun a slow fade in the 30s. By the mid-forties, there were perhaps two dozen big shows left, a tiny fraction compared to the shows' heyday.[1] Like a dying star, medicine shows had one last fiery explosion from 1949 to 1951. The fireworks emanated from the forceful personality of Dudley J. LeBlanc, a Louisiana Cajun who transformed the Bible Belt into the Hadacol Belt. Hadacol Caravans were extravaganzas that made Dudley LeBlanc a household name and gave delighted audiences much more than their money's worth. The shows were no less popular with their stars, who relished a visit to their vaudeville roots. LeBlanc's rise from backwoods businessman to high-profile impresario is the American Dream in Technicolor.

Dudley LeBlanc, or "Coozan" Dudley (every Cajun was somebody's cousin), was a politician, salesman, and medicine-show operator extraordinaire. Possessed of a natural inclination for hokum and a love of the spotlight, LeBlanc parlayed a $2,500 investment into an annual income of $24 million. Born in Youngsville, Louisiana, in 1894 to a family of sharecroppers, LeBlanc traced his ancestry back nine generations to Acadia and France. He spoke only the Cajun patois until he was ten, and later used his ethnicity to full effect in shaping a celebrity persona. He toiled for a time as a pants presser to pay for some education, served in World War I, then hit the road as a salesman of tobacco, shoes, and his own patent medicines: Dixie Dew Cough Syrup and Happy Day Headache Powder. He served on the Public Service Commission, beating a Huey Long–backed candidate for the post, and went on to serve in both houses of the Louisiana legislature, playing up his Cajun background.[2] In the 1920s, he sold burial insurance until Governor O.K. Allen, a Huey Long crony, pushed through the passage of stricter insurance laws. In 1932 LeBlanc ran for governor himself, promising to

Dudley J. LeBlanc.

put Long in the penitentiary if he won —
he didn't. Long accused LeBlanc of
transferring dead bodies out of expensive coffins and burying them in cheap
pine boxes, and LeBlanc was easily de-
feated in the primary.[3]

LeBlanc sold his insurance business
for $300,000 and promptly lost the pro-
ceeds in the stock market. His next move
was a return to patent medicine. Two
shipments of Dixie Dew Cough Syrup
and Happy Day Headache Powder were
seized by the FDA for fraudulent labeling, but that merely put a temporary
crimp in his career. LeBlanc had a more
serious obstacle ahead.

In the early 1940s, LeBlanc was
crippled by an ailment that swelled his
legs and big toe. Although he exhibited

classic symptoms of beri-beri
(a nerve disease caused by an
inability to assimilate thi-
amine), three doctors diagnosed his problem as either
severe gout or arthritis. None
of his doctors were able to
offer relief. As a last resort,
LeBlanc permitted a local
doctor to administer some
shots and within a week,
LeBlanc's symptoms had sub-
sided. Within ten weeks, he
was walking on crutches.
LeBlanc's curiosity was piqued.
He asked the doctor, "Doc,
wazzat stuff you got in dat l'il
ole bottle?" The doctor answered, "Dude, you crazy?
You think I give away my secrets to a man in the patent
medicine business?" When
LeBlanc returned several days
later for another injection,
the doctor was busy and
asked his nurse to do the honors. "She
wasn't so smart as him," LeBlanc reported years later. "Nor so careful either.
She left the bottle on the table. When
she finished I gave her that old Southern
Chivalry, you know, 'after you, Ger-
trude.' As soon as she turned her back I
shoved the bottle in my pocket."[4]
LeBlanc read the label and got some
books to figure out what it meant. The
active ingredients, he discovered, were
simply B vitamins.[5] After reading every
available book on vitamins, he analyzed
all the patent remedies on the market to
see what they contained and why. "Then
I figured," LeBlanc said, "this is it." The
Hadacol phenomenon was about to ex-
plode.

Working out of the barn on his farm in Erath, Louisiana, with "two pretty Cajun girls" for assistance, he stirred up noxious-smelling concoctions in wine barrels. The girls stirred the potions with boat oars and everybody else fled from the odor, variously described as ripe bananas and burning rope. When he was satisfied that he had found the right formula, he named it Hadacol. The name came from his old company, the Happy Day Company, with an L tacked on to represent his surname. He later joked about the name, saying, "I *hadda call* it *something.*"

Hadacol was no worse than the average nostrum and probably better than most, containing vitamins B1, B2, B6, nicotinic acid, pantothenic acid, iron, manganese, calcium phosphorus, hydrochloric acid, honey, citric acid, and 12 percent alcohol.[6] In short, with the exception of the alcohol, it was the sort of thing bought piecemeal today by thousands of consumers in health food stores.

LeBlanc gave samples to his neighbors, who reported that the formula made them feel good. He put it on the market, and it was an immediate success. Grateful consumers claimed that Hadacol relieved "anemia, arthritis, asthma, diabetes, epilepsy, heart trouble, high and low blood pressure, indigestion, eye and skin disorders, blindness, migraine, swelling, cataracts, gallstones, paralytic stroke, tuberculosis, and ulcers."[7] A Louisiana druggist recalls, "They came in to buy Hadacol when they didn't have money to buy food. They had holes in their shoes and they paid $3.50 for a bottle of Hadacol."[8]

The alcohol content in Hadacol gave some consumers and federal regulators pause. LeBlanc, like Lydia Pinkham before him, claimed that alcohol was a necessary preservative. Still, an eight-ounce bottle was the alcoholic equivalent of two stiff cocktails. That was nothing new for a patent medicine, but LeBlanc took matters a step further by marketing aggressively to children. LeBlanc invented a comic-book character, Captain Hadacol, who, in one issue, exhorts a boy to chug-a-lug eight bottles of the stuff for "immediate super strength." The alcohol in eight bottles of Hadacol equaled a pint of bonded whiskey, a dose more likely to induce a super case of alcohol poisoning than super strength — or at the very least, a head-pounding hangover. The saving grace of that marketing tactic was that the foul-tasting Hadacol was even less appetizing to children than spinach.

Some people who abstained from alcohol on moral or religious grounds readily indulged in Hadacol, just as they had done with other patent medicines. In dry counties in the midwest, druggists sold it by the shot. It was the beverage of choice at some high school parties. "Teenagers," one pillar of an Illinois town complained, "can get plastered on Hadacol."[9] Hadacol cost about one-quarter as much as a comparable amount of wine. It was, in short, a cheap, if not exactly palatable, way to get drunk. LeBlanc, whose preferred beverage was Old Forrester, laughed off suggestions that Hadacol was consumed for its intoxicating effect. He thought it tasted like dirt, but naturally had a convincing explanation: "It contained vitamins and they come from dirt and that's how it tasted."[10] A less enthusiastic taster described the flavor as "bilgewater."

While the medicine may have been inexpensive in comparison with liquor, the mark-up was nevertheless outrageous. It cost 21 cents per pint to produce and sold for $1.25. LeBlanc boasted in his advertisements that he paid $550 for a gallon of vitamin B6, but neglected to mention that the amount was stretched to cover 125,000 pints of Hadacol. A long course of treatment was recommended for everyone, which ensured continuing sales. Twelve weeks was the time it took, so the label said, to feel the full effect of the product. One pint lasted four days, so the average user spent $26.50 just to try the medicine.

LeBlanc tried without success to garner the approval of the medical community. Even though his advertisements stated that "Hadacol is recommended by many doctors," the only medical man in his employ was an L.A. Willey, who had been convicted in California for practicing medicine without a license. LeBlanc sent letters, with Willey's facsimile signature, inviting doctors to try Hadacol on their patients on a fee-per-patient basis. The ill-advised gesture brought the wrath of the American Medical Association (AMA) upon LeBlanc. An AMA investigator wrote in the association journal that

It is to be hoped that no doctors of medicine will be uncritical enough to join in the promotion of Hadacol as an ethical preparation. It is difficult to imagine how one could do himself or his profession greater harm, from the standpoint of the abuse of the trust of a patient suffering from any condition. Hadacol is not a specific medication. It is not even a specific preventive measure. It could not be eligible for serious consideration by the Council on Pharmacy and Chemistry.[11]

The AMA was unimpressed by Hadacol, but ordinary consumers continued to swallow both the advertising slogans and the product.

From the start of the Hadacol venture, LeBlanc understood the value of advertising. He started by collecting testimonials from his neighbors, on whom he had first tested the product. Testimonials made good advertising copy, and were also a clever way to get around governmental restrictions on fraudulent claims. Recipients of free samples also got a form on which they could enumerate the ills that Hadacol had cured. The label itself made the relatively conservative claim that Hadacol was good for nervousness, indigestion, insomnia, and other minor ills.

Users, in contrast, were free to claim cures of cancer and other life-threatening diseases. Outlandish testimonials came in by the hundreds.[12]

"I no longer suffer from asthma," wrote a man from Iowa, Louisiana. "Crippling rheumatism for 10 years long ... now I walk again," wrote a woman from St. Martinsville. "Was suffering terribly from a disease of the blood ... now back to work," wrote a man from New Orleans. "I do not have heart trouble anymore," wrote a woman from Port Arthur, Texas. "This is to certify," wrote a man from Arnaudsville, "that I ... was suffering from ulcers of the stomach... One doctor told me that I had cancer... I decided to be operated on and my wife persuaded me to take Hadacol.... I can now eat almost everything ... even pork. In fact, I feel perfectly well. I work hard in the field with no ill effect."[13]

Some praised the remedy in terms too vague to mean anything, like the customer who wrote, "I was disable to get over a fence. After I took eight bottles of Hadacol … I feel like jumping over a six-foot fence and I am getting very sassy."[14] Hadacol, according to its consumers, was good for everything from tuberculosis to delirium tremens. LeBlanc took elaborate measures to authenticate testimonials, sending a team of employees to the letter-writer's house. The team photographed the user, made audio recordings, and collected corroborating testimony from neighbors and relatives. The government couldn't challenge these heavily documented testimonials, to the great frustration of several Federal Trade Commission bureaucrats. They smelled something fishy in LeBlanc's operation, and it wasn't the Hadacol.

The Food and Drug Administration also kept a wary eye on LeBlanc's operation. Inspectors found no illegal statements on Hadacol labels, but thought that the slogans on Hadacol trucks crossed the line into fraud. LeBlanc agreed to repaint the trucks, and promised to stop saying that Hadacol would "restore youthful feeling and appearance," or ensure "good health." References to cancer were excised from company literature, and all that LeBlanc could claim was that "Hadacol was good for what ailed you, if what ailed you was what Hadacol was good for." His advertisements now whispered rather than trumpeted his message. One print ad depicted a man climbing over boulders labeled *fatigue, nervousness,* and *tiredness.* Small print at the bottom said, "when due to lack of Vitamins B1, B2, Niacin

and Iron."[15] By 1949, advertising had turned Hadacol from a moderately successful regional product with sales of $60,000 a year into a retail monster that produced $24 million in annual revenue.

By 1950, LeBlanc was pouring a million dollars a month into advertising, and recouping four times that amount in sales. On November 13 of that year, a memorable day for LeBlanc, orders came in for $1,570,000 worth of Hadacol. LeBlanc routinely bought print advertising in 700 daily and 4,300 weekly newspapers. More than 500 radio and television stations ran a million spots per year. Ads included sales figures, implying that millions of satisfied customers couldn't be wrong, so why not join the club? LeBlanc read testimonials in both English and French on Louisiana radio programs. The testimonials included such a wide sampling of the population that any listener could find someone with whom to identify.[16]

Promotional items, aimed mostly at children, blanketed the South. There were Hadacol Dolls, Hadacol Squirt Pistols, Hadacol Cowboy Holsters, and glow-in-the-dark Hadacol T-shirts that turned pint-sized wearers into nocturnal billboards. LeBlanc handed out Hadacol Lipsticks to pretty waitresses, saying, "Take this for your ruby lips, Honey, and give it back to me a little at a time." LeBlanc commissioned two songs, "Everybody Loves That Hadacol," and "Hadacol Boogie," which were placed in jukeboxes:

> Down in Louisiana in the bright sunshine
> They do a little boogie-woogie all the time

They do the Hadacol Boogie, Hada-
col Boogie
Hadacol Boogie, Boogie-woogie all
the time.
A-standing on the corner with a bot-
tle in my hand,
And up stepped a woman, said, "My
Hadacol Man."
She done the Hadacol Boogie, Hada-
col Boogie
Hadacol Boogie, Boogie-woogie all
the time.
If your radiator leaks and your motor
stands still,
A-give her Hadacol and watch her
boogie up the hill.
She'll do the Hadacol Boogie, Hada-
col Boogie,
The Hadacol Boogie makes you Boo-
gie-woogie all the time.[17]

LeBlanc even advertised for a parrot that
could say "Polly wants Hadacol." The
bird would be put up in a hotel and introduced to a pretty lady parrot. No such
bird was ever found, but the story made
the papers, which was more to the
point.[18] (P.T. Barnum would have approved.) Perhaps the most insidious
marketing gimmick was the issuance of
Hadacol credit cards to kids. The cards
entitled children to get a free bottle of
Hadacol from their local druggist, sell it,
and return with the money for more.
Hadacol boxtops could be traded for
things kids really wanted, like air rifles
and roller-skates.[19] LeBlanc knew that
the best sales representatives were the
ones who worked for free.

The more he advertised, the more
he sold; the more he sold, the more his
profits were taxed. LeBlanc needed to
find a way to both advertise and offset a
tax bill that at one point amounted to
over $300,000. As he fretted over the
problem one sleepless early morning, the
solution came to him in a brainstorm.

He jumped out of bed, jumped into his
Cadillac, and drove to his office eighteen
miles away to flesh out the plan. Thus
was born the Hadacol Caravan, the
largest medicine show ever produced.[20]

LeBlanc's scheme was to put on a
free show (admission was actually two
Hadacol boxtops). The show would provide a tax write-off and open up new territory at the same time. First, he had to
create a demand, so he blitzed the radio
waves with advertising that took the
form of a contest: The listener was invited to name a tune, usually something
simple like "Little Brown Jug." Winners
got certificates for a free bottle of Hadacol, available, according to the contest
promotion, at local drugstores. The
problem was, as LeBlanc well knew, that
drugstores in virgin territory didn't
stock Hadacol. Druggists all over the
country had to fend off hordes of mostly
middle-aged female customers who
marched from store to store in search of
their prize. When a Hadacol truck finally
appeared, druggists were willing to pay
whatever it cost to have the item on their
shelves. In Atlanta alone, ten trucks of
Hadacol were sold out in four days,
amounting to almost a quarter of a million dollars in sales. In Los Angeles,
LeBlanc hired legions of housewives to
canvass stores in order to create the perception that there was a demand for the
product.

The next step in the marketing plan
was to create anticipation for LeBlanc's
medicine show, the Hadacol Caravan.
Newspapers and radio programs saturated towns with ads for the event,
promising prizes and the appearance of
famous performers. After a location had
been primed, the Hadacol Caravan

rolled into town to close the sale and create a permanent market. The demand would probably have continued without the show, but the caravan solidified customer loyalty and gave LeBlanc a huge tax deduction. "I spent a cool half a million for talent and stuff on this tour," LeBlanc crowed, "but I sold more than three million bucks of Hadacol along the way."[21] The show was spectacular, and anticipation ran so high that, it was rumored, Hadacol boxtops were counterfeited in some areas. The Caravan had seventy trucks, twenty-five cars, two air-conditioned buses for the talent, a photolab truck, two beauty-queen floats, three sound trucks, three airplanes, two calliopes, and sometimes a train called the Hadacol Special. LeBlanc filmed the shows for the towns not fortunate enough to be on the route.

The best, most famous stars of the day hired on to flack Hadacol: George Burns and Gracie Allen, Bob Hope, Jack Benny, Mickey Rooney, Cesar Romero, Carmen Miranda, Dick Haymes, Connie Boswell, Chico Marx, Jimmy Durante, Dorothy Lamour, Rudy Vallee, Milton Berle, Minnie Pearl, Hank Williams and the Drifting Cowboys, and Roy Acuff and the Smokey Mountain Boys. Assorted acrobats, clowns, and dancing girls filled out the program. Many of the headliners had been in vaudeville before their successes on Broadway, radio, or film. Roaming the country doing sketch comedy and song-and-dance routines was a walk in the park to these seasoned troupers, who nicknamed the tour "The Gravy Train."[22]

The first tour in 1950 did one-night stands in eighteen cities. A typical Hadacol Caravan day started with a parade with floats and sound trucks. Most of the Hadacol executives were on board. At LeBlanc's insistence, they had left the operation of the business to a skeleton crew. The show preliminaries started about 7:30 P.M. in a large stadium where clowns and acrobats ran through the bleachers to entertain the crowd while the seats filled. One clown, dressed like a policeman, drank from a giant bottle of Hadacol. Every drink made his special glasses light up. "Coozan" Dudley not only made no bones about the intoxicating effects of Hadacol, but laughed about it openly. At 8 P.M., LeBlanc rolled into the stadium in his big white Cadillac.[23] He'd say a few words and then retire to his box for the rest of the show. George Burns and Bob Hope were alternating masters of ceremonies. The Tony Martin band started things with some Gershwin tunes, then the Chez Paree Chorus Line displayed bathing attire of yesteryear. The women were generally greeted with shouts of "Yahoo, Hadacol!" Another band would play, perhaps Sharkey Bonano and His Dixieland Band, followed by comedy routines that featured Hadacol jokes.

The humor in the show was suggestive. LeBlanc hinted broadly that Hadacol was an effective aphrodisiac, and any old joke that was remotely to the point was rewritten to include the product name. (Hadacol jokes became part of the national culture, which created a welcome diversion from the inflated health claims that had the FTC breathing down LeBlanc's neck.)[24] Singers and comics alternated; then toward the end of the show, the winners of the local beauty pageant took the stage with the winners of the boxtop drawing. A

Hadacol Caravan ad.

big finale featured everyone and, for the final flash, fireworks went off and a big electric sign came on that read, "HADA-COL FOR A BETTER TOMORROW."[25]

By the spring of 1951, LeBlanc was deluged with requests from performers to join his second show. He ensconced himself in a room at the Los Angeles Biltmore Hotel, where, surrounded by starlets, he heard every "wannabe" with a dog act or magic trick who managed to wangle an audition. Joining their ranks were real estate agents eager to broker the site of the next Hadacol factory. His stay in Los Angeles resulted in a radio broadcast that included the cream of Hollywood. When Groucho Marx asked what Hadacol was good for, LeBlanc retorted, "It was good for five and a half million for me last year."[26] The second

caravan started out in the late summer of 1951, touring the South and Midwest for crowds of ten to thirty thousand. Bob Hope, Jack Benny, and Milton Berle took turns as master of ceremonies. Hank Williams, very popular with the country music fans, performed in all the shows. The Hollywood and country music contingents got along very well.

The shows generated so many orders for Hadacol that the Lafayette factory went into constant production. LeBlanc's friends and relatives loaded and drove delivery trucks around the clock to meet the demand. The Hadacol operation was as informal as the Cajuns who ran it. Bookkeeping was spotty, and LeBlanc himself winked at employees who gave him ridiculously vague reports of orders and sales. Hadacol, LeBlanc assumed, would provide plenty of money for everybody.[27]

LeBlanc was a legendary profligate, buying yachts, taking friends on junkets to New York, handing out gold pen-and-pencil sets, and generally driving his business into the ground. While on the surface the second caravan was a big success, by September 1951 the company was deep in debt. To the shock of employees and investors both, LeBlanc sold the business for a mere $250,000. The new owners had the Hadacol name, $8 million in debt, and fourteen lawsuits.

LeBlanc made another run for governor, hoping his celebrity would translate into votes. He placed seventh in the race, and went home to Abbeville, Louisiana. The last, biggest medicine show was gone for good, and the form had passed into history.[28]

10

The Curtain Comes Down

By the 1930s, the law of supply and demand dictated that medicine showmen move on to other occupations. Rural consumers had other ways to get both headache remedies and shows. Drugstores, once rare, were now common, making proprietary and ethical drugs widely available. Formerly isolated farmers drove cars on paved roads to movie theaters, which exhibited the country's most popular entertainment. No single factor ended medicine shows, however. There were actually many reasons why medicine shows became extinct.

Legislation

Federal regulations governing medicine manufacture and advertising were the legislative wedge that was the beginning of the end of medicine shows. Such laws were a long time in coming, because the United States Congress had an institutional resistance to regulating the country's laissez-faire economy, or interfering with states' rights. As Georgia Congressman Herbert Spencer said, "The Federal Government was not created for the purpose of cutting your toe nails or corns."[1] Even Adam Smith, in the eighteenth century, argued against regulation of patent medicines. Toward the end of the nineteenth century, however, social Darwinism was countered by statesmen and philosophers who had a more humanitarian outlook. Legislation was the solution, in the minds of many social progressives, to the rapaciousness of the robber barons.

The first federal legislation to regulate medicine passed the Senate in 1892. A drug was deemed *adulterated* under the law if it fell below "the professed standard under which it was sold," a standard so vague it was unenforceable. Manufacturers, who were accustomed to setting their own standards, groused that the law was unconstitutional, unenforceable and irrelevant. Charles Fletcher, the maker of Castoria, fumed:

If the business were an underhanded one, or if in the preparation of these articles injurious substances were being used, or if there were anything in the nature of fraud in respect to a large proportion of the well-known proprietary articles, there might be some excuse for special legislation against the manufacturers. No such excuse now exists.[2]

Fletcher and his cohorts in the Proprietary Association, which was formed in 1881, lobbied successfully against the bill. The legislation died in the House, but opponents of quackery soldiered on.[3]

Various regulatory bills died aborning over the next several years, suffocated by the combined efforts of the Proprietary Association and the advertising industry. "When Missouri pharmacists sought a formula disclosure bill, 'it brought down on us,' asserted one druggist, 'all the patent medicine men in the state like a flock of wild pigeons.'"[4] Employing a similar flying-pest metaphor, a member of the Proprietary Association complained that "the crop of bills that has swept over the country ... has been like unto the locusts that spread over Egypt."[5]

By 1905, however, there were deep divisions within the Proprietary Association. One faction continued to resist all regulation, while another more compliant group was prepared to make concessions. In a combined effort to dampen their opponents' fervor, both factions voted to self-regulate alcohol content and refrain from "all over-statements" in their advertisements. Individually, proprietary makers continued to lobby members of Congress against regulations; but ultimately, their efforts were destined to fail.[6]

In 1906, after a long, acrimonious struggle between the Proprietary Association and Congress, President Theodore Roosevelt signed into law the Pure Food and Drug Act of 1906. The law merely required that all addictive drugs be listed on labels. Manufacturers, who had feared more stringent legislation than that which actually passed, cheerfully listed such ingredients as laudanum, cocaine, opium, morphine, and alcohol.

The law did not enjoin against adding narcotics to children's syrups, and consumers in 1906 were not in the label-reading habit. Winslow's Soothing Syrup, for example, was a syrup for teething babies that was advertised with idealized mother-and-child imagery. Anyone, teething or not, would have been soothed by Winslow's syrup: It was loaded with morphine. When a *Collier's* writer, Samuel Hopkins Adams, asked his maid how she could leave her small children alone at night, she replied, "Sure, they're alright. Just one teaspoonful of Winslow's an' they lay like dead until morning."[7]

The 1906 law applied to labeling, but not to advertising. Onstage, pitchmen were still free to make outrageous claims for their remedies. The statute's language that referenced "false and misleading" labels was amended in 1912 to read "false and fraudulent." Fraud is difficult to prove because it entails intent. Witnesses have been known to dissemble about their frame of mind in sworn testimony. Still, the law was a demoralizing setback for those in the trade, who had previously operated with no constraints at all.

Stung by the legislative defeat, the

Card advertising Mrs. Winslow's Soothing Syrup.

continued to flourish during the first two decades of the twentieth century, but the 1930s brought a flurry of proposed anti-quackery legislation. A propaganda war ensued between manufacturers on one hand and the newly formed Food and Drug Administration (FDA) and Federal Trade Commission (FTC) on the other. The FTC's interest was the elimination of false advertising claims and the FDA addressed itself to which kinds of drugs should be available over the counter. While the two agencies fought the quacks, they also wrangled with each other over jurisdiction. Allied with these federal agencies were the AMA and the American Pharmaceutical Association. In 1929, the first militant consumer's group, Consumer's Research, had joined the fray. All parties were egged on by a horde of muckraking journalists, who modeled their work on *The Jungle*, Upton Sinclair's exposé of the meat-packing industry. Gradually, the tumult reached the ears of consumers.

Proprietary Association decided once more to regulate itself. By 1914, narcotics for children and abortifacients had been taken out of production. The industry recovered its morale and puffed itself with an air of respectability. Association-member firms concentrated on remedies for non-life-threatening maladies such as halitosis, body odor, and fatigue. Small-time operators continued to do as they pleased, making claims for cancer and consumption cures. Association members took pains to distance themselves from their erstwhile brethren.[8]

The proprietary-medicine industry

By 1936, thirty-nine states had passed laws regulating drugs, but Congress equivocated on the issue until the Elixir Sulfanilamide fiasco. The elixir, diethylene glycol, was a lethal compound that had been tested for appearance, taste, and odor, but not toxicity. Sold as an anti-infection drug for children, it destroyed young kidneys and resulted in scores of lingering, painful deaths. The drug, which was more effective as a solvent, was taken off the market, but not every bottle was seized. It was rumored that the elixir was a cure for gonorrhea, and several afflicted people poisoned themselves with the under-the-counter supply. Even though Elixir Sulfanilamide was a prescription, not a proprietary drug, Congress was spurred to action and passed the Food, Drug and Cosmetic Act of 1938.[9]

For the first time, makers of proprietaries were compelled to list all active ingredients, make only supportable claims, refrain from creating medicines for life-threatening illnesses, and reveal all relevant facts. The element of fraud was not necessary to prove a violation. Medical devices, long big sellers in the medicine-show trade, were also regulated. Legislation, in combination with more sophisticated consumers, helped to bring the curtain down on medicine shows.[10]

Enter the Movies, Exit the Rube

Eventually, medicine shows no longer served a purpose. As the twentieth century wore on and transportation and communication developed, rural America broke out of its isolation and the "rube" became extinct. Without him, there could be no traveling medicine show. Toward the end of his career, Thomas Kelley noted the change:

> Progress is on the march to shatter the rural customs of yesterday; the natives are wiser now, here, there and everywhere in North America. Soon there

will be no such thing as a rube and if you think otherwise, you are only kidding yourself. A few more years and you are going to see an automobile in every barnyard, which will take the farmers and their families to the city lights of twenty and thirty miles away in less time than it formerly took to hitch up the old grey mare and drive to the crossroads…. The world is changing…. the presentation of theatrical entertainment is soon to change as sure as there is tea in China.[11]

Specifically, what Kelley predicted was the ascendance of motion pictures as the primary form of mass entertainment; he was, of course, correct. When motion pictures first came on the scene, they were one-reel shorts that were used as "chasers" in vaudeville houses to clear the auditorium for the next show. Kelley knew that motion pictures would expand to six and seven reels — a full evening's entertainment. He asked, "What chance has a med-man, with big expenses, tons of equipment, and seven to nine performers, against a fellow who comes along carrying his entire show in a tin can?"[12]

Indeed, the growth of the movie industry mushroomed. The first movie theater opened in McKeesport, Pennsylvania, in 1905, and by 1909 there were another 4,000 venues. By 1910, five million people a day were going to nickelodeons in any one of 12,000 locations. Medicine shows were not the only live entertainment threatened by these electric light-and-shadow plays. Vaudeville, burlesque, and legitimate theater all felt the squeeze. Theater operators had to charge $1.50 for live shows, but could easily meet expenses with a five-cent ticket for a film. One theater manager said, "The picture business is bound to grow because it furnishes satisfying entertainment to the masses at the lowest possible price of admission. In my opinion the best movement the regular manager can make is to enter the moving picture field themselves."[13]

Motion pictures were more convenient for both manager and audience. The former had less upkeep and audiences had many showings of early short films from which to choose. Americans were tiring of variety shows and melodrama, preferring the naturalism of the new medium. Cliff Mann's family adjusted to the trend:

> Well, I figured we might as well get in on the money, adapt movies to the medicine show. We could bring movies to those people, if that's what they'd rather see. In 1936, the last summer I traveled with my family's outfit, I talked Uncle Jude into building me a little projection room on a two-wheeled trailer. He bought me a sixteen-millimeter projector, some film and a big sheet. We took our traveling movies and our medicine down to those little towns in south Texas that still didn't have a movie theater, and we flashed films on the sheet in a tent. At first we just showed the movies between our regular shows, but the movies got to be more popular than the live entertainment.[14]

When Mann left his family to strike out on his own, he got a job sweeping a movie theater. He went on to manage movie theaters and used his experience with medicine-show ballyhoo to create promotions.[15] The old life was good preparation for several new careers. Many medicine show advance men were absorbed into politics as campaign workers, doing much the same kind of preparatory work as before. Well-known performers who perfected their craft on the medicine show platform are too numerous to mention.

Medicine shows also faced competition from other outdoor entertainments. Amusement parks, devised around the turn of the century, caught on quickly with the public. They were an unintended consequence of electric trolleys, which were invented to get workers to their jobs. All classes of people began riding them for fun, and soon parks sprang up at the ends of trolley lines. Roller skating and bicycle riding were other inexpensive activities that took audiences away from performers.

Economics

The years immediately following World War I put yet another crimp in the medicine-show business. Farmers saw the price of wheat fall from two dollars a bushel to sixty-seven cents, and couldn't pay the interest on their mortgages. Bankruptcies and foreclosures were epidemic years before the Great Depression.[16] Farmers who were under a financial strain did not favor pitchmen with an unnecessary purchase. Medicine men were reduced to performing in the smallest, most isolated southern villages, and literally chased a dollar by following government agents who handed out agricultural adjustment checks.[17] Local authorities grew more hostile to itinerant performers, charging as much as $1,000 for a license in some southern counties.[18]

Big traveling outdoor shows were dead by World War I. Cities were too congested with motor traffic to accommodate the grand horse-drawn parade. Ornamental wagons and calliopes held no charm for the ordinary family who got around in their own automobile.[19] What this combination of factors didn't kill, the Depression finished. Federal agents, who were charged with enforcing the 1938 Food and Drug Act, were all over the few remaining pitchmen. By the 1940s, there were only a few large medicine shows in operation, and even the street-corner pitchman was on his way to the history books. During World War II, gasoline rationing made touring impossible.[20] A few small family shows held on, but not for long.

Radio and Country Music

By 1920, radio took free programs right into farmers' living rooms. In the South, "The percentage of drugs and medicinal products ranged so high among hillbilly advertisers that it almost seemed as if the format of the old-time medicine show had been transferred to the hillbilly radio show."[21] Wine of Cardui and Black Draught, two of many staple nostrums in nineteenth century farm houses, continued to sell briskly. The products were advertised heavily on country music stations, according to the theory that country folk still disdained physicians and preferred to doctor themselves. Alka Seltzer, an unknown product in 1933, was introduced to rural audiences on the *National Barn Dance* broadcasts, extending the old medicine-show idea to a new remedy and the new medium.[22]

Indeed, country performers have been the caretakers of the last vestiges of the medicine show. As late as 1984, a popular country music performer known as "Doc" Tommy Scott toured with a show that combined variety entertainment with pitches for a liniment aptly named "Snake Oil."[23] In the same year, the *Los Angeles Times* ran a story about Michael Roe, who toured Southern California in a cattle truck selling his homemade medications. Dressed in a vest and top hat and billing his pitch as the Survival Magic Show, Roe sold medicine made from herbs he gathered himself. Taking a page from Healy and Bigelow, Roe says he gets his formulas from "old Indians and Mexicans." Roe complains that "People are over-entertained these days. You really need to get their attention before they'll listen to you."[24]

Cliff Mann would agree with Roe:

> I'd like to go back to the medicine show days, roll it back to say, 1937. We lived slower then. People those days had time to visit each other, to walk barefoot down the street, to run see a tramp medicine show, We've gotten off the track. People need to be a little dumb, not so worldly. It was better when a feller was a little more trusting and didn't think he knew everything. Because he don't anyway.[25]

Medicine-Show Traditions Live On

The medicine-show concept is evident in the structure of television programming, in which commercials are sandwiched between entertainment. Infomercials take the concept one step further: Trading on the current fascination for the private lives of celebrities, these half-hour-long (or longer) pitches blur the line between program and commercial. As faux talk shows, infomercials feature celebrities who willingly discuss their complexion, marital, and weight problems on-camera in order to entice the viewer to buy a product.

Another latter-day incarnation of the medicine show is the health expo— events that are held in hotels and convention centers. While FDA officials fume, sellers of everything from herbs to healing crystals, and yes, even electric belts, hawk their wares from portable booths. Some pitches, according to a 1985 FDA report, contain claims that sound as if they were written a century ago. One pitchman was heard to extol a fluid that would "cure cancer, kidney stones, multiple sclerosis, inflammatory illness, viral infections and bacterial organisms." A laboratory analysis found that the fluid was hydrogen peroxide. Like "an endangered species of migratory birds," a handful of pitchmen still work flea markets, and county and state fairs.[26]

Thomas Kelley said, "There is no such thing as a dyed-in-the-wool rube anymore. They see too much, hear too much; they've smartened up."[27] Perhaps not. Modern life, Cliff Mann argues, has not eliminated naiveté:

> People now are brainwashed from the time they are born. They're used to being persuaded by propaganda from the press, television and radio. Result, if you can convince people they'll be thinner, healthier, richer or live longer, they'll buy it. If you told people they'd be healthier by eating a certain kind of dirt, they'd eat it.[28]

Herbal medicine is at least as popular today as it was a hundred years ago.

As advertising critic Debra Goldman notes, "In a society obsessively focused on the future, herbal medicine harkens to the past, reaching back to medieval moms who soothed their babies' colic with dillweed." Today's advertising slogans for so-called natural products sound like ones used by scores of nineteenth-century pitchmen: "Quality Health from God's Pharmacy," "Trust the Leaf," "Put your faith in nature and your trust in Nature's Herbs." Goldman remarks that such ad copy "works as well on 1990s saps as it did on the 1890s kind."[29]

In the opinion of many former pitchmen, the only thing that has changed is the medium. Mae Noell says,

> Modern TV has perpetuated the old format. Just as we did in the old days, TV gives free entertainment sandwiched between sales talks. The difference is that we sold medicine whereas TV sells everything. Now, the announcer says, "we'll be right back, after this important message." Back then, we said, "right after this lecture we will present Terry the little wooden headed doll, so don't go away!" And like the old time medicine show, TV does "hold" the people as it comes back with more and more entertainment. But it jes' ain't the same![30]

Final Word (The Blow-off)

The great American medicine show has passed away. Its legacy is the convention of television programming that we take for granted: commercials sandwiched between cheesy dramas, situation comedies, and everything else that passes for entertainment on the tube.

Performers who made their livelihood selling remedies and telling jokes have, for the most part, gone to their re-ward. Today, there are very few people left who ever saw a medicine show. Sadly, there is almost no film of medicine shows, and a mention of them usually draws a blank stare. Even though many successful performers got their start in medicine shows, the shows themselves never got much respect. Ever the black sheep of the entertainment world, med-icine showmen were on a social par with thieves, prostitutes, and drunks. Of course, some of them were thieves, pros-titutes, and drunks, but they were tal-ented ones, and even law-abiding med-icine men were painted with the same brush. Despite their bad reputation, medicine pitchmen and performers were very hardworking and highly skilled. Anyone who had the nerve to get on a medicine-show platform had to deliver entertainment and sell the goods. Some of the best vaudeville and minstrel per-formers would have been hard-pressed to compete with medicine men on the basis of versatility. Medicine shows were a cultural sponge that absorbed every in-teresting thing that took place on a stage.

If not for the medicine show, life in rural America would have been much more dreary than it was. Medicine shows went where many circus, vaudeville, and legitimate stage productions couldn't or wouldn't go. Medicine show performers were determined to prosper in an un-forgiving environment, and they suc-ceeded for the better part of a century. They embodied the romance of the road, and had the quintessentially American attitude that anything is possible.

The medicines they sold were mostly worthless and usually harmless. Perhaps the shortcomings of the medicines were balanced by the salutary effects of a good time. Medicine show audiences were ei-ther determined or forced to doctor themselves, and would have bought patent remedies one way or another.

Medicine shows were perfectly suited to isolated rural audiences that liked uncomplicated entertainment. As America became more citified, tastes and leisure time choices changed. Paved roads and motor cars enabled farmers to break out of their isolation. Bicycles, amusement parks, movies, roller skates, and beach resorts were all within reach of the ordinary consumer. No one had to wait for entertainment to come to them. The shows that did go to the au-dience reached right into the living room; radio and television delivered the top acts of the day, every day. There was no longer a reason to gather in a tent or open field for amusement.

The melodramas and pratfalls of an earlier era were no longer interesting to audiences who now had a wider view of the world. Movies and radio were capa-ble of creating sophisticated fantasies that were not possible on the medicine platform. The rube and the medicine man disappeared together.

Rural Americans not only joined their city cousins as the new century progressed, they also became more global in outlook. World War I was a sobering event that altered the Ameri-can mind-set and the American econ-omy. Later, the Great Depression ren-dered medicine shows uneconomical for both producers and consumers. The array of over-the-counter remedies in modern drugstores made the traveling nostrum seller irrelevant.

The twentieth century is gone, and

medicine shows have receded further into history. When the twenty-first century brings us holograms, 500 channels that interact on our home computer, and other wonders not yet dreamed of, the old shows will seem impossibly archaic. Technology will bring its changes, but one thing will stay the same — entertainment sells!

Appendix *I*

"All Run Down"

(a vaudeville monologue — abridged)

Character: E.Z. MARK, a victim of flivvers and doctors

No scenery required

Costume: straight or eccentric

Time: About ten minutes (unabridged)

E.Z. Mark (*facing audience and looking very woebegone and downtrodden*): I was standing on the corner waiting for a chance to cross the street. The traffic officer went, "Phew! Phew!" (*whistle*) and I ran over the crossing. A flivver went, "Honk! Honk!" and ran over me. As I was lying on my back in the middle of the street, wondering what had happened, a policeman came along and pinched me for parking more than six feet from the curb.

Then I went home and crawled into bed; but I must have caught cold, because when I woke up the next day I was a little hoarse. So I went to a horse doctor.

A horse doctor is a man who knows all about cows.

The horse doctor was sitting in his house all alone. A horse doctor never has much office practice. I lived next door to a horse doctor for seven years, and never once did I see a horse enter his office.

"What do you want?" said the doctor.

"I'm sick," said I.

"Can you eat and sleep?" said he.

"Not at the same time," said I.

"You have hoof and mouth disease," said he.

"I have not," said I. "I was run down by an automobile."

"I can do nothing for you," said he. "I am a horse doctor and know nothing about automobiles."

Then I asked him if he couldn't give me something to relieve the pain. He said that he could, went over to a shelf, and took down a large bottle of some sticky-looking stuff, which he handed to me. I took out the cork and — wow! That was the worst smelling stuff I ever came in contact with. It was awful. When I got my breath back, I gasped, "What is it, Doc?"

"It's a lotion," said he. "Just before you retire tonight, rub yourself from head to foot with this lotion. Use plenty of it; then get into bed. At nine o'clock tonight the pain will leave you; at twelve o'clock tonight the soreness will leave you —"

"Yes," said I, handing back the bottle, "and at six o'clock in the morning my wife will leave me. Good-bye, Doc."

Then I went to a general practitioner. A general practitioner is a man who is generally practicing.

When I limped into his office, he said, "Ah, you're a little stiff. You have the rheumatism."

I said, "You're a big stiff, and I haven't got the rheumatism."

"Excuse me," said he. "You were walking lame, and naturally I thought that it was the rheumatics. I now see that the trouble with you is that your kidneys are in your feet instead of your back."

He then took a telephone and listened in on my chest.

"I was mistaken," he said. "The trouble is in your appendix. You will have to cut out smoking."

"You are wrong again," said I. "The appendix is in the back of the book, whereas the pain I have is on the contrary."

"You know a lot about the appendix, don't you?" sneered the doctor.

"I know all about the appendix," I replied. "To begin with, the appendix has two plurals — appendixes and appendicitis."

"You will have to have an operation."

"How much will it cost?"

"Five hundred dollars."

"Five hundred dollars! Suffering cats! They opened up the Panama Canal for less than that."

"This is a major operation," said the doctor.

"A major operation," I said, "for five hundred dollars! It ought to be a major-general operation. The operation is out."

Then I went to the family doctor.

A family doctor is a man who gets up in the middle of a cold winter's night, climbs into a flivver, and drives seven miles through the snow and slush because you telephone him that you have a pain in your jaw. The family doctor is the first one you call for and the last one you pay.

"What's the matter?" said Doc, when I walked into his office.

"I don't know," said I. "I sleep all right, and I eat all right, but I have no desire to work. I just sit around on the bed all day."

"That's a common complaint," said he. "I will inoculate you with a gland."

"A monkey gland?" said I.

"No, an elephant gland," said he.

And he did. Now I don't sit around on my bed anymore. I sit around on my trunk.

Appendix *II*

"Heart Failure"

Is as Rapid and Fatal in its Action as a Stroke of Lightning (Advertising copy from the *Kickapoo Dreambook*, a Healy and Bigelow pamphlet)

The daily press is constantly announcing deaths of people, more or less prominent, from heart-failure. They were well, as they thought, a few hours before — "never felt better" than just previous to the attack — and yet in a few hours are dead. What does it mean? What is the reason? Simply, that from inattention they have allowed their systems to get run down, have let their blood become weak and impure, and the result is a sudden and fatal illness.

Nature has been at work silently and unfelt, until from some slight exertion the weak parts of the human engine break down, and the end overtakes the sufferer almost before he knows he is sick. If a little more care had been taken to keep the system "toned up" and in perfect condition, and, above all, the blood pure, these sudden collapses could be avoided. For this purpose there is no remedy on earth so efficient as Kickapoo Indian Sagwa, made as it is from roots, barks, herbs and gums of the forest. This remedy is without parallel for keeping the body strong, healthy and well. Sagwa accomplishes its wonderful results by purifying the blood and regulating the stomach, liver and kidneys. It should be taken regularly at this season of the year, when all nature is undergoing a change, as it will prevent the blood from becoming vitiated.

The Indians have used it successfully for centuries. Their continual perfect health and longevity, and the fact that sudden strokes, such as heart failure, apoplexy and kindred ailments are unknown to them, is due to the fact that from their birth they have used Kickapoo Indian Sagwa. If you are not feeling just right, and cannot locate the trouble, take this wonderful medicine before it is too late. You do not know what minute you may be overtaken by some dire calamity. Health attends its use always. All druggists sell it. $1 a bottle; six bottles for $5.00.

Appendix III

Temperance Songs

From *Anti-Saloon Campaign Songs* (Chicago: Hope Publishing Co., ca. 1910).

Free Your Town

(Tune — Yankee Doodle)
Words: Rev. E[lisha] A. Hoffman

We'll vote the curse of liquor down,
   The People's ruination
We'll vote the evil from our town,
   And from our noble nation

(Chorus)

We've resolved to free the town,
   And to free the nation,
From the curse that causes only Crime
   and ruination.

We to the polls will early go,
   The friends of Prohibition,
Assured we have the people's votes
   To carry its adoption

(Chorus)

'Tis not the man of the saloon
   We temp'rance folks are after,
It is the traffic we condemn,

A robber and a grafter

(Chorus)

For men who like ourselves have
souls
   We have a kindly feeling,
But we are tired of the saloon,
   The trade in which they're dealing

(Chorus)

Too long we have submitted
   to the traffic's domination,
At last we hurl at the saloon
   Our wrath and condemnation

(Chorus)

The Skies Are Bright

(Tune — When Johnny Comes
Marching Home)
Words: Rev. Elisha A. Hoffman

The skies are very bright at last,
   Hur-rah! Hur-rah!

The hour of doubt is overpast,
   Hur-rah! Hur-rah!
We have the votes to win the day,
The folks have come to think our way,
They will cast their votes
   to put the saloon away.

We knew when people came to think,
   Hur-rah! Hur-rah!
They would destroy the curse of
drink,
   Hur-rah! Hur-rah!
They've done some thinking,
   sure, of late,
And learned the evil thing to hate,
And to drive it out with
   ballots they only wait.

This enemy of land and home,

Hur-rah! Hur-rah!
Will at last be overcome,
   Hur-rah! Hur-rah!
Its death is up in heav'n decreed,
And local option will succeed,
And to cast their votes is all
   that the people need.

Then one more song of hope and
cheer,
   Hur-rah! Hur-rah!
The better day is drawing near,
   Hur-rah! Hur-rah!
For glorious victory we pray,
We'll win the fight, it looks that way,
In a few more days we'll
   put the saloon away.

Chapter Notes

Chapter 1

1. Some writers differentiate the medicine pitchman from the showman in that they regard the former as a small-time con artist and the latter as a theatrical producer. I see the difference as one of degree and shifting circumstance, and use the terms interchangeably.

2. David Cohen and Ben Greenwood, *The Buskers: A History of Street Entertainment* (North Pomfret, Vermont: David and Charles, 1981), 87.

3. Bim Mason, *Street Theatre and Other Outdoor Performances* (New York: Routledge, 1992), 16.

4. Cohen and Greenwood, 21.

5. Samuel McKechnie, *Popular Entertainment Through the Ages* (New York: Benjamin Blom, 1969), 1.

6. Grete de Francesco, *The Power of the Charlatan* (New Haven: Yale University Press, 1939), 1.

7. *Ibid.*, 4.

8. *Ibid.*, 124.

9. *Ibid.*, 12.

10. *Ibid.*, 18.

11. A similar situation exists today on the internet. The World-Wide Web provides instantaneous access to all sorts of information, much of it unverified and of dubious origin. Those predisposed to a certain school of thought can easily obtain "data" to bolster their point of view. We find the eighteenth-century belief in alchemy quaint today, but the notion of instantaneous transformation persists; look at any infomercial, UFO Web site, health food–store catalog, or ad for a psychic hotline.

12. de Francesco, 18–19.

13. Owen Stratton, *Medicine Man* (Norman: University of Oklahoma Press, 1989), 39.

14. de Francesco, 23.

15. McKechnie, 56–57.

16. Robert B. Cialdini, *Influence: The Psychology of Persuasion* (New York: William Morrow, 1984), 239.

17. McKechnie, 58.

18. Cohen and Greenwood, 76.

19. de Francesco, 90, 100.

20. *Ibid.*, 104–5.

21. *Ibid.*, 77, 91.

22. Roy Porter, *Health for Sale: Quackery in England, 1660–1850* (Manchester: Manchester University Press, 1989), 117.

23. de Francesco, 80.

24. Brooks McNamara, *Step Right Up* (Garden City, New York: Doubleday and Co., Inc., 1976), 3.

25. Cohen and Greenwood, 74.

26. Kenneth MacGowan, *The Living Stage: A History of World Theater* (New York: Prentice-Hall, 1955), 107.

27. David Armstrong and Elizabeth Metzger Armstrong, *The Great American*

Medicine Show (New York: Prentice Hall, 1991), 174.

28. C.J.S. Thompson, *The Quacks of Old London* (London: Brentano's Ltd., 1928), 140.

29. Cohen and Greenwood, 91.

30. *Ibid.*, 89.

31. Thompson, 25.

32. de Francesco, 106–7.

33. Porter, 97.

34. *Ibid.*, 105.

35. *Ibid.*, 35

36. *Ibid.*, 30

37. *Ibid.*, 1

38. *Ibid.*, 2

39. *Ibid.*, 5

40. *Ibid.*, 36

41. *Ibid.*, 25

42. *Ibid.*, 5

43. *Ibid.*, 33

44. Armstrong, 9.

45. The archaic term *patent medicine* refers only to royal patronage, not the U.S. Patent Office.

46. Porter, 28.

47. *Ibid.*, 37

48. *Ibid.*, 38–9

49. *Ibid.*, 45

50. McKechnie, 58–59.

51. McNamara, *Step Right Up*, 9.

52. Constance Rourke, *American Humor: A Study of the National Character* (Tallahassee: Florida State University Press, 1931), 107.

53. There were some medicine shows in the New York and Boston areas, but for the most part they occurred in rural areas.

54. McNamara, *Step Right Up*, 6.

55. *Ibid.*, 8

56. *Ibid.*

57. Richardson Wright, *Hawkers and Walkers in Early America* (Philadelphia: J. B. Lippincott Co., 1927), 198.

58. *Ibid.*, 198.

59. *Ibid.*, 57.

60. Rourke, 19.

61. *Ibid.*, 33.

62. *Ibid.*, 26.

63. *Ibid.*, 39.

64. *Ibid.*, 54.

65. *Ibid.*, 54–55.

66. *Ibid.*, 52–58.

67. *Ibid.*, 59.

68. Thomas P. Kelley, Jr., *The Fabulous Kelley: Canada's King of the Medicine Men* (Don Mills, Ontario: General Publishing Co. Ltd., 1974), 104.

69. Violet McNeal, *Four White Horses and a Brass Band* (Garden City, New York: Doubleday and Co., 1947), 75.

70. Russel Blaine Nye, *Society and Culture in America, 1830–1860* (New York: Harper and Row, 1974), 137.

71. A. H. Saxon, *P.T. Barnum: The Legend and the Man* (New York: Columbia University Press, 1989), 81.

72. James Twitchell, "The Annals of Advertising," *Ad Age's Creativity* (6 June, 1998, vol. 6, no. 50), 6.

73. Saxon, 30.

74. *Ibid.*

75. *Ibid.*, 11–12.

76. *Ibid.*, 11.

77. *Ibid.*, 55.

78. *Ibid.*

79. *Ibid.*, 51.

80. *Ibid.*, 67.

81. Burton Raffel, *Politicians, Poets and Con Men: Emotional History in Late Victorian America* (Hamden, Connecticut: Archon, 1986), 177.

Chapter 2

1. Madge E. Pickard and R. Carlyle Buley, *The Midwest Pioneer: His Ills, Cures and Doctors* (New York: Henry Schuman, 1946), 103.

2. Don B. Wilmeth, *Variety Entertainment and Outdoor Amusements* (Westport, Connecticut: Greenwood Press, 1982), 48.

3. Joseph Kett, *The Formation of the American Medical Profession* (New Haven: Yale University Press, 1968), 9.

4. *Ibid.*, 5–6

5. *Ibid.*, 10, 13.

6. *Ibid.*, 30, 67.

7. *Ibid.*, 30.

8. Armstrong, 5.

9. *Ibid.*, 5–7.

10. *Ibid.*, 8.

11. Pickard and Buley, 11.

12. Armstrong, 3.

13. *Ibid.*, 4.

14. *Ibid.*, 7.

15. Pickard and Buley, 28.
16. Armstrong, 9–10.
17. Pickard and Buley, 15–16.
18. *Ibid.*, 13.
19. *Ibid.*
20. *Ibid.*, 21–22.
21. *Ibid.*, 24.
22. *Ibid.*, 16–17.
23. *Ibid.*, 17.
24. *Ibid.*, 26, 27.
25. *Ibid.*, 47.
26. This notion was recently mirrored in a commercial for Robitussin cough syrup featuring a character called "Dr. Mom."
27. These healing superstitions were often very specific: "Corn beef and cabbage is good for a blacksmith with cramps, but ain't worth a damn for cramps in a minister." Pickard and Buley, 75.
28. Winifred Johnston, "Medicine Show," *Southwest Review*, 21.4 (July 1936), 253.
29. Pickard and Buley, 63.
30. *Ibid.*, 41, 43.
31. Armstrong, 16–17.
32. Porter, 1.
33. Pickard and Buley, 98–100.
34. Kett, 48.
35. Armstrong, 3.
36. Johnston, 257, 288.
37. Pickard and Buley, 119.
38. Armstrong, 10.
39. Pickard and Buley, 169.
40. *Ibid.*, 169–72.
41. Kett, 107.
42. Armstrong, 11.
43. Kett, 106.
44. Pickard and Buley, 243.
45. *Ibid.*, 181.
46. *Ibid.*, 289.
47. *Ibid.*, 262.

Chapter 3

1. Here is a further clarification of terminology: *Patent* and *proprietary* have been used interchangeably although there are subtle differences. The word *patent* has nothing to do with the United States Patent Office. It's a holdover from the British monarchy, as in "a patent of royal favor." A more accurate term, used by industry professionals, is *proprietary* medicine, meaning sold over the counter, without a doctor's prescription. *Proprietary* carries the important connotation that the medicine is the invention and exclusive property of the manufacturer. Patenting a formula was not in the manufacturer's interest, as it would necessitate publishing a list of ingredients. Further, a patented formula devolves to the public domain after seventeen years. More practical than a patent was a trademark, which medicine manufacturers registered with the U.S. Patent Office and used year after year to market their product. Formulas changed, but logos and trademarks were sacrosanct. For example, all the ingredients in Lydia Pinkham's Vegetable Compound have changed since 1899, but as of 1990, the label had not been altered. A. Walker Bingham, *The Snake-Oil Syndrome: Patent Medicine Advertising* (Hanover, Massachusetts: The Christopher Publishing House, 1994), 5–6.
2. Charles Goodrum and Helen Dalrymple, *Advertising in America: The First 200 Years* (New York: Harry N. Abrams, 1990), 17.
3. Armstrong, 162.
4. McNamara, *Step Right Up*, 11.
5. Bingham, 11.
6. *Ibid.*, 7
7. James Harvey Young, *American Self-Dosage Medicines: An Historical Perspective* (Lawrence, Kansas: Coronado Press, 1974), 4.
8. The debate about self-dosing is ongoing. For example, CNN news story on 9/16/98 asserted that St. John's Wort and other herbs may be harmful or useless.
9. James Harvey Young, *The Toadstool Millionaires* (Princeton, New Jersey: Princeton University Press, 1961), 169–70.
10. Bingham, 9–10.
11. Arthur Cramp, M.D., *Nostrums and Quackery and Pseudo-Medicine* (Chicago: The American Medical Association, 1936), 22–23.
12. Bingham, 67–68.
13. Gerald Carson, *One for a Man, Two for a Horse* (Garden City, New York: Doubleday and Co., 1961), 33.
14. Armstrong, 162.
15. *Ibid.*, 163.
16. Dorothea D. Reeves, "Come for the Cure-All: Patent Medicines, Nineteenth Century Bonanza," *Harvard Library Bulletin*, 15.3 (July 1967), 255.

17. Young, *American Self-Dosage Medicines*, 6.
18. Armstrong, 165.
19. Carson, 18.
20. Reeves, 256–7.
21. Bingham, 85.
22. *Ibid.*, 49.
23. Reeves, 258.
24. Carson, 30, 49.
25. Bingham, 113.
26. *Ibid.*, 141.
27. James Cook, *Remedies and Rackets: The Truth About Patent Medicines Today* (New York: W. W. Norton and Co. Inc., 1958), 26.
28. Goodrum and Dalrymple, 17–18.
29. Bingham, 113.
30. The device is still in use, as in the commercial that says "works fast, fast, FAST!"
31. Young, *The Toadstool Millionaires*, 166.
32. Goodrum and Dalrymple, 24.
33. Bingham, 114.
34. Before the age of *People* magazine, crowned heads and U.S. senators were the best Barnum could do for a little star power.
35. Goodrum and Dalrymple, 20.
36. Young, *The Toadstool Millionaires*, 185, 188.
37. Bingham, 95.
38. *Ibid.*
39. Goodrum and Dalrymple, 29.
40. *Ibid.*
41. Carson, 73.
42. Reeves, 261.
43. Bingham, 101.
44. Young, *The Toadstool Millionaires*, 184.
45. *Ibid.*, 181.
46. Greil Marcus, "Where Are the Elixirs of Yesteryear When We Hurt?" *The New York Times*, Jan. 26, 1998.
47. *Ibid.*
48. Young, *The Toadstool Millionaires*, 181.
49. Reeves, 263–4.
50. Young, *The Toadstool Millionaires*, 180–1.
51. *Ibid.*, 174–5.
52. McNamara, *Step Right Up*, 13.
53. Cook, 18.
54. Young, *The Medical Messiahs* (Princeton: Princeton University Press, 1967), 307.
55. *Ibid.*
56. Cook, 26.

Chapter 4

1. Popular taste did not necessarily keep pace with standards of morality, however. Ordinary people often resisted efforts to have high culture rammed down their throats, behaving boorishly at events like classical music concerts. Lewis J. Atherton, *Main Street on the Middle Border* (Bloomington: Indiana University Press, 1954), 127.
2. *Ibid.*, 113–7.
3. Saxon, 90.
4. Bluford Adams, *E Pluribus Barnum: The Great Showman and the Making of U.S. Popular Culture* (Minneapolis: University of Minnesota Press, 1997), 76–7.
5. *Ibid.*, 80.
6. Tracy C. Davis, *Actresses as Working Women* (London: Routledge, 1991), 69.
7. Wilmeth, 93.
8. Saxon, 92–4.
9. Wilton Eckley, *The American Circus* (Boston: G.K. Hall and Co., 1984), 10.
10. Saxon, 77.
11. Adams, 83.
12. M.R. Werner, *Barnum* (Garden City, New York: Garden City Press, 1926).
13. *Ibid.*, 80.
14. Adams, 77.
15. *Ibid.*, 83–5.
16. *Ibid.*, 98.
17. *Ibid.*, 99.
18. *Ibid.*, 78.
19. Saxon, 96.
20. *Ibid.*, 112
21. Adams, 80.
22. *Ibid.*, 79.
23. Bernard Sobel, *A Pictorial History of Vaudeville* (New York: The Citadel Press, 1961).
24. McNamara, *Step Right Up*, 40.
25. Young, *The Toadstool Millionaires*, 183
26. McNamara, *Step Right Up*, 42.
27. Young, *The Toadstool Millionaires*, 183.
28. George L. Chindahl, *A History of the Circus in America* (Caldwell, Ohio: The Caxton Printers, Ltd., 1959), 1.

29. Atherton, 131.

30. *Ibid.*

31. Chindahl, 1–3.

32. *Ibid.*, 5.

33. Eckley, 2.

34. *Ibid.*

35. Nye, *Society and Culture*, 189.

36. Chindahl, 192–3.

37. Atherton, 132.

38. Chindahl, 20.

39. Eckley, 12–14.

40. *Ibid.*, 17.

41. Wilmeth, 52.

42. Chindahl, 152.

43. Nye, *Society and Culture*, 191.

44. Saxon, 117.

45. *Ibid.*, 101.

46. *Ibid.*, 100.

47. *Ibid.*

48. Kristine Fredriksson, *American Rodeo: From Buffalo Bill to Big Business* (College Station: Texas A&M University Press, 1985), 10–11.

49. Nye, *Society and Culture*, 149.

50. Don Russell, *The Wild West* (Ft. Worth, Texas: Amon Carter Museum of Western Art, 1970), 1.

51. *Ibid.*, 11.

52. Fredriksson, 140.

53. *Ibid.*

54. Nye, *Society and Culture*, 191–2.

55. *Ibid.*, 192.

56. Fredriksson, 141.

57. Russell, 19.

58. *Ibid.*, 26–7.

59. Dee Brown, *Bury My Heart at Wounded Knee* (New York: Holt, Reinhart and Winston, 1971), 427.

60. Russell, 21.

61. Arts and Entertainment Network television program, *The Story of the Gun*, 1998.

62. B.A. Botkin, *A Treasury of American Folklore* (New York: Crown Publishers, 1944), 68.

63. *The Story of the Gun.*

64. Russell, 118.

65. Nye, *Society and Culture*, 193.

66. Christina C.Z. Jensen, "Indian John: Prairie Medicine Man," in *Mystic Healers and Medicine Shows*, ed. Gene Fowler (Santa Fe: Ancient City Press, 1997), 97.

67. McNamara, *Step Right Up,* 80–1.

68. Brooks McNamara, "The Indian Medicine Show," *Educational Theatre Journal* (Dec., 1971), 431–2.

69. Armstrong, 178.

70. McNamara, *Step Right Up,* 84.

71. *Ibid.*, 81–4.

72. *Ibid.*

73. *Ibid.*, 85.

74. *Ibid.*

75. *Ibid.*

76. Cialdini, 17.

77. McNamara, *Step Right Up,* 88.

78. Armstrong, 178.

79. McNamara, *Step Right Up,* 87–90.

80. McNamara, "The Indian Medicine Show," 436.

81. McNamara, *Step Right Up,* 97.

82. *Ibid.*

83. Armstrong, 180.

84. *Ibid.*, 180.

85. McNamara, *Step Right Up,* 102–3.

86. Young, 193.

87. McNamara, "The Indian Medicine Show," 441.

88. Sisley Barnes, "Medicine Shows: Duped, Delighted," *Smithsonian* 5 (Jan. 1975), 52.

89. McNamara, "The Indian Medicine Show," 441.

90. Carson, 62.

91. Harlowe R. Hoyt, *Town Hall Tonight* (Englewood Cliffs, New Jersey: Prentice-Hall, Inc., 1955), 247.

92. McNamara, *Step Right Up,* 95.

93. McNamara, "The Indian Medicine Show," 438.

94. Carson, 62.

95. Armstrong, 179.

96. McNamara, *Step Right Up,* 106.

97. George Jean Nathan, "The Medicine Men," *Harper's Weekly* 55 (Sept. 1911), 23.

98. McNamara, *Step Right Up,* 106–9.

99. Ann Banks, *First-Person America* (New York: Alfred A. Knopf, 1980), 30.

100. *Ibid.*, 31.

101. *Ibid.*

102. *Ibid.*, 32.

103. McNeal, 35–6.

104. David Edstrom, "Medicine Man of the '80s," *Reader's Digest* (June, 1938): 77.

105. Stewart H. Holbrook, *The Golden Age of Quackery* (New York: The MacMillan Co., 1959), 205.

106. McNamara, *Step Right Up,* 120–25.

107. *Ibid.*, 128.
108. Mary Calhoun, *Medicine Show: Conning People and Making Them Like It* (New York: Harper and Row, 1976), 5–7.
109. *Ibid.*, 8.
110. *Ibid.*
111. *Ibid.*, 8–11.
112. *Ibid.*, 11.
113. *Ibid.*, 20.

Chapter 5

1. Minstrel show revenues declined steadily for professional troupes in the 1880s, but the form was a mainstay of amateur groups until 1940 or so. Gary D. Engle, xiv.
2. Nye, *Society and Culture*, 3.
3. Martin Banham, ed., *The Cambridge Guide to Theatre* (Cambridge: Cambridge University Press, 1992), 50.
4. Richard C. Toll, *Blacking Up: The Minstrel Show in Nineteenth-Century America* (New York: Oxford University Press, 1974), 17.
5. *Ibid.*, 18.
6. *Ibid.*
7. Dale Cockrell, *Demons of Disorder: Early Blackface Minstrels and Their World* (Cambridge: Cambridge University Press, 1997), 32–33.
8. *Ibid.*, 36.
9. *Ibid.*, 69.
10. Toll, 15.
11. *Ibid.*, 13.
12. Engle, xxv.
13. *Ibid.*
14. *Ibid.*, xxvii.
15. Toll, 18.
16. Wilmeth, 119.
17. Carl Wittke, *Tambo and Bones* (New York: Greenwood Press, 1968), 145.
18. Toll, 4–5.
19. Russel B. Nye, *The Unembarrassed Muse: The Popular Arts in America* (New York: Dial Press, 1970), 162.
20. Cockrell, 75.
21. *Ibid.*, 89.
22. *Ibid.*, 90–91.
23. *Ibid.*
24. Toll, 30–31.
25. The medicine show "professor" is a version of the interlocutor.

26. Engle, xviii.
27. Toll, 55.
28. Wittke, 156.
29. Banham, 682.
30. Nye, *The Unembarrassed Muse*, 164–5.
31. Engle, xix.
32. Toll, 67.
33. While the black man was fair game, white minstrel shows never parodied the African American woman.
34. Toll, 57.
35. One of the few exceptions was Bert Fields, a black minstrel who performed in white companies with the likes of Al Jolson (Wittke, 145).
36. Banham, 682.
37. Nye, *The Unembarrassed Muse*, 166.
38. Engle, xiv.
39. Wilmeth, 121.
40. Toll, 146.
41. Wittke, 113.
42. *Ibid.*, 124.
43. *Ibid.*, 127.
44. *Ibid.*, 138.
45. McNamara, *Step Right Up*, 19–22.
46. Bernard Sobel, *A Pictorial History of Vaudeville*, 22–24.
47. London's Palace Theater had first presented "Living Pictures" in the late 1700s. These were reproductions of famous sculptures with live models that caused an uproar in Parliament. The Palace, under considerable public pressure, withdrew the piece. Susan Pennybacker, "'It Was Not What She Said, But the Way She Said It': The London City Council and the Music Halls," in *Music Hall, the Business of Pleasure*, Peter Bailey, ed. (Stony Stratford: Open University Press, 1986), 120–3.
48. Douglas Gilbert, *American Vaudeville: Its Life and Times* (New York: Dover Publications, 1940), 4.
49. John E. DiMeglio, *Vaudeville, U.S.A.* (Bowling Green, Ohio: Bowling Green University Press, 1973), 71.
50. Sobel, 37.
51. Banham, 993.
52. *Ibid.*, 1037.
53. Gilbert, 11.
54. Wilmeth, 131.
55. Gilbert, 10.
56. *Ibid.*, 6.
57. *Ibid.*, 198.

58. DiMeglio, 72.
59. Gilbert, 62.
60. Wilmeth, 133.
61. Sobel, 59–60.
62. DiMeglio, 119.
63. Sobel, 57.
64. Gilbert, 135.
65. DiMeglio, 187.
66. *Ibid.*, 186.
67. *Ibid.*, 107.
68. McNamara, *Step Right Up*, 132.
69. *Ibid.*, 140.
70. McNeal, 24.
71. *Ibid.*, 25.
72. Another cast member was Joseph Keaton, nicknamed "Buster" by Houdini.
73. Milbourne Christopher, *Houdini: The Untold Story* (New York: Thomas Y. Crowell and Company, 1970), 26–30.
74. DiMeglio, 16.
75. Bill C. Malone, *Country Music, U.S.A.* (Austin: University of Texas Press, 1985), 6.
76. *Ibid.*, 78–79.
77. McNamara, *Step Right Up*, 134.
78. When Houdini and his wife were with Dr. Hill, they were grateful for the steady twenty-five-dollar-a-week salary. McNamara, 136.

Chapter 6

1. Banham, 655.
2. "Afterpiece" is something of a misnomer, because they came to be placed all through the shows.
3. Jeffrey D. Mason, *Melodrama and the Myth of America* (Bloomington: Indiana University Press, 1993), 62.
4. Nye, *Society and Culture*, 48–49.
5. Mason, 61
6. *Ibid.*, 85
7. William H. Smith, *The Drunkard: Or the Fallen Saved* (New York: Samuel French, 1844), 50.
8. *Ibid.*, 51–52.
9. William W. Pratt, *Ten Nights in a Barroom* (New York: Samuel French, 1854), 5.
10. *Ibid.*, 44.
11. Nye, *The Unembarrassed Muse*, 154
12. Banham, 1011.

13. Nye, *The Unembarrassed Muse*, 154–5.
14. William Lawrence Slout, *Theatre in a Tent: The Development of a Provincial Entertainment* (Bowling Green Ohio: Bowling Green University Press, 1972), 53.
15. *Ibid.*
16. Catherine Yronwode, *Hoodoo: Definition and History* (http://www.sonic.net/yronwode/hoodoo.html, Jan. 18, 1999), 1–3.
17. Catherine Yronwode, *High John the Conqueror* (http://www.luckymojo.com/johntheconqueror.html), 1, 5.
18. Banks, 186.
19. *Ibid.*, 186–7.
20. *Ibid.*, 187.
21. McNamara, "The Medicine Show Log," *The Drama Review*, 28.3 (Fall 1984), 85.
22. *Ibid.*, 23.
23. Twitchell, 4.
24. Jim Tully, "The Giver of Life," *American Mercury* (1928): 157.
25. *Ibid.*, 155.
26. *Ibid.*, 159.
27. *Ibid.*, 160.
28. Stratton, 34.
29. Hoyt, 247.
30. Stratton, 34–35.
31. Hoyt, 245-6.
32. Stratton, 39.
33. McNeal, 144.
34. Calhoun, 37–38.
35. Carson, 43.
36. McNeal, 57.
37. *Ibid.*, 56–57.
38. McNamara, *Step Right Up*, 68.
39. Calhoun, 39.

Chapter 7

1. McNeal, 101.
2. McNamara, *Step Right Up*, 21–22.
3. McNeal, 59.
4. *Ibid.*, 61–62.
5. *Ibid.*, 62–64.
6. *Ibid.*, 66.
7. McNeal, 65–66.
8. *Ibid.*, 37–39.
9. McNeal, 104.
10. *Ibid.*

11. Cialdini, 172.

12. McNeal, 94.

13. The term comes from "skid road," the street in a logging town where the logs were slid to the water to be "rafted" to the mill or market.

14. McNeal, 29.

15. *Ibid.*, 52.

16. *Ibid.*, 132.

17. *Ibid.*, 125.

18. Women worked in blue-collar jobs under mostly dire conditions, doing tasks that no middle-class white woman would consider.

19. Mary Frank Fox and Sharlene Hesse-Biber, *Women at Work* (Mayfield Publishing Co, 1984), 19. This notion does not apply to farm women, whose status and usefulness were on a par with men's.

20. Kathleen DeGrave, *Swindler, Spy, Rebel* (Columbia: University of Missouri Press, 1955), 55.

21. Stratton, 4.

22. *Ibid.*, 30.

23. *Ibid.*, 42.

24. *Ibid.*, 97.

25. *Ibid.*, 99.

26. McNeal, 54–55.

27. William P. Burt, "Backstage with a Medicine Show Fifty Years Ago," *The Colorado Magazine* (July 1942): 128.

28. *Ibid.*, 132.

29. *Ibid.*

30. McNamara, *Step Right Up*, 71.

31. Hoyt, 250.

32. *Ibid.*, 248.

33. McNamara, *Step Right Up*, 75–76.

34. *Ibid.*, 77.

35. Malcolm Webber, *Medicine Show* (Caldwell, Ohio: The Caxton Printers, Ltd., 1941), 223.

36. *Ibid.*, 53.

37. *Ibid.*, 21.

38. *Ibid.*, 25–26.

39. *Ibid.*, 47.

40. *Ibid.*, 164–7.

41. *Ibid.*, 28.

42. *Ibid.*, 52.

43. *Ibid.*, 28.

44. *Ibid.*, 53–54.

45. *Ibid.*, 243.

46. *Ibid.*, 88–91.

47. *Ibid.*, 93–99.

48. *Ibid.*, 30–34.

49. *Ibid.*, 111–3.

50. *Ibid.*, 109.

51. *Ibid.*, 102, 130–4.

52. *Ibid.*, 150.

53. *Ibid.*, 163.

54. *Ibid.*, 158.

55. *Ibid.*, 257.

56. William Price Fox, "The Late, Great Medicine Show!" *Travel and Leisure*, 4 (Dec. 1974): 6, 10, 14.

57. Kelley, 4.

58. *Ibid.*, 7.

59. *Ibid.*, 45.

60. *Ibid.*, 8–11.

61. *Ibid.*, 4.

62. *Ibid.*, 16.

63. *Ibid.*, 14–17.

64. *Ibid.*, 27.

65. *Ibid.*, 38.

66. *Ibid.*, 30.

67. *Ibid.*, 34.

68. *Ibid.*, 35.

69. *Ibid.*, 40.

70. *Ibid.*, 41.

71. *Ibid.*, 84.

72. *Ibid.*, 85–86.

73. *Ibid.*, 93–94.

74. *Ibid.*, 93.

75. *Ibid.*, 96.

76. *Ibid.*, 102.

77. *Ibid.*, 110.

78. *Ibid.*, 138–9.

Chapter 8

1. Arthur H. Lewis, *Carnival* (New York: Trident Press, 1970), 116.

2. *Ibid.*, 140–1.

3. *Ibid.*, 243.

4. A "tip" is a small crowd; a "push" is a large one.

5. Cialdini, 21, 64, 118.

6. Lewis, 254.

7. *Ibid.*, 115. In addition to selling medicine and running jam auctions, the Noells traveled around with the ever-popular animal exhibit. Out of a converted Blue Ribbon beer truck, they showed a chimp, a deformed rooster, white rats, and opossums. None of the animals were exotic, but the Noells convinced their backwoods crowds that they were seeing something special.

Traveling through North Carolina and Virginia, the Noells eked out a living on nickel and dime "donations." When medicine shows died out, Anna Mae and Robert ran "Noell's Ark" on the carnival circuit. "Noell's Ark" was an ape exhibit with the added attraction of an ape-wrestling contest. From the "bally platform," Robert talked chumps from the crowd into getting into the cage with a chimp. Ticket sales and betting were brisk for "man versus chimp." Even against trained athletes, the chimp was always triumphant. Arthur Lewis, on viewing Noell's chimps, expressed his reservations that such small, mild-looking creatures would be a match for a large man. Noell replied with a laugh, "That's what they all think till they get in the ring with 'em. But I say there ain't no refunds no matter if the fight lasts one minute or ten.... Whatever happens they get a good show, sumpin' they can't see no other place in the world, and that's the truth, mister!"

8. Banks, 32.
9. McNamara, *Step Right Up*, 35.
10. Kelley, 5.
11. Banks, 39.
12. Gilbert, 202.
13. *Ibid.*, 203.
14. *Ibid.*
15. *Ibid.*
16. Irving Zeidman, *The American Burlesque Show* (New York: Hawthorne Books, Inc., 1967), 198.
17. McNamara, *Step Right Up*, 44.
18. Kelley, 71.
19. McNeal, 70.
20. Kelley, 72–73.
21. Carson, 89.
22. Armstrong, 175.
23. Stratton, 65.
24. Carson, 91.
25. McNeal, 70.
26. Carson, 91.
27. Barnes, 50.
28. The fear of parasites persists, even in this age of USDA-inspected meat. *Ad Age's Creativity* for August 1997 noted this e-mail "Spam of the Month":

Shocking News!!! This information could save your life!! Parasities [*sic*] may be eating you alive. 85 percent of North Americans have parasites [*sic*] living inside of

them. Who's getting to your supplements first? The parasites or YOU?"

The testimonial that followed read:

I had not gotten results from other parasite cleansing products. Two days after taking Awareness Products, I passed a seven-inch tape worm!! — Ben Walburger, Colon Therpist [*sic*].

29. McNamara, *Step Right Up*, 30.
30. Calhoun, 77.
31. Stratton, 6.
32. *Ibid.*, 6–11.
33. McNeal, 183.
34. *Ibid.*, 159.
35. Thomas J. LeBlanc, "The Medicine Show," *American Mercury* 5 (June, 1925): 232.
36. McNamara, *Step Right Up*, 28.
37. *Ibid.*
38. *Ibid.*, 28–30.
39. Doc Miller, "Medicine Show Tonight!" *Bandwagon* 16 (July-August 1972): 21.
40. Dennis Goodwin, *Brass Bands and Snake Oil Stands*, (Chicago: Adams Press, 1993), 3.
41. McNamara, *Step Right Up*, 33.
42. McNeal, 68.
43. Hoyt, 246.
44. Gene Fowler, "The Diamond King," in *Mystic Healers and Medicine Shows*, 69.
45. Burt, 128.
46. Webber, 78.
47. *Ibid.*, 83–84.
48. Armstrong, 180.
49. *Ibid.*
50. *Ibid.*, 180–1.
51. McNeal, 122–26.
52. Stratton, 47.
53. *Ibid.*, 47–49.
54. McNamara, *Step Right Up*, 39.
55. *Ibid.*
56. Mae Noell, "Some Memories of a Medicine Show Performer," *Theatre Quarterly*, 4.14 (May-July 1974): 29.
57. M.R. Werner, *Barnum*, 52–53.
58. McNeal, 152.
59. *Ibid.*, 152–53.
60. McNamara, *Step Right Up*, 24.
61. Calhoun, 47–48.

62. Hoyt, 244.
63. Cialdini, 117.
64. Calhoun, 57.
65. McNeal, 119.
66. McNamara, *Step Right Up*, 142, 147.
67. Kelley, 70–71.
68. McNeal, 97–98.
69. *Ibid.*, 121.
70. *Ibid.*, 96–97.
71. Hoyt, 245.
72. McNamara, *Step Right Up*, 23.
73. Stratton, 81, 90.
74. McNeal, 106.
75. Stratton, 54–60.
76. W.A.S. Douglas, "Pitch Doctors," *American Mercury* 10 (February 1927): 223.
77. McNeal, 69.
78. *Ibid.*
79. Calhoun, 18.
80. Slout, 22.
81. Kelley, 30.
82. *Ibid.*, 31.
83. *Ibid.*, 35.
84. Noell, 25.
85. Calhoun, 16.
86. *Ibid.*, 15–16.

Chapter 9

1. McNamara, *Step Right Up*, 165.
2. Young, *The Medical Messiahs*, 318.
3. J.D. Ratcliff, "The Hullaballo About Hadacol," *The Reader's Digest* 41.49 (July 1951): 12.
4. Young, *The Medical Messiahs*, 317.
5. *Ibid.*
6. Jerry C. Brigham and Karlie Kenyon, "Hadacol: The Last Great Medicine Show," *Journal of Popular Culture* 10:3 (Winter 1976): 517.
7. Young, *The Medical Messiahs*, 320.
8. *Ibid.*, 317.
9. *Ibid.*, 325.
10. *Ibid.*, 325–26.
11. *Ibid.*, 327
12. Brigham and Kenyon, 520–26.
13. Young, 320
14. Ron Raynolds and T. George Harris, "Yahoo Hadacol," *Life* 29.12 (Sept. 18, 1950): 31.
15. Young, *The Medical Messiahs*, 321–22.
16. *Ibid.*, 322–23.
17. Floyd Martin Clay, *Coozan Dudley LeBlanc* (Gretna, La.: Pelican Publishing, 1973) 167.
18. Brigham and Kenyon, 526.
19. Ratcliff, 13.
20. Clay, 69.
21. Young, *The Medical Messiahs*, 324.
22. McNamara, *Step Right Up*, 167.
23. LeBlanc bought Cadillacs compulsively. He was fond of saying, "Got rid of the old one because the ashtrays got full." Raynolds and Harris, 34.
24. Young, *The Medical Messiahs*, 325.
25. Brigham and Kenyon, 529.
26. *Ibid.*, 530.
27. Clay, 173.
28. Brigham and Kenyon, 231–32.

Chapter 10

1. Young, *Self-Dosage Medicines*, 5.
2. *Ibid.*, 8.
3. *Ibid.*
4. *Ibid.*, 9.
5. *Ibid.*
6. *Ibid.*, 10.
7. *Ibid*, 12. *Collier's* hired Adams to write a series of muckraking articles about the patent-medicine business. The magazine's hostile stance toward the proprietary industry is somewhat peculiar, as it was created specifically as a vehicle for advertising, and nostrums accounted for a quarter of its revenue (Pavese, 30).
8. *Ibid.*, 12–18.
9. *Ibid.*, 25–26.
10. Clever pitchmen like Violet McNeal and Milton Bartok, the Health Evangelist, got around the law and continued to ply their trade for many years. Bartok never claimed that his medicine cured anything, pointing out that "Nature heals. There is no medicine that heals anything; it helps Nature. Nature does the curing." McNamara, *Step Right Up*, 163.
11. Kelley, 113.
12. *Ibid.*, 114
13. Slout, 33.
14. Calhoun, 117.
15. *Ibid.*, 117–19.

16. Slout, 70.
17. Johnston, 396.
18. Calhoun, 109.
19. Russell, 85.
20. Armstrong, 182.
21. Malone, 101.
22. *Ibid.*
23. *Ibid.*, 6.

24. Armstrong, 184.
25. Calhoun, 121.
26. Armstrong, 183.
27. Kelley, 139.
28. Calhoun, 121.
29. Debra Goldman, "Herbal's Essence," *Ad Week* (Dec. 7, 1998): 58.
30. Noell, 30.

Bibliography

Adams, Bluford. *E Pluribus Barnum: The Great Showman and the Making of U.S. Popular Culture*. Minneapolis: University of Minnesota Press, 1997.

Armstrong, David and Elizabeth Metzger Armstrong. *The Great American Medicine Show*. New York: Prentice Hall, 1991.

Atherton, Lewis J. *Main Street on the Middle Border*. Bloomington: Indiana University Press, 1954.

Banham, Martin, ed. *The Cambridge Guide to Theatre*. Cambridge: Cambridge University Press, 1992.

Banks, Ann. *First-Person America*. New York: Alfred A. Knopf, 1980.

Barnes, Sisley. "Medicine Shows: Duped, Delighted." *Smithsonian* 5 (January 1975): 50–54.

Bingham, A. Walker. *The Snake-Oil Syndrome: Patent Medicine Advertising*. Hanover, MA: The Christopher Publishing House, 1994.

Botkin, B.A. *A Treasury of American Folklore*. New York: Crown Publishers, 1944.

Brand. J. "Picturesque Medicine Shows Combined Entertainment with Salesmanship." *Missouri Historical Review* 45 (July 1951): 374–76.

Brigham, Jerry C. and Karlie Kenyon. "Hadacol: The Last Great Medicine Show." *Journal of Popular Culture* 10–3 (Winter 1976): 520–533.

Brown, Dee. *Bury My Heart at Wounded Knee*. New York: Holt, Rinehart and Winston, 1971.

Burt, William P. "Back Stage with a Medicine Show Fifty Years Ago." *The Colorado Magazine* (July 1942): 127–36.

Calhoun, Mary. *Medicine Show: Conning People and Making Them Like It*. New York: Harper and Row, 1976.

Carson, Gerald. *One for a Man, Two for a Horse*. Garden City, New York: Doubleday and Co., 1961.

Chindahl, George L. *A History of the Circus in America*. Caldwell, Ohio: The Caxton Printers, Ltd., 1959.

Christopher, Milbourne. *Houdini: The Untold Story*. New York: Thomas Y. Crowell and Company, 1970.

Cialdini, Robert. B. *Influence: The Psychology of Persuasion*. New York: William Morrow, 1984.

Clay, Floyd M. *Coozan Dudley LeBlanc: From Huey Long to Hadacol*. Gretna, Louisiana: Pelican Publishing, 1973.

Cockrell, Dale. *Demons of Disorder: Early Blackface Minstrels and Their World*. Cambridge: Cambridge University Press, 1997.

Cohen, David and Ben Greenwood. *The Buskers: A History of Street Entertainment*. North Pomfret, Vermont: David & Charles, 1981.

Cook, James. *Remedies and Rackets: The Truth About Patent Medicines Today*. New York: W.W. Norton and Co., Inc., 1958.

Cramp, Arthur, M.D. *Nostrums and Quackery and Pseudo-Medicine.* Chicago: The American Medical Association, 1936.

Davis, Tracy C. *Actresses as Working Women.* London: Routledge, 1991.

de Francesco, Grete. *The Power of the Charlatan.* New Haven: Yale University Press, 1939.

De Grave, Kathleen. *Swindler, Spy, Rebel.* Columbia: University of Missouri Press, 1955.

DiMeglio, John E. *Vaudeville, U.S.A.* Bowling Green, Ohio: Bowling Green University Press, 1973.

Douglas, W. A. S. "Pitch Doctors." *American Mercury* 10 (February 1927) 222–6.

Eckley, Wilton. *The American Circus.* Boston: G.K. Hall and Co., 1984.

Edstrom, David. "Medicine Man of the '80s." *Reader's Digest* (June, 1938): 77–78.

Fowler, Gene, ed. *Mystic Healers and Medicine Shows: Blazing Trails to Wellness in the Old West and Beyond.* Santa Fe: Ancient City Press, 1997.

Fox, Mary Frank and Sharlene Hesse-Biber. *Women at Work.* Mayfield Publishing Co., 1984.

Fox, William Price. "The Late, Great Medicine Show!" *Travel and Leisure.* (Dec. 1974): 4.

Fredriksson, Kristine. *American Rodeo, from Buffalo Bill to Big Business.* College Station: Texas A&M University Press, 1985.

Gilbert, Douglas. *American Vaudeville: Its Life and Times.* New York: Dover Publications, 1940.

Goldman, Debra. "Herbal's Essence," *Adweek* (Dec. 7, 1998): 58.

Goodrum, Charles, and Helen Dalrymple. *Advertising in America: The First 200 Years.* New York: Harry N. Abrams, Inc., 1990.

Goodwin, Dennis. *Brass Bands and Snake Oil Stands.* Chicago: Adams Press, 1993.

Harris, Neil. *Humbug: The Art of P.T. Barnum.* Chicago: University of Chicago Press, 1973.

Harrison, Sally. "Vi-ton-ka Medicine Show Plays NY." *USITT Newsletter* 21.1 (Winter 1983–4): 16.

Haugaard, Kay. "Medicine Show." *True West* 46 (Jan–Feb 1964): 26–27.

Henry, O. *The Gentle Grafter.* The McClure Co., 1908.

Holbrook, Stewart H. *The Golden Age of Quackery.* New York: The MacMillan Co., 1959.

Hoyt, Harlowe R. *Town Hall Tonight.* Englewood Cliffs, New Jersey: Prentice-Hall, Inc., 1955.

Hutton, Laurence. *Curiosities of the American Stage.* New York: Harper and Bros., 1891.

Jensen, Christina C.Z. "Indian John, Prairie Medicine Man," in *Mystic Healers and Medicine Shows,* Gene Fowler, ed. Santa Fe: Ancient City Press, 1997.

Johnston, Winifred. "Medicine Show." *Southwest Review* 21.4 (July 1936): 390–399.

Kelley, Thomas P., Jr. *The Fabulous Kelley: Canada's King of the Medicine Men.* Don Mills, Ontario: General Publishing Co. Ltd., 1974.

Kett, Joseph. *The Formation of the American Medical Profession.* New Haven: Yale University Press, 1968.

LeBlanc, Thomas J. "The Medicine Show." *American Mercury* 5 (June 1925): 232–7.

Lewis, Arthur H. *Carnival.* New York: Trident Press, 1970.

MacGowan, Kenneth, *The Living Stage: A History of World Theater.* New York: Prentice Hall, 1955.

Malone, Bill C. *Country Music, U.S.A.* Austin: University of Texas Press, 1985.

Marcus, Greil. "Where Are the Elixirs of Yesteryear When We Hurt?" *The New York Times,* Jan. 26, 1998.

Mason, Bim. *Street Theatre and Other Outdoor Performances.* New York: Routledge, 1992.

Mason, Jeffrey D. *Melodrama and the Myth of America.* Bloomington: Indiana University Press, 1993.

McHargue, Georgess. *Facts, Frauds and Phantasms: A Summary of the Spiritualist Movement.* Garden City, New York: Doubleday and Co., 1972.

McKechnie, Samuel. *Popular Entertainment Through the Ages.* New York: Benjamin Blom, 1969.

McNamara, Brooks. *Step Right Up.* Garden City, NY: Doubleday and Co., Inc., 1976.

_____. "The Indian Medicine Show." *Educational Theatre Journal* (December 1971): 431–445.

_____. "Medicine Shows: American Vaudeville in the Marketplace." *Theatre Quarterly* 4.14 (May–July 1974).

_____. "The Medicine Show Log: Reconstructing a Traditional American Entertainment." *The Drama Review* 28.3 (Fall 1984): 74–97.

McNeal, Violet. *Four White Horses and a Brass Band.* Garden City, NY: Doubleday and Co., Inc., 1947.

Miller, Doc. "Medicine Show Tonight!" *Bandwagon* 16 (July–August 1972) 20–22.

Nathan, George Jean. "The Medicine Men." *Harper's Weekly* 55 (September 1911): 24.

Nicoll, Allardyce. *Masks, Mimes and Miracles.* New York: Cooper Square Publishers, Inc., 1963.

Noell, Mae. "Some Memories of a Medicine Show Performer." *Theatre Quarterly* 4.14 (May–July 1974): 25–30.

Nye, Russel Blaine. *Society and Culture in America, 1830–1860.* New York: Harper and Row, 1974.

_____. *The Unembarrassed Muse: The Popular Arts in America.* New York: Dial Press, 1970.

Pennybacker, Susan. "'It Was Not What She Said, But the Way She Said It': The London City Council and the Music Halls," *Music Hall, the Business of Pleasure,* Peter Bailey, ed. (Stony Stratford: Open University Press, 1986), 120–3.

Pickard, Madge E. and R. Carlyle Buley. *The Midwest Pioneer: His Ills, Cures and Doctors.* New York: Henry Schuman, 1946.

Porter, Roy. *Health for Sale: Quackery in England, 1660–1850.* Manchester: Manchester University Press, 1989.

Pratt, William W. *Ten Nights in a Barroom.* New York: Samuel French, 1854.

Raffel, Burton. *Politicians, Poets and Con Men: Emotional History in Late Victorian America.* Hamden, Connecticut: Archon, 1986.

Ratcliff, J.D. "The Hullabaloo About Hadacol." *The Reader's Digest* 41.49 (July 1951): 12–13.

Raynolds, Ron and T. George Harris. "Yahoo Hadacol." *Life* 29.12 (Sept. 18, 1950): 23–34.

Reeves, Dorothea D. "Come for the Cure-All: Patent Medicines, Nineteenth Century Bonanza." *Harvard Library Bulletin* 15.3 (July 1967): 253–272.

Rourke, Constance. *American Humor: A Study of the National Character.* Tallahassee: Florida State University Press, 1931.

Russell, Don. *The Wild West.* Ft. Worth, Texas: Amon Carter Museum of Western Art, 1970.

Saxon, A.H. *P.T. Barnum: The Legend and the Man.* New York: Columbia University Press, 1989.

Slout, William Lawrence. *Theatre in a Tent: The Development of a Provincial Entertainment.* Bowling Green, Ohio: Bowling Green University Press, 1972.

Smith, William H. *The Drunkard: Or the Fallen Saved.* New York: Samuel French, 1844.

Sobel, Bernard. *A Pictorial History of Vaudeville.* New York: The Citadel Press, 1961.

Stratton, Owen T. *Medicine Man.* Norman: University of Oklahoma Press, 1989.

Thompson, C. J. S. *The Quacks of Old London.* London: Brentano's Ltd., 1928.

Toll, Richard C. *Blacking Up: The Minstrel Show in Nineteenth-Century America.* New York: Oxford University Press, 1974.

Tully, Jim. "The Giver of Life." *American Mercury* (1928): 154–160.

Twitchell, James. "The Annals of Advertising." *Ad Age's Creativity* 6:50 (1998): 3–6.

Webber, Malcolm. *Medicine Show.* Caldwell, Ohio: The Caxton Printers, Ltd., 1941.

Werner, M. R. *Barnum.* Garden City, New York: Garden City Publishing, 1926.

Williamson, Sonny Boy, "Hoodoo Hoodoo," audio recording, Chicago, Illinois, August 6, 1946.

Wilmeth, Don. B. *Variety Entertainment and Outdoor Amusements.* Westport, Connecticut: Greenwood Press, 1982.

Wittke, Carl. *Tambo and Bones.* New York: Greenwood Press, 1968.

Wright, Richardson. *Hawkers and Walkers in Early America.* Philadelphia: J.B. Lippincott Co., 1927.

Young, James Harvey. *American Self-Dosage Medicines: An Historical Perspective.* Lawrence, Kansas: Coronado Press, 1974.

_____. *The Toadstool Millionaires.* Princeton: Princeton University Press, 1961.

_____. *The Medical Messiahs.* Princeton: Princeton University Press, 1967.

Yronwode, Catherine. *Hoodoo: Definition and History.* http://www.sonic.net/yronwode/hoodoo.html, Jan. 18, 1999.

_____. *High John the Conqueror.* http://www.luckymojo.com/johntheconqueror.html

Zeidman, Irving. *The American Burlesque Show.* New York: Hawthorne Books, Inc., 1967.

Index